choration

Light Houses already built

for the Bishop Rock

ALKERS REPORT
PAY 6

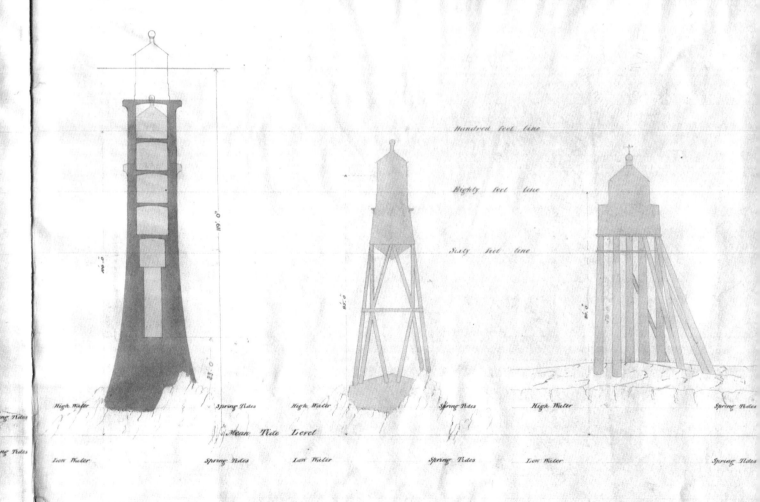

Hundred feet line

Eighty feet line

Sixty feet line

High Water   Spring Tides   High Water   Spring Tides   High Water   Spring Tides

Spring Tides   Mean Tide Level

Spring Tides   Low Water   Spring Tides   Low Water   Spring Tides   Low Water   Spring Tides

20½ Miles   Bishop (proposed)   Bishop (proposed)   Smalls

17½ Miles   design B   16½ Miles   16 Miles

wofeet

The
Lighthouses
of Trinity House

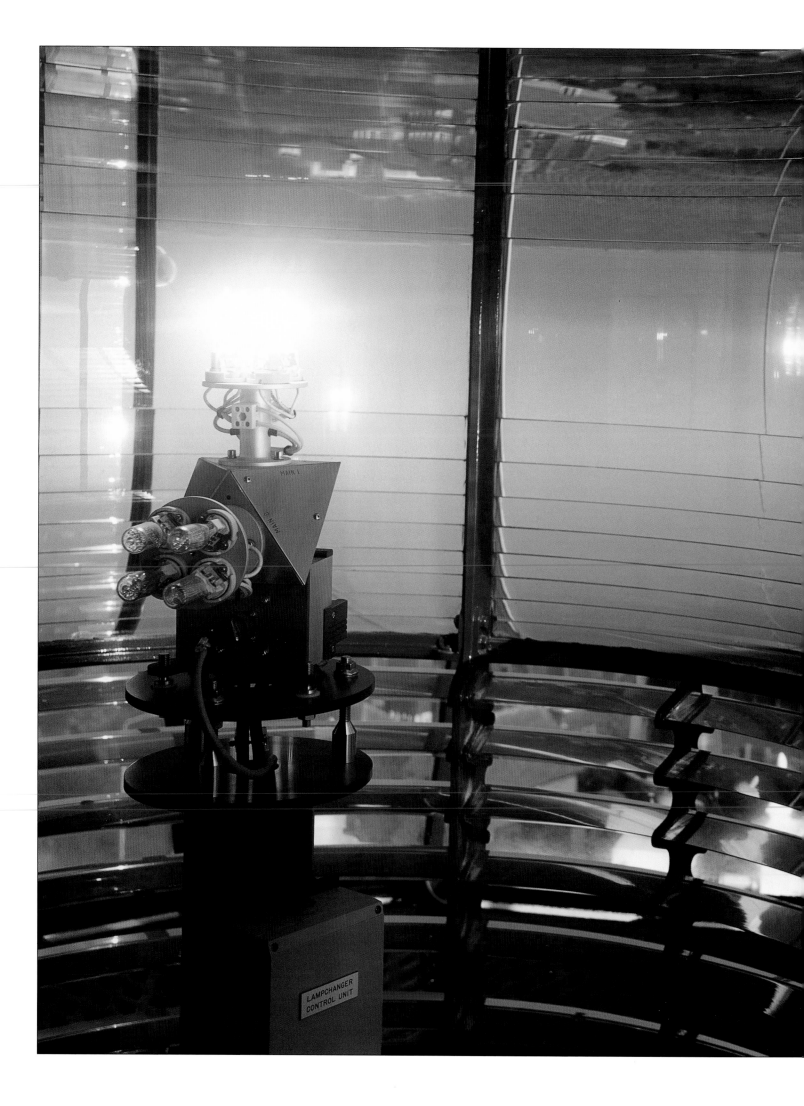

The Lighthouses of Trinity House

Thomas Reed Publications
A Division of the ABR Company Limited

Published by Adlard Coles Nautical
an imprint of A & C Black Publishers Ltd
36 Soho Square, London W1D 3QY
www.adlardcoles.com

First published in Great Britain by Thomas Reed Publications 2002
Reprinted by Adlard Coles Nautical 2004, 2009

British Library Cataloguing-in-Publication Data.
A CIP catalogue record for this book is available from the British Library.

Text by Richard Woodman and Jane Wilson
Edited by Jenny Bennett
Design and Layout by C E Marketing

Printed and bound in China by 1010 Printing International Ltd

ISBN 978-1-9040-5000-1

Half Title Page: Trinity House Coat of Arms

Title Page: The optic in North Foreland Lighthouse

Above: Mumbles Lighthouse

Facing: South Lundy Lighthouse

Following: Start Point Lighthouse

Contents

Foreword

M ost of the lighthouses around the coasts of England, Wales, the Channel Islands, and Gibraltar were built and are operated by The Corporation of Trinity House, a self-governing institution established by King Henry VIII. For some 500 years their lights provided the primary navigation aids for seafarers in our coastal waters. Then came the introduction of powerful fog signals, radio aids, and, more recently, electronic response beacons. Although the development of satellite global positioning systems has given many ships the ability to navigate more accurately, lighthouses remain as positive confirmation of positions.

For most of their history, lighthouses have been individually manned by resident keepers, but recent advances in technology have made it possible for operation by electronic communication from the remote Operational Control Centre supported by local attendants and specialist maintenance teams.

In 1998 the departure of the last resident lighthouse keepers from North Foreland Lighthouse marked a significant change in the working practices of Trinity House. This publication pays a well-deserved tribute to the generations of lighthouse keepers who served the mariner faithfully and reliably for so many centuries. The book also describes the special difficulties and triumphs in designing and building these magnificent and historic structures. The lighthouses of Trinity House will continue to provide a valuable service to mariners for the foreseeable future, but I am sure that readers will be intrigued by this retrospective review of the Trinity House Lighthouse Service.

HRH The Prince Philip, Duke of Edinburgh KGKT
Master of the Corporation of Trinity House

The History of Trinity House

The origin of the Corporation of Trinity House is obscure, but it derives from those associations of tradesmen that emerged as guilds in the medieval epoch. These organisations were intended to spiritually and materially nurture the practitioners of a certain craft and were under the protection of the universal church. They sought to exclude interlopers, to promote proper standards through the informed acquisition of knowledge and skills, and acted as proto-trade unions in regulating remuneration. Grades of skill and 'cunning', most commonly from the day-working journeyman to master-craftsman, were regulated and rewarded by a 'court' presided over by an elected master, whose rule, subjected only to the hand of God, was absolute. The members of these early Trinity Houses were 'shipmen' and pilots; the former being the masters, or commanders of merchant vessels, the latter men employed as reliable guides for the entry and exit of vessels to specific channels, rivers and ports. In those primitive times ship-management was unregulated and hazardous, partly because of the risks of bad weather, faulty and inaccurate navigation, and an imperfect knowledge of natural dangers, but also by virtue of command owing more to nepotism than expertise. It became obvious that the safe navigation of a vessel out of the environs of a port and into the safer waters of the open sea was something that those with local knowledge could best achieve. Proper pilotage significantly reduced the dangers of stranding and wrecking. Similarly, when laden with cargo, any reduction of the risks increased the prospects of a profitable voyage; ships were replaceable and seamen came cheap, but the commodities borne as lading were often valuable.

Trinity Houses are known to have existed in Dundee, Leith, Newcastle-upon-Tyne and Kingston-upon-Hull as well as in London. Remnants of these early establishments survive; those at Newcastle and Hull remain as constituted bodies with residual, largely charitable, responsibilities in their localities, but the London 'house' has transformed itself from its early beginnings. Connections with Stephen Langton, Archbishop of Canterbury during the reign of King John, are conjectural but probable. Certainly the See of Canterbury would have extended its influence over the Trinity House established at Deptford on the south bank of the Thames a couple of miles below London Bridge. Here it enjoyed links with the parish church of St Clement, an early Christian martyr who had been thrown into the Black Sea from a cliff, weighted down, appropriately enough, by an anchor. The fraternal guild was well established by the time of the first Tudor monarch, when the coronation of Henry VII put an end to the internecine strife that had tormented England for several generations. Henry's successor perceived a greater role for his kingdom, rivalling that of France, and for this he required a navy. Henry VIII was the first English monarch who realised the potential of sea power and, in addition to establishing the beginnings of a standing navy, saw in the brethren of Trinity House a ready-made and useful source of both funding and expertise.

The relationship of Trinity House with the nascent Royal Navy was close. For pilotage of the king's ships, Henry naturally turned to the master and brethren at Deptford. The then master of the guild, Thomas Spert, was appointed sailing master of two royal vessels, the *Mary Rose* and later the magnificent *Henri Grace á Dieu*, for which services he was knighted. Spert's fellows received similar postings and their duties included supervision of the loading and 'burthen' of the king's ships. Most significantly their prime function was the 'conduct' of the vessel; this included pilotage and manoeuvring, tasks that required a thorough knowledge of seamanship.

At this time the court of Trinity House was petitioning the king to prohibit unqualified pilots with insufficient experience from practising on the River Thames, claiming that their use endangered shipping. These young men, Trinity House alleged, were unwilling to take the labour and adventure of learning their craft on the high seas and were therefore unfitted to seek employment as ship's guides. The Brethren also warned of the dangers of allowing foreigners, particularly

Facing: An early form of parabolic reflector from the late Eighteenth Century 'spangle light' at Lowestoft. Glass facets make up the reflective surface.

'Scotts, Flemmyngs and Frenshman', to 'knowe yor stremes and the daungers and secrets of the same contrary to yor olde lawes and customes…', meaning the outer channels of the Thames Estuary, thereby betraying an enduring fear of invasion.

Above: The Roman lighthouse, or pharos, within the castle walls at Dover.

Facing: An illuminated page from The Benefactors' Roll showing King Henry VIII granting the charter.

On 20 May 1514, Henry reacted by granting a charter 'to our trewe and faithfull subjects, shipmen and mariners of this Our Realm of England' to 'begyn of new and erecte and establish a Guild or Brotherhood of themselves or other persons as well men as women, whatsoever they be…'. Setting aside the interesting allusion to women, which suggests the past was in some ways more advanced in its thinking than we imagine, this empowered 'The Master, Wardens and Assistants of the Guild or Fraternity of the Most Glorious and Undividible Trinity and St Clement in the Parish of Deptford Strond' to regulate pilotage as they desired. In charging his faithful shipmen to 'begyn of newe' Henry not only swept aside all previous, and clearly long-standing arrangements, but stamped his royal authority on the affairs of the Guild. During the Commonwealth the business of Trinity House continued under a Select Committee but, some years after the restoration of the monarchy, Charles II confirmed all previous charters. Thereafter supplemental charters of confirmation and incorporation were granted by successive monarchs. Significantly these modifications governed the numbers of brethren assisting the master and wardens, confirming the title of 'Elder Brethren' upon the assistants and allowing a pool of 'Younger Brethren' to be elected, but to remain at sea as associates from which the Elders might be drawn in due course. With some subsequent adjustments, this pertains to the present day, the Master being HRH The Prince Philip, Duke of Edinburgh, with a Deputy Master undertaking the day-to-day responsibilities of Executive Chairman presiding over two boards, one entrusted with managing the affairs of two charities and the other responsible for the function of the Lighthouse Service, both accountable to the Court. Outside the immediate circle of Trinity House a number of

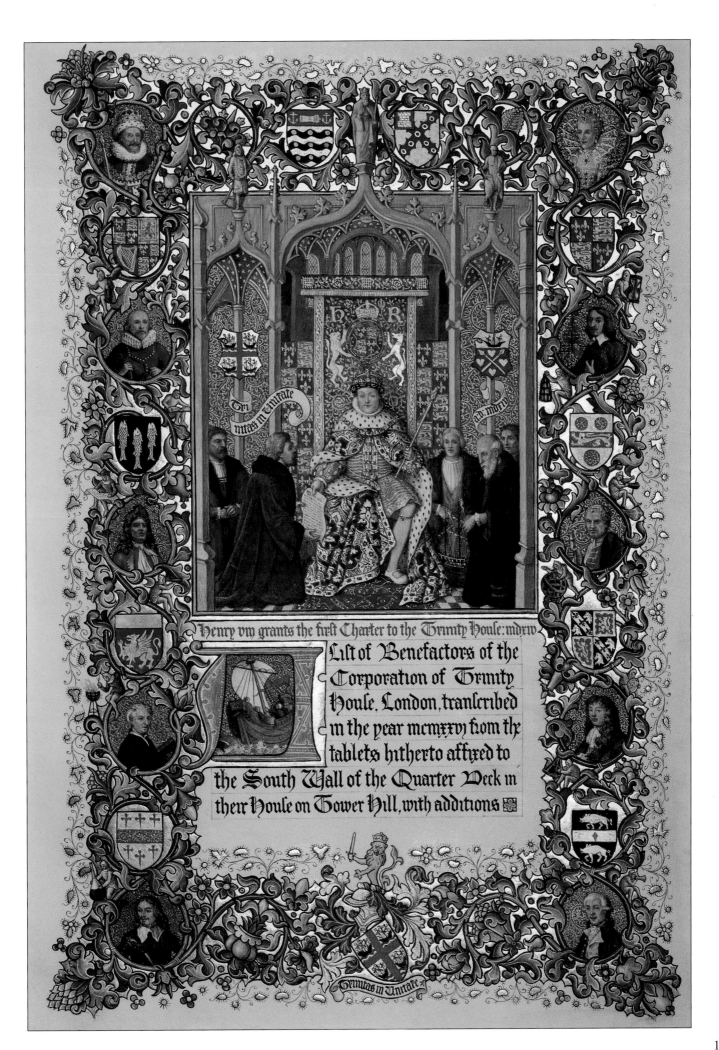

Henry vııı grants the first Charter to the Trinity House: mdxv

List of Benefactors of the Corporation of Trinity House, London, transcribed in the year mcmxxvı from the tablets hitherto affixed to the South Wall of the Quarter Deck in their House on Tower Hill, with additions

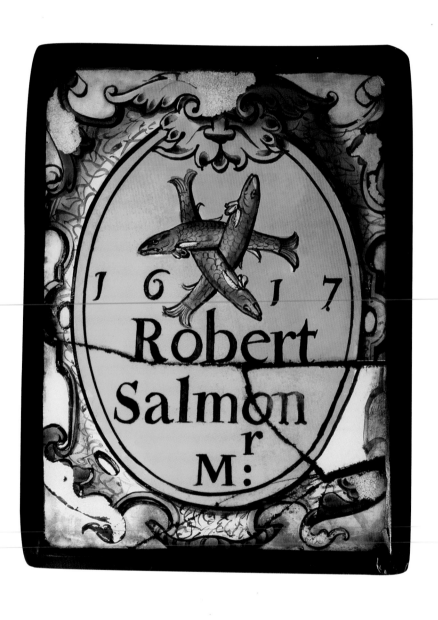

experienced sea officers in both the Royal Navy and the Merchant Service are elected as Younger Brethren.

The confrontation with Spain during the reign of Elizabeth I brought Trinity House into greater prominence, when the Brethren apparently acted as agents to raise auxiliary support to the queen's small fleet, and provided portolans and charts. More significant during this period was the increase in sea-borne trade and merchant shipping. Sadly this came with a consequent loss of ships by stranding and, in 1566, Parliament charged Trinity House with the duty of erecting seamarks, to act as conspicuous supplements to the church towers, hillocks, castles, and prominent trees that pilots used to navigate along the English coast and which were mentioned in portolans. Though it seems little was actually done beyond the provision of a few beacons, demand for more of these rose rapidly, far exceeding the pockets of the Brethren at Deptford, who rather reprehensibly dragged their feet over the matter. This problem was solved when, on 11 June 1594, the Lord High Admiral of England, Lord Howard of Effingham, surrendered his traditional rights to the perquisites arising from selling dredged ballast to sailing vessels discharging their cargoes in the port of London. This revenue was sensibly diverted to the Trinity House, which took over the task of dredging shingle from the bed of the River Thames and selling it to the masters of vessels requiring ballast.

As early as the beginning of the Seventeenth Century the march of technology had revived the ancient concept of the lighthouse. But it was not until losses of merchant ships engaged in the East Coast coal trade from Newcastle to London began to reach unacceptable financial levels in the early 1600s, that Orders in Council were directed by the Crown to Trinity House to erect lighthouses and carry out the duties laid upon them by the Act of 1566. These Orders, dated January 1606, May 1607, and May 1609 required the Brethren to build lighthouses on the East Anglian coast, to guide vessels through the maze of sandbanks between Happisburgh and

The Ballast Office

A 'warden' was put in charge of the operations of the Ballast Office, its dredgers, lighters, and water- and lightermen. The activities of the Ballast Warden and his staff had two important consequences in the succeeding 250 years. The first was to vastly enrich the Corporation due to the huge expansion of London as a port; far exceeding the demands of buoyage and beaconage, surplus profits were diverted to the almshouses maintained by Trinity House for 'decayed mariners'. But by the end of the Eighteenth Century most of the shingle had been lifted from the Thames and ships' bilges were being filled with the stinking ooze dredged from the river that had long since become an open sewer and the depository for London's filth. This encouraged rot in both ships and seamen and, despite the charity shown to their own kind, the Brethren acquired a reputation for malpractice, particularly among the common seamen who lay outside the scope of their largesse.

Happily for both parties, the practice of ballasting by the means of riparian deposits rapidly declined in the Nineteenth Century when cargoes were increasingly sought for both inward and outward voyages, and ended altogether with the introduction of iron and steel ships and the provision of double-bottomed hulls capable of holding sea water as ballast. At this time the Ballast Office was closed, the fleet of dredgers and lighters was scrapped, their crews paid off and the post of Ballast Warden abolished.

Above: The medieval chapel at Ilfracombe with its restored lantern tower which once exhibited a light to guide mariners.

Facing: This stained glass coat of arms of Mr Robert Salmon can be found in the Library in Trinity House.

13

Early Lights

The ancient world had devised the idea of an elevated fire to mark a port; the best known were the Colossus of Rhodes and the great Pharos of Alexandria. Throughout their empire, the Romans built numerous lights, of which those at Dover and La Coruña remain extant. In England, early medieval lighthouses existed at the Cinque Port of Winchelsea in 1261, on the Ecrehou Reef in the Channel Islands in 1309, at St Catherine's Head on the Isle of Wight in 1323 and on the Yorkshire coast at Spurn Head in 1427. With the exception of the last named, which was the responsibility of the Trinity House at Kingston-upon-Hull, these were usually maintained by monks and hermits as acts of charity.

Lowestoft. Difficult or impossible to see, set along an almost featureless low coast above which only the occasional church lifted its tower, these complex shoals bedevilled the passage of

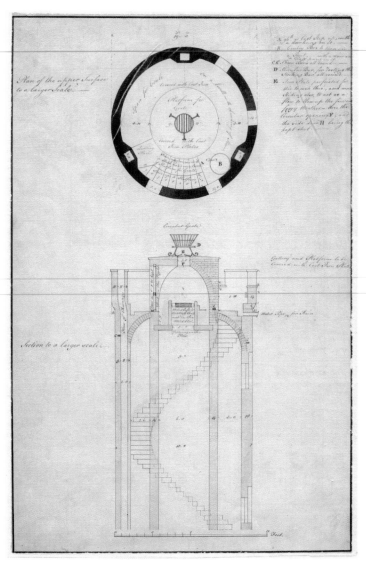

ships. Unstable in character, they took a terrible toll of ships and seamen which, year after year, ran aground and broke up in heavy weather. Many of these were colliers, bringing 'sea-cole' from the north East Coast to the fires of London and, in one particular gale, over six hundred small merchant vessels were lost. Although the death toll was appalling, it was the loss of investment and deprivation of goods, coal included, that stirred the influential merchants in London to action. The king was petitioned and the Orders in Council directed Trinity House to remedy the deficiency.

To maintain these proposed new lighthouses, a levy of twelve pence per ton was imposed on all ships leaving the ports of Newcastle, Hull, Boston and King's Lynn, This was collected by the officers of the King's Custom House and sent to London 'to support the buoys and beacons between Leistoff [Lowestoft] and Winterton'. This principle of payment by the user has remained the state's preferred method of funding the lighthouse authorities, but this is also an early reference to buoys which formed a supplementary aid to the dangerous navigation on the East Anglian coast.

Lowestoft was the earliest to benefit from one of these first lighthouses but Trinity House was curiously reticent about establishing more. One reason was that to reduce navigational difficulties would discourage shipmasters from taking pilots, and thus interfere with the livelihoods of many of the Corporation's members. Another was that it exposed those 'secrets' of navigating coastal channels to the king's enemies. Yet a third argued that the levy would discourage trade.

Initially then, the Elder Brethren contented themselves with the management of three East Anglian lighthouses, devolving their powers to erect more lighthouses elsewhere. Instead they merely advised the Crown when and where it was appropriate for a petitioning speculator, usually a landowner, to erect a lighthouse. This prevented a rampant proliferation of lights, but it was not long before private lighthouses began to earn their owners a reputation for greed and, regrettably in many cases, for inefficiency – a curious situation that resonates with modern arguments about the advantages and disadvantages of privatisation. While the number of lighthouses grew slowly and some were conscientiously run, others were not, being regarded by their owners simply as a means of making money after an initial outlay. Part of the investment was spent on a patent, obtained with the consent of Trinity House and upon which a fee was paid to either the Crown or the Corporation. This was combined with an annual rent to the Corporation for the term of the patent, which now became a form of lease. Thus the Corporation grew wealthy and unpopular amongst both seamen and shipowners. In common with many other contemporary institutions, Trinity House was no longer open and had become hermetically exclusive.

These drawings (left and facing) are of the early coal-fired light at Dungeness.

Top of Platform

Roof Covered with Slate

15

Another weakness of the system of private lights was that, with the exception of the East Anglian lighthouses, only the commercially-inspired initiative of a speculator resulted in the establishment of a lighthouse. The unhappy result was thus an inconsistent service to the mariner. Whilst philanthropic individuals pioneered construction in the most inhospitable environments, such as on the Eddystone Rocks, off Plymouth, and the Smalls reef off Pembrokeshire, whole tracts of coast remained as dangerous as they had been in the Dark Ages – particularly on the West Coast of England and along the entire coast of Wales. The Elder Brethren of the day retreated behind their outmoded argument as to the importance of ships taking proper pilots and of the protection of the coast's navigational secrets, while uncooperative landowners and the majority of their impoverished tenants preferred the occasional bonus of a richly laden wreck to ease the discomforts of an English winter.

Clearly this situation was anachronistically opposed to the changing temper of the times as, by the latter half of the Eighteenth Century, not only was British trade increasing dramatically, but so, too, was the power of the mercantile classes. This, combined with losses of naval vessels, isolated the archaic concepts of the Elder Brethren. But the constitution of the Corporation was itself changing as the expertise of shipmasters experienced in the Far East and West Indian trades infused new blood into its own ranks. These men brought a new vision of the opportunities open to British trade and they found allies among the handful of influential naval officers that the Brethren had elected, in part, to maintain royal interest. This collective change of heart swiftly removed much of the parochial and introverted thinking of their own Court, and produced men of a remarkably innovative turn of

mind. Parallel changes were occurring in the Royal Navy itself as it, too, expanded under the imperatives of protracted wars with France and her allies. Professional skill, rather than birth and influence, was increasingly raising competent men to positions of authority. As Britain developed into the world's first industrial economy and acquired her maritime supremacy at the end of the Napoleonic War, the Elder Brethren were faced by an ironic consequence of their predecessors' lack of foresight: the original patents granted to the erectors of private lights were always for a finite period, usually a century; consequently the first of these leases began to expire in the first decade of the Nineteenth Century and in 1807 Trinity House took over the management of the Eddystone, the world's first true rock lighthouse.

In the succeeding thirty years, the entire complexion of lighthouse organisation under the Corporation changed radically. In 1836, the last year of the 'sailor-king' William IV's reign and just before Queen Victoria came to the throne, matters were transformed. Following earlier provisions to make lighthouse management a matter for state commissioners in Ireland and Scotland, an Act of Parliament was passed by which the remaining private lights in England, Wales, and the Channel Islands could be compulsorily purchased and placed under the management of Trinity House. Effectively this was an act of nationalisation. Despite the payments of annual rents to Trinity House, private owners had often made substantial sums from the light-dues that their agents levied upon passing ships when they reached port. Whiffs of scandal surrounded these sums; in his novel, *Nicholas Nickleby*, Charles Dickens, the social commentator of his age, has a lunatic propose marriage to Nicholas's widowed mother; pretending great wealth the lunatic pleads he has jewels and a lighthouse!

Notwithstanding rumoured riches, other owners made little profit from their investments and the standard of lighthouse keeping varied

enormously. Whereas the Corporation's own lighthouses at Lowestoft and the Eddystone could be regarded as being at the cutting edge of contemporary technology, the light at St Bee's remained a smoky coal fire which, though it might burn well in a gale, nearly killed its keeper and his wife as they toiled up flights of stone steps to feed it with coal. This inconsistent service to the mariner was out of step with the spirit of the age and was one of the reasons why shipowners petitioned the government to do something, but it was met with opposition from the successful lighthouse owners who, concerned by their loss of income, vociferously counter-lobbied. The 1836 Act therefore compensated owners on the basis of their receipts from light-dues. In some cases the sums were considerable, reaching almost half a million in the case of the Skerries lighthouse off Anglesey, fully bearing out Dickens's contention.

The change was timely, however, occurring as it did with the advent of steam power, an expansion in universal trade, and the tremendous increase in mechanical and engineering skills during the period. Building on methods pioneered by Smeaton and by Stevenson, the engineer to the Commissioners for Northern Lights, the Victorian lighthouse became an icon of its age, a standing synonym for utter reliability.

In the half century to 1854, when Parliament passed a ground-breaking Merchant Shipping Act, the whole spectrum of maritime endeavour had altered and with it the character of Trinity House and the highly motivated public service that it now oversaw.

Above: A painting by Thomas Butterworth (1768-1842) of Trinity House yachts visiting Smeaton's Eddystone, c.1815.

Facing: A silver model of Smeaton's Eddystone by Edward and John Barnard, which dates from the second part of the Nineteenth Century.

Trinity House

No plans or drawings survive of the Brethren's original home at Deptford but in 1618 there was a move to Ratcliffe and, in 1660, another relocation to Stepney – where a building was leased and used for meetings until 1670 – and to Water Lane, in the City. The Stepney building was in fact destroyed in the Great Fire of London in 1666 and when, in 1790, it was found that the building in Water Lane also now required extensive repairs, the Corporation moved its headquarters to the present, purpose-built site.

The Trinity House building on Tower Hill was designed and built in 1794-1796 by Samuel Wyatt. It was partially destroyed in 1940 when a German firebomb lodged in the roof of the stairwell and, once the ensuing

flames had been extinguished, all that was left of the building was the Trinity Square facade. The house was completely rebuilt under the direction of A.E. Richardson and the interior was reconstructed almost exactly in its original form. Today the Trinity House building is home to some of the most remarkable works of maritime art and artefacts – both originals and replicas.

Facing top: The present Trinity House.

Facing bottom: The main staircase.

Left: The 'Quarterdeck' at Trinity House with Gainsborough Dupont's group portrait of the Elder Brethren at the time of Trafalgar dominating the head of the staircase.

Below: The courtroom of Trinity House. Over the door at the far end hangs a portrait of King Henry VIII. He is flanked by the 'Sailor King', William IV, and his consort, Queen Adelaide.

Managing the Offshore Lights

The first lightvessel appeared at the Nore in the Thames Estuary as the result of a private venture in 1732. Initially Trinity House opposed this impudent act but the Admiralty soon received reports as to its value and paid for the establishment of several more, particularly near the Goodwin Sands. Since ships of the Royal Navy often anchored in the Downs, and a whole squadron had been lost there in the great gale of November 1703, their Lordships persuaded Trinity House to assume management of these lightvessels. Thus, by about 1810 Trinity House was appointing local agents who employed their own tenders to service the buoys, lightvessels, and lighthouses in their locality, and to maintain buoys and moorings ashore. In due course, these local agents were to become District Superintendents, Captains in the Trinity House Service. These men employed the crews of their District Tender (each of which was in the charge of a Commander), the lightsmen aboard the lightvessels, the keepers of the lighthouses, and the labourers and specialist tradesmen such as radio-mechanics, masons, carpenters, and blacksmiths who worked in the buoy-yards at the District Depots, or were sent to carry out maintenance work on station, offshore.

Below: A painting by Roland Langmaid (1897-1956) of the Trinity House lightvessel laid off Juno beach for the D-Day operations in June 1944. The THV Warden, in wartime grey, approaches from the left, while cruisers shell German positions ashore.

Remnants of the old Trinity House remained however. Although the Elder Brethren had, by 1800, moved their headquarters from Deptford, first to Water Lane, near where the Custom House now stands, and then to Tower Hill in the City of London, they retained their almshouses in east London. Today the charitable side of their original work continues and the Corporation runs a home for elderly and infirm master mariners at Walmer in Kent. Moreover, the Corporation continues to actively encourage maritime education and safety at sea, and grants scholarships to cadet officers in an attempt to provide against the lack of young people going to sea in a much shrunken British merchant fleet.

This adaptability of the Corporation has proved the key to its durability. During the reigns of James I and James II, the number of Elder Brethren was increased and has fluctuated ever since. In recent years, reflecting management changes throughout all organisations, the numbers of active, salaried, Elder Brethren have fallen sharply. Such rationalisation is found elsewhere in the modern Trinity House Service, which has grown from that pivotal Act of Parliament of 1836 and the more recent establishment of the statutory powers of the General Lighthouse Authorities under the Merchant Shipping Act of 1995. The great expansion of technological processes which constitute the legacy of the Industrial Revolution are, in fact, still in motion and ever since Trinity House assumed full responsibility for the entirety of a service providing seamarks for mariners in 1836, the Corporation has kept a constant and measured pace with changes and improvements.

The self-sufficient lighthouse – at The Mumbles solar panels power the light of the Twenty-First Century.

HURST HIGH LIGHTHOUSE
PROPOSED NEW TOWER & ADDITIONS to DWELLINGS

— North East Elevation —

II 485

Scale 4 feet to 1 inch

Jas. N. Douglass
12th February 1867

22

Lighthouse Construction and Equipment

The Colossus of Rhodes and the great Pharos of Alexandria were understandably marvels of the ancient world, but the early proto-lighthouses of the medieval period ranged from the lamps exhibited from chapel towers and maintained by hermits, to the wood- and coal-fuelled braziers, sometimes known as chauffers, erected on beacons or swapes. These were not particularly effective, being erratic in brilliance and highly dependent upon human assiduity. Moreover, while they provided dim glimmers of reassurance to the worried mariner, they rarely gave him more than an indication of his position and rarely truly marked a danger. It was not until Henry Winstanley built his first lighthouse actually upon the top of the dangerous Eddystone Rocks, that the concept of the lighthouse as we have come to understand it in its primary function, was born. As will be seen, Winstanley's technique was flawed, but he was followed by other innovators who literally and metaphorically laid the foundation for the golden age of lighthouse construction.

Although the civil engineers of the Victorian era were to perfect the methodology of constructing stone towers upon tide-swept rocks, the pioneering groundwork had been achieved in 1759 by Smeaton on the Eddystone and, in 1812, by Stevenson on the Bell Rock in the Firth of Forth. These men had progressively devised a means by which each course of stones interlocked with its neighbours, enabling the building of the classic granite 'rock-tower lighthouse'. As will be seen, other methods were tried and failed.

After the construction of the lighthouse itself came the all-important provision of adequate lighting apparatus. When Trinity House took over Smeaton's lighthouse in 1807, the tower was lit by a candelabra, its range limited and its miserable luminosity scarcely worthy of the splendid tower which supported it. Smeaton had tried oil lamps, but found them self-defeating, producing far too much soot. Trinity House removed the candles and replaced them with 'Argand' lamps. These had been developed by the Swiss inventor Ami Argand, who discovered the increased illumination conferred by burning an oil wick in a glass tube. Creating its own Venturi

Facing: The proposed new tower for Hurst Point, late 1860s.

Below: The light mechanism and optic for Les Hanois Lighthouse.

Following: The first High Light at Hurst Point and plans for additional accommodation at the same. The pink colour in the floor plan denotes the new proposed extension.

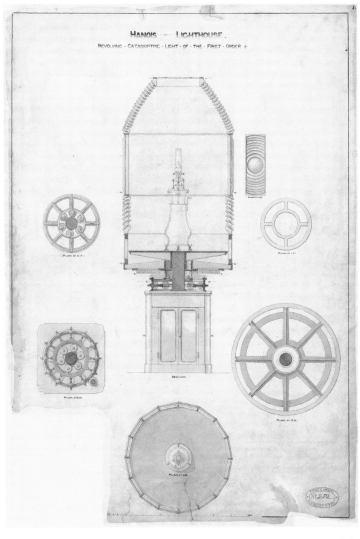

PLANS

of the

HIGH LIGHT HOUSE

HURST

1828

HIGH LIGHT. DESIGN FOR DWELLINGS

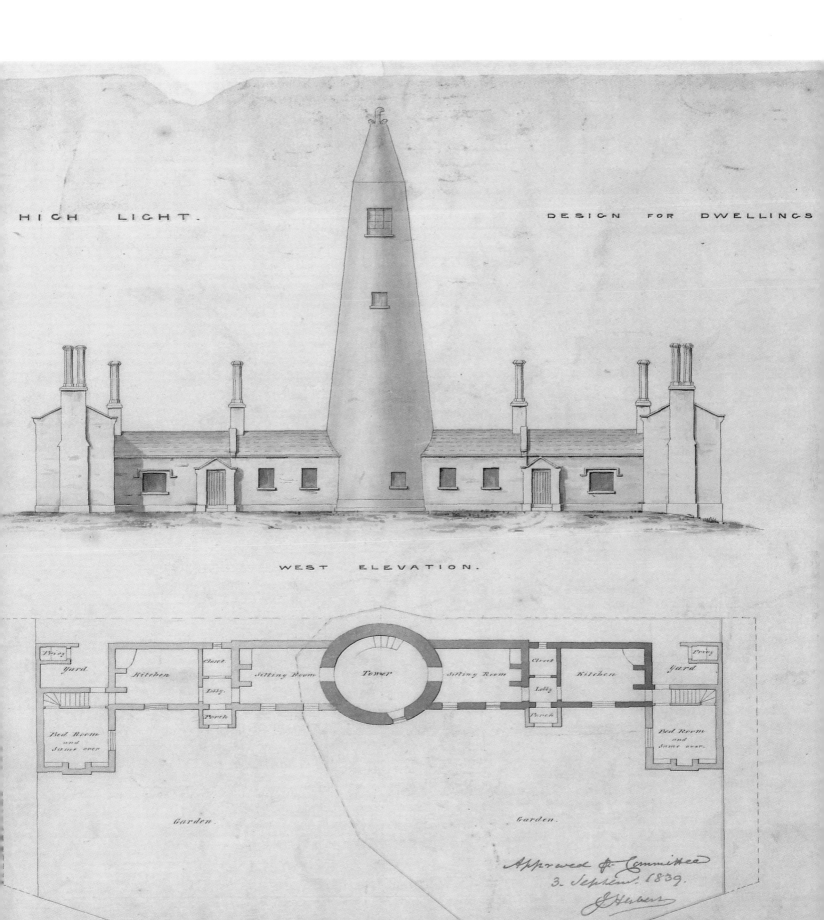

WEST ELEVATION.

PLAN.

Approved y Committee
3. September. 1839.

Above: The optic in Round Island Lighthouse.

Facing: A typical rotating mechanism seen here at Sark Lighthouse.

this was indistinguishable from another, the precise definition of his location, relied upon a mariner knowing roughly where he was as he approached a coast after a long sea passage. In the days of sail, before the widespread use of the chronometer made the determination of longitude possible, this was less easy than might be supposed.

Difficulties were compounded in areas such as the western approaches to the British Isles. Strong gales and overcast skies denied the mariner any astronomical observations, while calm was often accompanied by dense fog. The danger of making a landfall by dead reckoning was particularly acute in the chops of the English Channel. It had been addressed but not solved in the Seventeenth Century by providing the area's three main lighthouses with distinguishing characteristics. These consisted of a differing number of coal fires, so that the lighthouse on St Agnes in the Isles of Scilly displayed one fire on a single tower, and that at the Lizard in Cornwall, two, each on a distinct and separate building. On the opposite side of the Channel on the Casquets Rocks north of the Channel Islands, three towers were built, each burning a bright light. The difficulty of maintaining three fires in so remote a location as the Casquets does not need emphasising, while the wide disposition of these crucial lighthouses gives us some idea of the technical difficulties confronting the mariner of those days, along with the risks he ran in his daily life.

Not surprisingly ship losses continued, including that of the first-rate man-of-war, HMS *Victory*, which, despite the three lights, was cast ashore on the Casquets in 1744 with the loss of Admiral Balchen and all hands. Suffice to say that the system was much improved by Nordqvist's invention, for now a whole range of characteristics was available, and adjacent lighthouses could be made, if not unique, then distinguishable from their immediate neighbours.

Thereafter improvements in glass lenses followed. The dioptric system gathered the maximum of light rays from the source and concentrated them in a horizontal beam to become the norm in lighthouses. Lightvessels, however, limited in the lantern space available, retained an improved form of the catoptric reflector. Better quality fuels followed sperm oil, but it was 1901, when vaporised paraffin oil was burned in a mantle to produce an incandescent light, before a really powerful illuminant was found. This was retained as economically efficient in many stations, although electrical power had been selectively introduced after the first installation at South Foreland in 1867. The reliability and performance of independent incandescent oil burners ensured they remained in service until 1977 when the last in the Trinity House service at St Mary's Bay, Tynemouth, was replaced.

Today, Trinity House's offshore lighthouses run on electrical power generated on station either by diesel generators or solar energy. In the case of land-based lights power is taken directly from the National Grid. In all cases there is a fail-safe provision which produces a light of equal intensity to the primary light source, along with an emergency system of reduced battery-power available as a last resort.

effect, the extra air drawn up the tube produced a flame of significantly increased brilliance. Later combination of the Argand lamp with the cleaner-burning sperm oil further improved the quality of the light emitted.

Attempts to gain even greater intensity from a light source had been made by creating reflectors. One method was to polish a brass sheet that had been shaped into a hollow parabola; another was the so-called 'spangle light' made by pressing small facets of glass into a parabolic concavity of clay mounted in a wooden frame. By the beginning of the Nineteenth Century a Swede named Johan Nordqvist, had invented a revolving apparatus, thus enabling lighthouses to exhibit flashing lights, either singly or in groups. The apparatus was powered by clockwork driven, like a massive long-case clock, by a heavy weight descending an iron tube in the centre of the light tower.

This was a major breakthrough, for in the days of the coal chauffer, only a single burning light could be shown. As

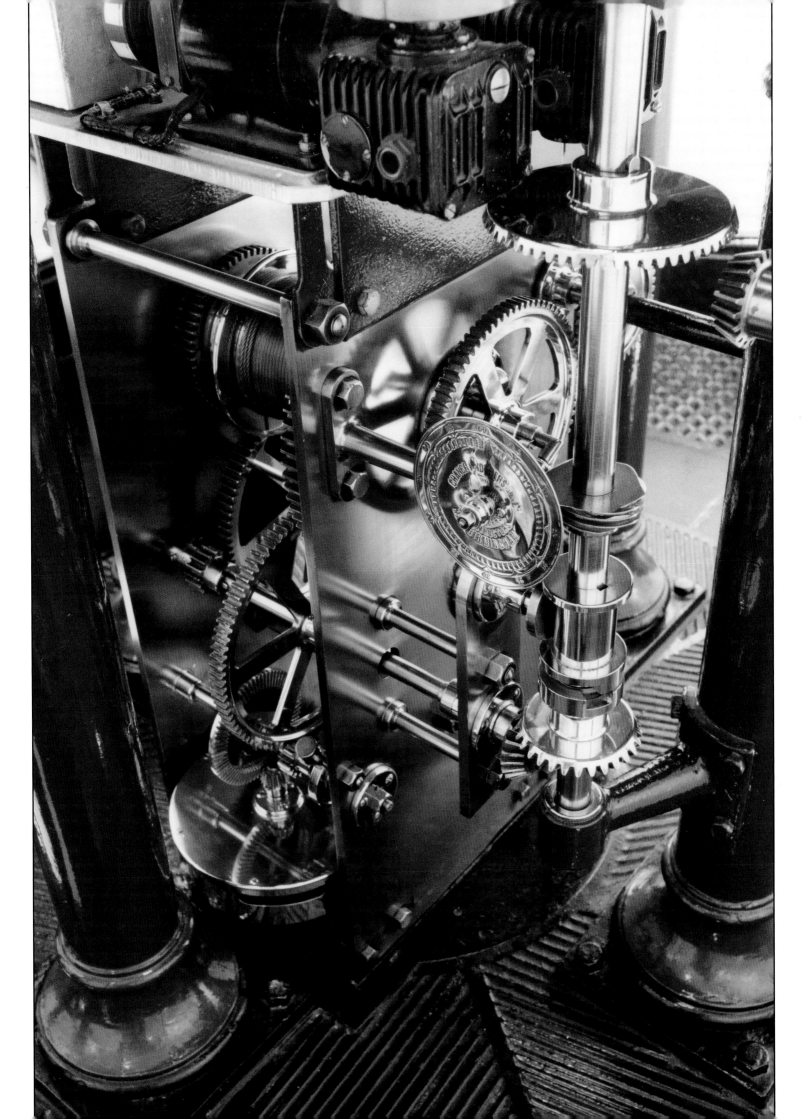

The Drawing Archive

The headquarters of Trinity House has been badly damaged or destroyed by fire three times, in 1666, in 1714, and again in 1940. It is remarkable, therefore, that any of the Corporation's artefacts and collections have survived through the centuries; that so much of the drawing archive exists is extraordinary.

Like all major new buildings the construction of a lighthouse required backing, consultation, approval. In the earliest days the relationship would have been between landowner and builder but, with the formation and development of Trinity House as an overseeing body, the collaboration shifted first to the Corporation consulting with the petitioning landowner and his representative designer and then, latterly, to the Brethren working with their own appointees.

Drawings were produced for manifold reasons: to launch a campaign for support by giving financial backers visual images from which they could appreciate the magnitude or beauty of the undertaking; to illustrate diverse schemes in the early days of planning a lighthouse's construction or redevelopment; to act as instruction manuals for the on-site workers; to trumpet the magnificence of a lighthouse once it had been built.

In many cases it is difficult to say who was the individual designer responsible for a lighthouse's construction. The records are muddied by the use of different terms for different individuals: designer, engineer, architect, builder, superintendent of works. Furthermore it is often the case that one name will be attributed to the lighthouse while others will appear in the drawings of that same building. With the Eddystone, for instance, there exist published drawings depicting the structure of Rudyerd's tower (1709) and the building techniques of Smeaton's tower (1759) that are unattributed – in the first instance it is not clear who generated the draft from which the engraving was worked, in the second it

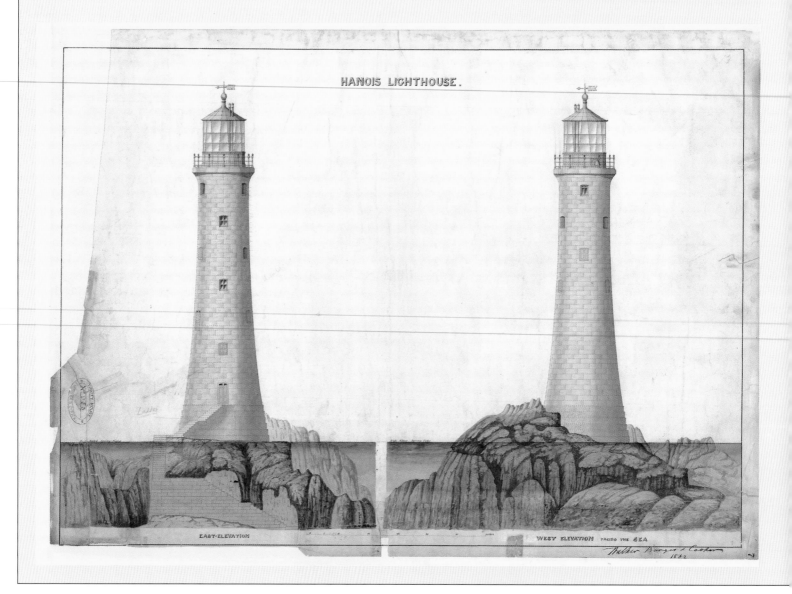

HANOIS LIGHTHOUSE.

EAST ELEVATION

WEST ELEVATION FACING THE SEA

was almost certainly Smeaton himself who did so.

From the late 1700s Trinity House appointed its own engineers and designers. Samuel Wyatt was consultant engineer from 1776 to 1807 when he was succeeded by Daniel Alexander; in 1839 Nicholas Douglass came to Trinity House as a constructional engineer and eventually rose to superintendent engineer; Sir James Douglass was Engineer-in-Chief from 1863 to 1892; Philip Hunt held the same post from 1951 to 1967. Structural engineers of extreme talent, all these men would have produced their own drawings but all would have had assistants to tidy up rough drafts, expand plans to show detail for workers, or produce copies for other interested parties. However, no matter who was responsible for them, many of the drawings are beautiful documents often showing exacting details and occasionally revealing insights at first not recognised: many earlier plans, for instance, are colour-coded for the benefit of illiterate on-site workers.

Despite its gaps, the archive that remains in the Trinity House collection is a fascinating documentation of the development in construction technology and illustrates the extraordinary engineering involved in building great towers in some of the most inhospitable places around our coasts.

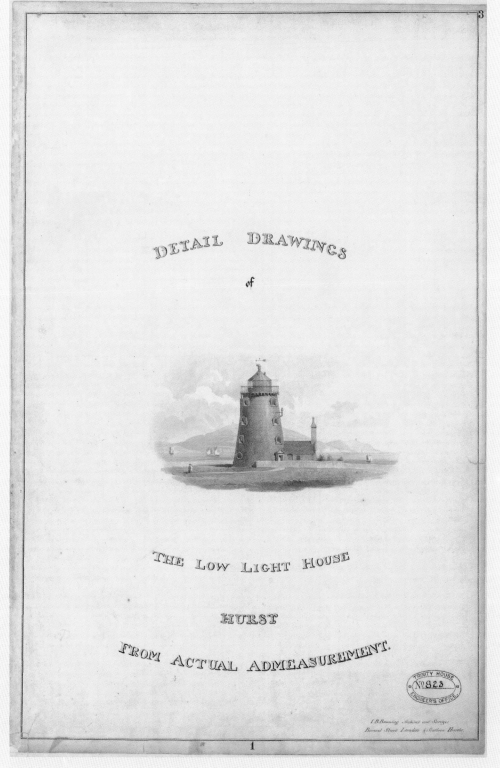

Most of the drawings in this book, like this of Les Hanois (facing), have been in the public domain for some time, but those of Hurst Point (seen here and on pages 22 and 24), have only just come to the attention of Trinity House and are here reproduced for the first time. They are all now catalogued and held in the extensive Trinity House Archive.

Unfortunately the best light cannot penetrate fog, an all-too-common phenomenon on the British coast, and early fog signals relied upon the making of loud noises. Like the lights, these became coded, to identify the emitting lighthouse. Early attempts were somewhat erratic: carronades (small, short-barrelled cannon) were discharged. Later, electrical impulses were used to detonate charges of mercury fulminate, but these were dangerous to handle and, like the cannon, required much tedious labour, labour that was apt to lag behind the advertised intervals between explosions. Early lightvessels employed hand-turned emitters that blew a mournful blast by passing air across a reed. These were larger though similar to the fog signals then used by sailing ships. (Steamships could operate steam whistles and sirens.) It was the great physicist William Thomson, first Baron Kelvin who, as scientific adviser to Trinity House, suggested the use of compressed air. Under his guidance, a huge iron trumpet was installed at Trevose Head in north Cornwall in 1913, and the success of the instrument led to the development of the diaphone, an ear-splitting emitter that provided the basic fog signal during much of the Twentieth Century. From about

1965, this was partly superseded by multiple broadcasting electrical fog signals.

However, the demands of the modern ship require a better warning than a sound signal, which is only audible when within relatively short range of the emitting station and even then may be lost in the background rumble of a modern diesel engine and the noises of electronic equipment on the ship's bridge. The true fog signal has only been possible since the advent of radar during the Second World War and is provided by a device called the 'racon', a contraction of 'radar beacon'. The racon is an electronic responding device stimulated by an incoming signal from a ship's radar. The incoming signal triggers a transmission from the racon which, on the radar screen of the vessel, shows up as a dash or a series of dots and dashes to form an identifying code, indicating the object from

Facing top: A lightvessel's lantern curtained off during daylight hours.

Facing bottom: The sound emitter at St Bee's, once vital for navigation in fog.

Below: Compressed-air reservoirs at Portland Bill, now open to the public.

which it emanates. Thus, it is possible to characterise not merely an isolated lighthouse, but a lightvessel or buoy perhaps surrounded by anchored ships, fishing vessels, or other obstructions. Moreover, since the racon is passive until activated, it is extremely efficient in its use of power.

For the greater part of their history, most of these devices, whether lighting apparatus or fog signal, have required the hand of man to ensure they worked reliably. Initially the job of a lighthouse keeper meant the humping of coal and the stoking of a fire. A man and his wife lived on a station and toiled every night, come wind, rain, or fog for the ultimate financial benefit of an absentee owner and in the pious hope of providing the passing mariner with a warning of danger. In addition to the benefit of their accommodation they received a pittance by way of a wage. The gradual introduction of lightvessels and offshore lighthouses with increasingly sophisticated equipment under the proper management of Trinity House, bred a new profession with its own high standards, imbued with the virtues of service to the public good. Many land-based lights continued to be run by a husband and wife until the advent of automation and, indeed, were comfortable stations offering a pleasantly quiet way of life for senior lighthouse keepers.

Offshore the keepers and lightsmen worked under a more rigorous roster system, punctuated by the active flurry of 'the relief'.

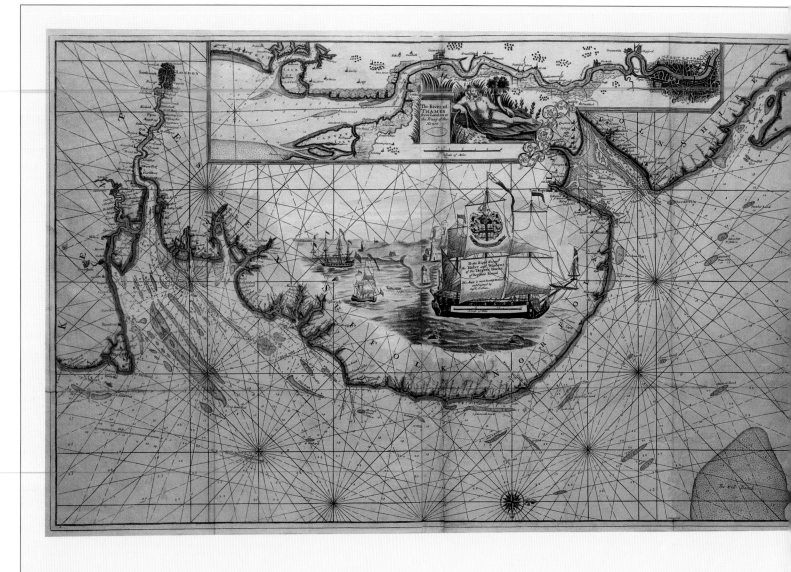

Charting the British Coast

Late in the Seventeenth Century, when Samuel Pepys was Secretary to the Admiralty and Master of Trinity House, remarkably little surveying had been carried out in British waters. To partially address this in 1681 the Admiralty commissioned a complete survey of all the coasts around Great Britain and appointed Captain Greenvile Collins to carry out the work. Collins was a Younger Brother of Trinity House and he was supported by the Corporation.

By 1688 120 plans of harbours and coastal areas had been prepared. Five years later forty-eight of the plans had been engraved and published in *Great Britain's Coasting Pilot* – it was the first English-language pilot book to cover the whole British coast including the offshore islands of Orkney, Shetland and Scilly. Fourteen editions were published over the next hundred years but, in spite of its many inaccuracies, few changes were made.

Perhaps seeking to improve matters both at home and abroad, by 1740 the Admiralty had appointed a drawing master at Portsmouth. In 1754 *The Elements of Navigation*, a seminal textbook on the subject was published and included a section on the surveying of coasts and harbours. At last, in 1795, the Admiralty established the Hydrographers' Department and Alexander Dalrymple was appointed as the first 'Hydrographer to the Board of Admiralty'. Dalrymple was not a naval officer but the distinguished hydrographer to the Honourable East India Company. Upon his death in 1808 Captain Thomas Hurd was appointed to the position and it was he who set up a regular system of nautical surveys from which, in 1811, the Hydrographic Office published a series of charts of the English Channel.

In 1848 the Department reported to Parliament that, since its earliest days, it had been progressing with its remit to produce charts of British waters around the world but that, in the previous decade in particular, the work load had been greatly increased, that the department had then employed 1,227 personnel and that large tracts of the British coasts had been surveyed. In later detail, the same report revealed

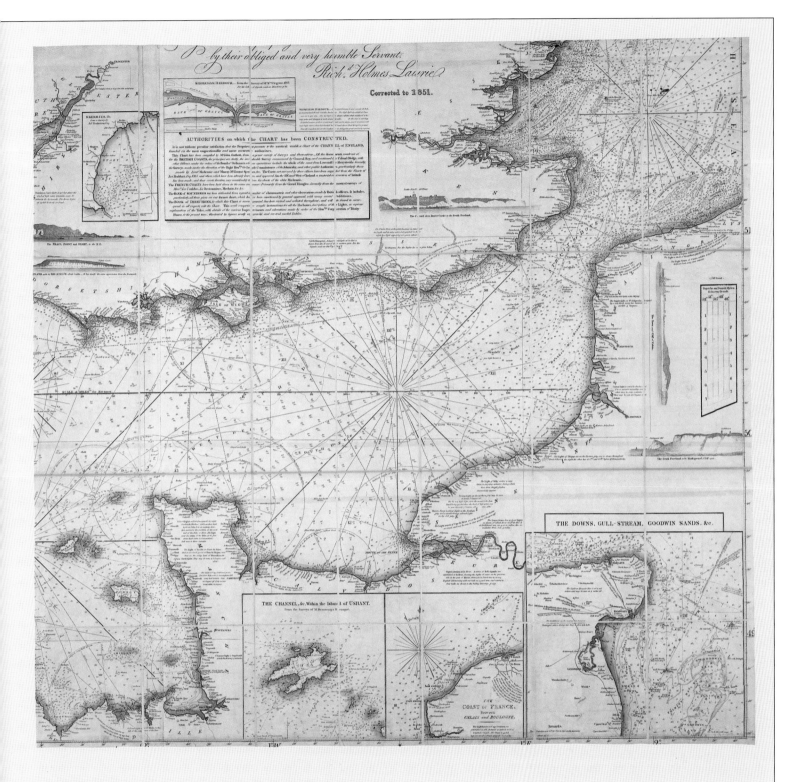

that for most of the South Coast of England few charts had any 'of that accurate detail' that the Admiralty considered necessary. Updates and amendments were required and, indeed, were made. *Notices to Mariners* had begun in 1834 with the support of the then Hydrographer Sir Francis Beaufort. The *Notices* are still published and allow the Hydrographic Department to make public note of changes around the coast

without having to print new charts every year. Today some 3,000 *Notices* are published annually to which Trinity House contributes regularly.

In addition to the Royal Navy's work, many commercial charts were produced in the Nineteenth Century by private companies for merchant shipping. Some such companies still exist and their charts are used by many of today's yachtsmen.

Facing: A curiously orientated chart of the East Anglian coast and the River Thames, dedicated to Trinity House but the cartographer Captain Greenvile Collins.

Above: A mid-Nineteenth-Century commercial chart of the English Channel and Strait of Dover by Henry Laurie.

This transfer of lighthouse keepers by sea, begun in the days of sail, was ongoing until comparatively recent times. The entire manpower for a District's offshore stations was embarked in the local tender and then transferred to each light by the vessel's motor launch. Subject to the weather, late reliefs of lighthouse keepers were not unknown, particularly on such difficult and dangerous locations as the Wolf Rock, exposed as it was to the full fury of the Atlantic. Even on a relatively calm day, the low Atlantic ground swell, generated by a depression perhaps many hundreds of miles out to the west, could suddenly sweep across the small landing to dash men from their footholds and swamp any boat in the vicinity. Overdue reliefs caused domestic disharmony and occasionally malnutrition, with lighthouse keepers running out of the rations they had to provide for themselves. The commitment to a relief also tied up the tenders, whose buoy-maintenance programmes could fall behind if such a delay was prolonged.

In 1969 the first experimental reliefs were carried out on the West Coast of England and Wales using a helicopter. The success of these trials initiated a programme of fitting a helipad to every lightvessel as it came in for routine dry-docking and to the providing of a similar facility at each

Left: The powerful electric lamps in this lighting unit at Pendeen are backed up by a reserve acetylene burner seen here between them.

Facing: Attendant Peter Williams and the light in St Ann's Head Lighthouse

Tower-Top Helipads

To modernise lighthouses with helipads required some ingenious engineering. The helipads were fitted above the lanterns; complex helical lattices of steel supports were grounded in the upper courses of stonework and extended upwards around the lantern to provide the structural strength for a flat platform. The lattice had to coincide exactly with the lantern astragals, so that the intensity of the light remained unimpaired. The design of such a contrivance had to take into consideration the stresses induced by strong winds blowing across the horizontal plane of a pad high above sea level. Such strains on the structure of the tower were unforeseen by the original lighthouse builders and so the horizontal plating was held in place by sacrificial bolts that, in storm-force winds, sheered off and jettisoned small sections of the pad, leaving it useable and largely intact. The loss of such plating in a gale is not uncommon.

Smalls Lighthouse

lighthouse. In many cases it was possible to clear an area of rock and top it off with a levelled concrete landing pad, but in the case of the remote rock towers, such as the Wolf Rock and the Eddystone, this was not possible and helipads had to be built atop the lighthouses themselves.

By the last quarter of the Twentieth Century, the possibilities of electronics were suggesting more innovations in the efficient provision of aids to navigation – even at sea in an environment intrinsically inimical to electronics. Early experiments in automation were not without their setbacks, however. The first major project was the Large Navigational Buoy, known by its acronym: Lanby. This was an unmanned buoy of 40 feet diameter, exhibiting a light of power comparable to a lightvessel and also fitted with a fog signal and, if required, a racon. Its purpose was to replace the conventional lightvessel hull with concomitant savings on maintenance. Initial trials in 1971 proved a degree of feasibility and a succession of modifications followed. These, however,

were running alongside a programme of lightvessel automation.

Simultaneously, concerted efforts were in hand not just to provide a remote automatic aid to navigation, but also to build an intelligent unit, capable of reporting back to a base station if all was not well. Such an installation could obviously be fitted to either a floating or a fixed aid, and as electronic control systems proliferated and developed quickly, a series of Lanbys and automatic lightvessels appeared. Oddly, but perhaps unsurprisingly, it was the original sea-kindly lightvessel hull that proved the most enduring practical platform on which to deploy the latest generation of remote, electronic packages. By the end of May 1989 the last manned lightvessel had been withdrawn from the Channel station and thereafter groups of offshore lights, whether borne by a lightvessel, lighthouse, or Lanby, were grouped under a controlling area base station ashore. These area base stations were situated in major coastal lighthouses, so that the keepers were now

Navigational Buoys

In the Nineteenth Century, the first buoys were unlit, but a century later first carbide, then oil gas and, finally, acetylene, operating a sophisticated automatic flasher, provided a floating buoy with a characteristic light pattern of its own. Such buoys could even be fitted with coded fog signals, first by means of a carbon-dioxide-powered bell, later by small electric fog signals. In addition, lower and more random technology was available from either a wave-activated bell, or whistle. Twentieth Century electronics also enabled racons to be fitted to buoys, but the replacement of acetylene by electrical power was always frustrated by the lack of endurance in battery capacity. However, by the beginning of the 1980s, even in the temperate zones of the world, solar power was beginning to be a realistic option, with solar panels capable of recharging batteries upon which a regular, deep-cyclical demand was made. At the same time battery technology facilitated the adoption of solar energy for the illumination of buoys by providing cells with sufficient reserves to survive and produce power during the short days and long nights of medium- to high-latitude winters. Further endurance was required for possibly prolonged periods of overcast skies during anti-cyclonic high-pressure weather systems; that these often occur in winter only compounded the problem. Trinity House adopted an ambitious, rolling programme which was not without its set-backs in successive gloomy winters, but ultimately triumphed. The end-product, the self-sufficient solar-powered lighted buoy, unlike its acetylene predecessor, requires only one annual visit to inspect its moorings as well as its steel body.

Right: A 10-tonne Class One buoy is lifted aboard a Trinity House Vessel for servicing.

Facing top: A working party from THV Mermaid attend a fault on the North Shipwash buoy.

Facing bottom: The East Channel light-float.

Above: A series of photographs taken during the building of Beachy Head Lighthouse in 1901.

Facing: The accommodation block and light-tower prefabricated ashore at Newhaven for the Royal Sovereign lies on its camels, ready for moving into position offshore, 1971.

responsible not just for a single station, but for a group of them. This 'grouping' marked the high-water mark of the lighthouse keeper's professional development. Like all high waters, it did not last long, for the remorseless advances in technology were already past the experimental stage.

Solar power, first used by Trinity House on navigational buoys, was becoming increasingly reliable and was clearly capable of greater exploitation. Many lighthouses possessed areas capable of supporting solar panels. Moreover, lightvessels too, were large enough to be fitted with an array of solar cells and, as a result of widespread conversion, major savings in fuel have been achieved.

Such radical changes in the provision of aids to navigation could not be made without a widespread consultative exercise. Known as the 'Navaid Review', this was carried out in 1987 and reported an over-provision of aids to navigation in the waters of the United Kingdom. It suggested that a slight drop in the number of stations was possible, with small reductions in light ranges within a philosophy of general rationalisation. It coincided too, with government strictures on the spending of public bodies. While Trinity House, as one of three General Lighthouse Authorities in the British Isles, derived its income by the continuing levying of light-dues upon ships visiting English, Welsh, Scottish, and Irish ports, it was clear that reductions in running costs were a necessity to avoid expenditure exceeding income. The possibilities of cost savings on manpower were already impacting on all areas of the Trinity House Service. By 1986 solar power had enabled the number of Trinity House Vessels to be reduced to two large, multi-functional tenders, whose operation with helicopter support had become very efficient. On the industrial front, an overhaul of working practices in the various buoy-yards, the introduction of mechanised scaling

and shot-blasting, and the application of modern epoxy protective coatings to buoys, had resulted in a steady erosion of the workforce.

By the early 1990s the final phase of automation began as the studies of fuller remote control began to bear fruit. It was intended to remove any vestige of local control from the area base stations; thus 'grouping' was doomed and with it the profession of lighthouse keeper. Control would be achieved by centralising operations at a single place, an Operational Control Centre (OCC) at the primary depot of the Trinity House Service at Harwich in Essex. Out on site, each lighthouse, now known as an 'out-station', would be looked after on a periodic basis by a part-time 'attendant'.

The development work necessary to bring this to fulfilment required the provision of a system that not only reported in from every station under the surveillance of the Operational Control Centre when a defect had arisen, but also 'talked and shook hands'. This system would establish that all was operating normally and that the communication link between the outstation and the Operational Control Centre was fully maintained.

The Work of the Trinity House Vessels

Before the introduction of a Service helicopter to carry the keepers and maintenance personnel to and from lighthouses, all offshore operations were carried out by District Tenders. Formerly Trinity House Depots existed at Holyhead, Swansea, Penzance, East Cowes, Harwich, and Great Yarmouth, with industrial workshops at Blackwall on the Thames; with the exception of the last, each was supported by a tender. In fact, owing to the workload in the outer Thames Estuary and the Strait of Dover, four tenders were based at Harwich.

lightvessel on station; tanks of fresh water or oil to be pumped ashore into a lighthouse; stores bound for a difficult and often damp landing at a lighthouse. They also conveyed the keepers and their provisions to and from their lighthouses, a duty that called for perfect local knowledge, cool heads and a high standard of seamanship from the crews.

In addition to their boat-handling skills at lighthouses, the maintenance of buoys engaged the tender crews in some hair-raising

The ship's crew, too, demonstrated considerable skill in such operations, the lowering and recovery of the launch required fine judgement on the part of all hands, and the ship would give what protection she could while the much smaller motor launch was in the water.

Although Trinity House Vessels were fitted with helicopter decks by which means stores, oil, and water were transferred to lighthouses in the later years of their service, the *Winston Churchill* and her three sisters *Mermaid*, *Siren* and *Stella*, proved too small to handle the largest class of buoy, especially after the introduction of the universal standards of the IALA Buoyage System were introduced in 1977. Thus, this class of vessel was gradually phased out, along with the old, 1938-built *Patricia*, to be replaced by two multi-functional tenders of over 2,000 tons.

Despite many changes in technology, buoy maintenance remains the bread-and-butter work of Trinity House Vessels. It can be undertaken in surprisingly poor conditions and occasionally, as when a new and dangerous wreck requires urgent buoying to warn shipping of its uncharted presence, buoys are laid in extreme weather. It is not unknown for a 10 tonne buoy, with a 5 tonne cast-iron sinker and 100 metres of heavy steel chain to be laid in wind strengths of Force 9. Such dangerous operations require the closest co-operation between the vessel's Commander, his Navigating Officer, and the seamen on the buoy-deck working under the direction of the First Officer.

THV *Winston Churchill* was the last of a class of four diesel-electric-powered vessels built between 1959 and 1964. Originally based at East Cowes, the steady contraction of the fleet saw her finish her service on the West Coast, where she was responsible for all aids to navigation between the Solway Firth and Lyme Bay. She was of 1,430 gross registered tons and equipped with two heavy motor launches capable of carrying two tons deadweight. The launches handled a variety of cargoes: a 15 fathom 'shackle' of heavy anchor cable to replace a worn length in a

enterprises. In the days of oil-gas and acetylene buoys, the occasional extinguishing of a lantern in extreme weather required the prompt attention of a Trinity House Vessel. Often lowered in appalling, storm-force conditions, the motor launch's coxswain would lay his boat as close to the bucking buoy as he dared. An officer and a seaman would then jump on to the defective buoy and rectify the fault, after which came the difficult job of withdrawing the men without injury. This process might take over an hour and require the transfer of equipment to and from the ship.

As well as the obvious attributes of motor launches, a 20 tonne derrick and heavy duty capstans, the modern Trinity House Vessels *Patricia* and *Mermaid* carry sophisticated manoeuvring systems comprising twin screws, twin rudders, and an azimuthal bow-thruster. They are also fitted with a range of electronic instrumentation that includes ARPA radar, GPS, Sonar and

This page clockwise from top left: The second Patricia was built in 1938. Her extended quarterdeck was originally fitted as a gun mounting on the outbreak of WWII.
She remains afloat as a night-club in Stockholm.
An Elder Brother's cabin.
The Elder Brethren's smoking room.
The foredeck.

Facing: THV Patricia, built in 1982, is the third vessel to bear the name.

Below Left: THV Winston Churchill, built in 1964, is shown here in about 1980 after modifications for operating with a helicopter. She has since been sold out of service.

Below: The Elder Brethren of Trinity House exercising their prescriptive right of preceding HM The Queen in the Royal Yacht Britannia in UK pilotage waters.

high-grade echo-sounding equipment.

Prior to the decommissioning of HMY *Britannia*, it was the prescriptive right of the Elder Brethren to escort HM The Queen to sea in Home Waters. The workmanlike *Patricia* thus annually preceded the Royal Yacht out of Portsmouth, the only vessel allowed to do so, seeing the *Britannia* clear of the dangers of land before detaching and executing a smart 'steam past', her crew at the rail, the Elder Brethren paraded on her helicopter flight deck. This little ceremony was invariably acknowledged by Her Majesty in person.

As had occurred with the introduction of previous innovations, specialised training was necessary. The concept of centralised operational superintendence had been the task of the Operational Control Centre for over a decade. What the new system did was to combine all the new technologies and fully orchestrate hands-on control from this single facility, which was fully commissioned by 1991. The duty officers manning the Operational Control Centre today are all master mariners with considerable sea-experience, and they remain the full-time link between the Trinity House Service and the mariner at sea. But they are now supplemented by a roster of 'monitoring officers', whose task continues to be keeping watch on all the lighthouses and lightvessels under the management of Trinity House. It is these men and women, with their banks of screens and keyboards, together with specialised maintenance teams, and attendants, who today 'keep' the lighthouses of Trinity House.

At the turn of the millennium, the lighthouse remains an important aid to navigation. While the mariner enjoys the assistance of electronic aids on the bridge of his ship, and while these include the impressive and highly accurate Global Positioning System (GPS), a failure of any of these can prove disastrous. Should such an event occur, either from external causes such as the destruction of the GPS satellite constellation, or an internal cause such as a power failure, the lighthouse remains as a fail-safe and reliable seamark. Few other 'inventions' have such a long history, for the lighthouse is almost as old as that of seagoing ships themselves.

The medieval lighthouse in England was usually in the charge of a lonely recluse, an anchorite or hermit who endured his self-imposed exile for spiritual reasons. Centuries later, in the high age of Victorian achievement, the lighthouse keeper had a job that, in its way, was at the cutting edge of technology. Today, the keeper has gone, swept aside by the very systems he helped to nurture; his ancient calling has been reduced to a handful of shore-bound watch-keepers who sit at the centre of an electronic web, watching for and reacting to problems as and when they arise.

Technical staff carry out planned preventative maintenance and are on call to be dispatched when trouble occurs. They are flown out by helicopter, transported by launch, or conveyed by a Trinity House Vessel, depending upon the nature and location of the task, to join the attendants appointed to each lighthouse who make periodic visits to keep things tidy and who undertake the 'light house-keeping' of the old joke.

For the most part, however, the remote rocks and skerries have passed back to the guillemots and the razorbills, the puffins and the gulls. Where the Atlantic grey seals lumber ashore to keen in the wind, adopting the posture that the ancients thought of as mermaids, there is still the surge of the sea and the passing of the winds. Man has retreated, returning to the land whence he came, but he has left behind him the great, granite monolith of his passing, and it still hums with power. Communicating with its unseen controller many miles away, it still shines its warning to the mariner at sea.

Though unmanned, the lighthouses on the British coast are still a reassuring sight for today's mariners.

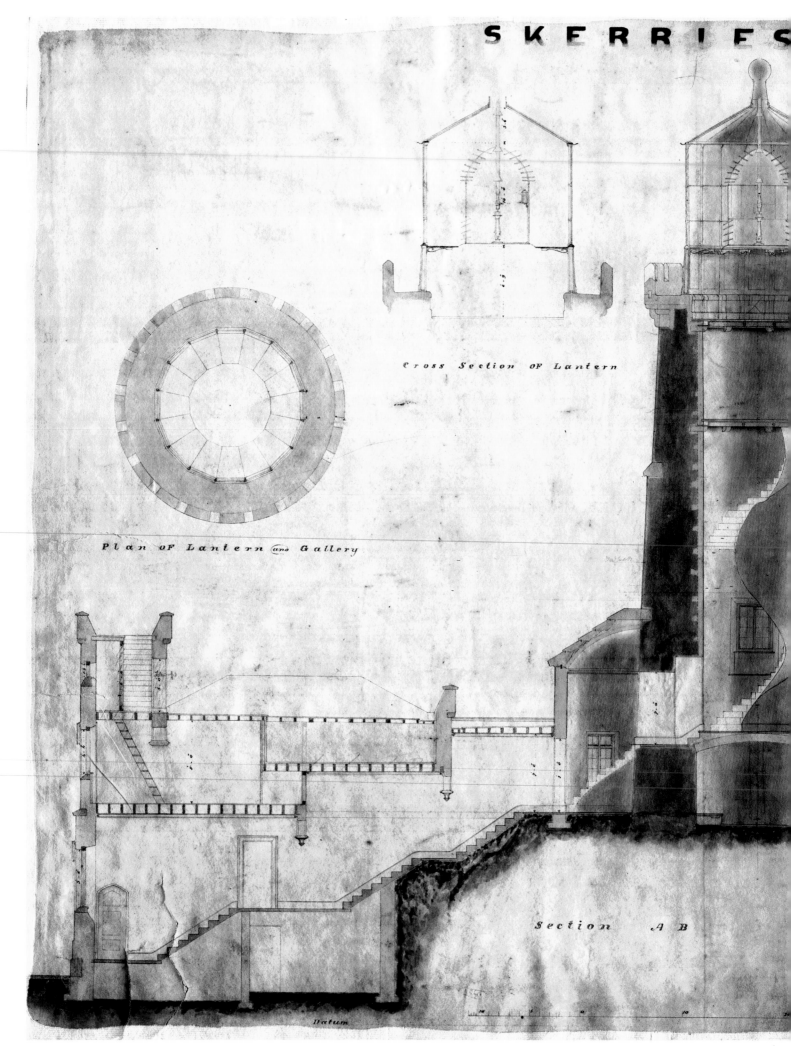

SKERRIES

Cross Section of Lantern

Plan of Lantern and Gallery

Section A B

Datum

44

Section E F

No 1777

Datum

Section C D

The Lighthouse Keepers

then. And he would get up and have his breakfast and then you would start cooking the dinner.

Going back a few years you might have had the old Hamco oil stove for cooking on. I mean they were a bugger, keeping the bloody same temperature – a pain in the bum! In fact really the old coke ones were better, you knew where you were. But in the last fifteen years or whatever, it was all electric so there was no problem. You would cook the dinner; usually on the table for about 12.30pm.

Terry Johns: And after dinner the two who hadn't cooked used to toss a coin for jobs:

whoever wins is all right, the one who loses has to do the washing up. I mean, it sounds stupid when you hear it, but it was a bit of fun to keep the place going.

Bill Arnold: After that we'd have a game of cards or something, then about 1.30pm you'd go and get your head down. So there was only a couple of hours around lunchtime when there wasn't anybody in bed. Then you might get up again about 6pm so there would be nobody in bed from 6pm till about say 10pm – when the bloke who was on at midnight would go and get his head down for a couple of hours and that's how it went on….

A melding of the old and the new: Nash Point lighthouse as a base monitoring and control station in 1992. The Principal Keeper, Mr Nat Illston, calls up an out-station report on his VDU.

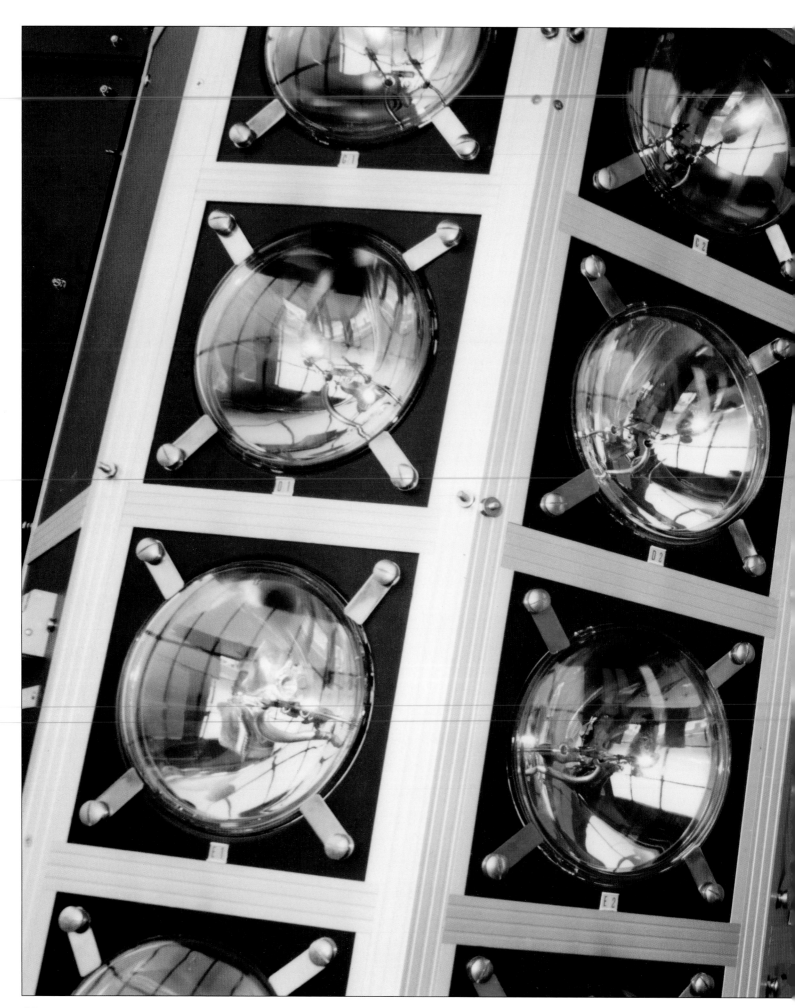

Eddie Matthews: Of course there are other little rules and routines. Like, for example, every middle watch, that is 12 to 4, which is every third day, the other two men would be in bed, and that's your turn to have a bath. And you never came down if you knew the man was in the bath – things like that.

All the comforts of home

The domestic facilities of lighthouses were little changed from their Nineteenth Century state until their automation in the 1980s. The lighting equipment may have been altered over the years but the structure and fittings and the daily way of life for the keepers did not really change until the relief by helicopters began. John Ball's account of the Longships in 1896 is remarkably similar to the recent keepers' reminiscences of their early days on the rock towers of the 1960s and 1970s.

John Ball: On entering the bottom room, you see ropes & landing gear stowed away ready for use, also the tank for keeping the [light]house supplied with water, that having to be brought from the shore. Then comes the coal room, in which there is a pump, for pumping water from the lower room up to a tank in the kitchen, then comes the store room, in which there are roomy cupboards for each keeper, also a cask for each man to keep potatoes in. Then there is also a Magazine for storing our fog signal explosives. We next come to our oil room, where we have large tanks for oil, also our lifeboat signals; next we come to our kitchen or living room, then

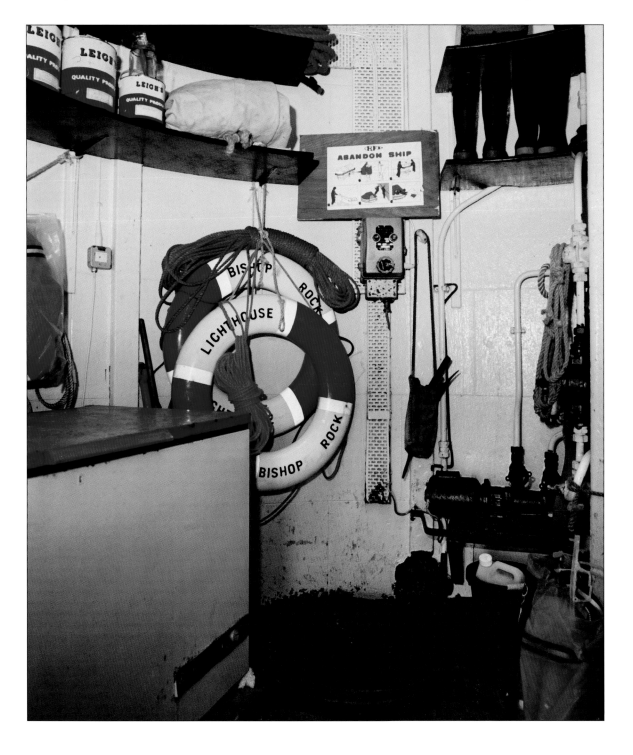

Storage space was always at a premium in a rock tower. From freezer to seaboots, essential items are neatly stowed in the entrance at Bishop Rock. Note the manhole leading down into the water reservoir.

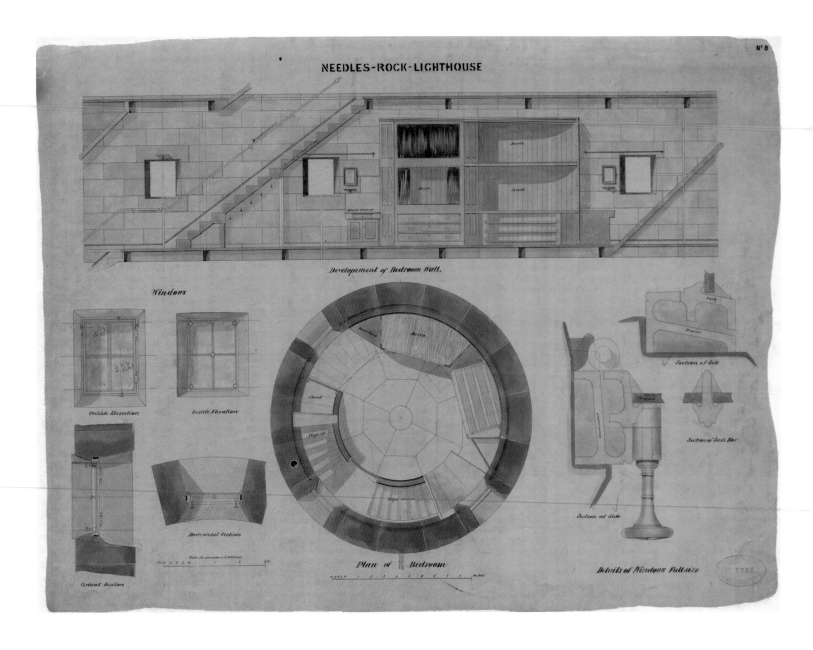

Developement of Bedroom Wall.

Windows

Outside Elevation

Inside Elevation

Horizontal Section

Vertical Section

Plan of Bedroom

Section of Sill

Section of Sash Bar

Section at Side

Details of Windows Full-size

The bedroom area in the Needles Lighthouse.

comes our bedroom in which there are five bunks, the two top ones being used for any Mechanic that may have to be here. We have also a cupboard here, in which we have a good supply of tinned meat kept in reserve, then comes the service room and lantern, in which everything looks bright and clean; how nice everything is, yes, but there are times when things do not look so pleasant, and that is when there is a change coming, then they would see the walls and the floors running with water, and everything you touch feeling cold and clammy. Then again with a heavy sea on (and we do get some heavy seas now and then, I have seen it myself come down the chimney and on to the kitchen range), and all the shutters closed up, making the [light]house look very dark and miserable. Or then again when there is a thick fog on for a couple of days not being able to get out, and one continual booming going on with

the fog signal, sleep then being out of the question, they would then see that we have a few discomforts to put up with, and that everything was not always so nice as it looked. But give us fine weather so that we can get out for exercise and fresh air, and also good cheerful mates then we are as happy and comfortable as can be.

Bill Arnold: The lights vary but in general you've got the lantern, underneath the lantern you've got what they used to call a service room, and then under the service room would be a bedroom, and then under the bedroom would be the kitchen. The bedroom would have five bunks – three on the bottom, two on the top. So you could have two visiting Mechanics or Electricians [to carry out routine plant maintenance]. During automation we even had a bloody camp bed on what little bedroom floor there was as well, so we had six. And at one

point on the Bishop [Rock] we had seven – seven blokes on there! With three of you it can be hard going, but when there's seven!

Eddie Matthews: Those banana beds – you've got the curve of the lighthouse, you see. You get used to it, you bend into the curve. Some people got back problems, especially the taller ones. I am only a short arse so I was OK and I was in charge so I had the privilege of the middle bed – because that was the biggest one. But the taller lads had to scrunch up a bit and that wasn't so funny. The bunks are all curtained off so basically when you get into bed you are on your own. And of course everybody learned, in later years, to sneak around on tiptoe because the doors have to be left open because it got so damn hot from the engines.

There was very little heating – paraffin and, of course, you got those Tilley lamps. The

continuous hiss of those things; very smelly too; everything smelt. If you came ashore – my god, you'd take your uniform off and it was still stinking of diesel.

Dermot Cronin: The heating that you had was a solid-fuel burner in the kitchen, inside the wall itself, and that took the chill off the bedroom. That was it. You had to keep the condensation down, keep it dry. You'd batten down, which you had to do in winter times in stormy weather, and then the condensation would run on the inside of the tower so you had to keep the windows open for ventilation. Now in latter years, places like the Bishop Rock where…you were running an engine, the heat of the engine would go up through the tower and warm the place, just take the edge off.

You didn't have a lot of light to read by. There was no light back in the early days, no electric lighting. I was on the Smalls in 1966 where we had a generator which charged a set of batteries which ran battery lights. You had a battery light on each floor, but I don't think you had one at each bunk and you only had one in the kitchen. But the warmest place on the station was up in the light room when the paraffin light was in at night. That was the place to go and read as well – you could read up there with perfect light!

A la carte

In the basic conditions on an offshore lighthouse food was a comfort. When keepers joined in the Fifties and Sixties the ways of cooking and preserving meat had changed little since the late Nineteenth Century. The keepers were taught to bake bread and preserve meat in jars. Proper dinners of meat and vegetables were produced at midday – a valuable ritual when the keepers could all get together. Later fridges and freezers and new foods came in, bringing changes, so this ritual faded away in some stations.

Eddie Matthews: There's three stages to do with food which show how things have changed. When I first started I went aboard with my fresh meat and vegetables. The meat would last two days and then I would have to cook it, pickle it and put it in a jar for the rest of the time. The fresh veg would go into the open window for two or three days and you could eat it for four days. Now the second stage was when we were given paraffin fridges; you had to watch them or they'd end up defrosting on you. Then, of course, the next stage was when the engine rooms came in, then there were freezers so there was no problem. And those three stages took over forty years!

Dermot Cronin: When I first joined fresh food would only last you possibly ten days or a fortnight. Then you would have to go onto tinned [supplies]. A lot of tinned food. In those days you didn't even have dried milk – you had condensed milk. One particular keeper did not even put it in his tea, he would spoon it out or make sandwiches out of it. Everybody to his own way. I was on the Holyhead [Breakwater] light for five years when I first joined and there was a grocer called Davey Green [in the town], he did a service for Morecambe Bay [Lightvessel], Skerries, Bardsey, South Stack, South Bishop, Smalls, and all those lighthouses. Every month he would do food for the keepers in a wooden box. He was very good but there was only one thing, supposing you

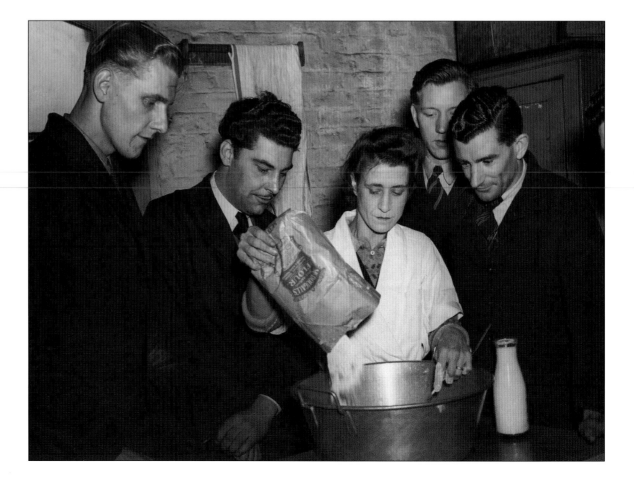

Supernumerary Keepers undergoing training at Blackwall Workshops in the 1950s. The lesson in bread making seems to be absorbing the attention of the trainees!

asked for a packet of biscuits and he didn't have it – he might put in a packet of toothpaste instead.

Bill Arnold: I always made sure I ate well. It was better after freezers came in. For twenty-eight days I would take seven lamb chump chops, seven pieces of chicken, seven pork chops and some beef, and a bit of steak and some liver, and the standard couple of pounds of sausages to fill in, and bacon, and I always used to take myself a treat – because there were times when you were out there and you thought, I just fancy a bar of chocolate, or something, and you couldn't nip down to the shop. It's those little things that you miss if you don't take them. And going back before that, I mean before my time, the keepers used to pot their own meat. They would take the meat out with them and then, within the first couple of days, they would boil it all up and bloody stick it in jars and pour fat over it and seal it and then just open it up as-and-when they wanted it.

We had to take all this food and stuff out with us, of course. You used to pack it all in these red plastic boxes which Trinity provided.

You could get nine of them in the back of a helicopter – three each for the keepers – so that was it really for your grub, plus a sack of spuds or whatever, and the chopper would end up doing a couple of trips to get all your gear up. And you knew that if you didn't take it with you, you wouldn't have it. But you always kept in your own cupboard emergency rations and tins of this and that, that you could open if you were overdue [being relieved].

The midday meal was a time for all the keepers to gather together – although the variable quality of the cooking caused some problems.

Bill Arnold: Every third day you were cook. But remember, there were some good cooks and some bloody awful cooks! Some really couldn't boil a bloody egg. And when it was their turn to cook you made sure that one of you was handy to make sure that you got a dinner. It wasn't unusual to have your dinner served up to you as burnt offerings. But the standard thing at dinner time was thick onion gravy. You just added to whatever gravy was left over from the day before.

Although fitted with a helipad, relief of the Needles Lighthouse was generally carried out by local boat from Yarmouth, Isle of Wight. Here stores are passed ashore.

Dermot Cronin: Funnily enough in those days you didn't have many vegetarians and most people smoked. I will always remember one Principal Keeper, Bob Ratty, who was well known for his puddings. He would tell you exactly what to bring out to the rock – apples etc – and if you didn't make a pudding he would make it for you – apple crumble, I remember. Very good.

Mike O'Sullivan: Discipline was very, very strict even as far as cooking was concerned. We used to cook every third day and some cooks were terrible. If lunch or dinner wasn't ready at a certain time you could be in trouble. In those days the food never changed, it was the same basic thing every day: meat, vegetables and potatoes, followed by a great big steam duff. A lot of PKs insisted on this steam duff and some of the supernumerary would say, 'we don't know how to make this stuff', and the PK would say, 'then you'd better learn quick!'

Then a big change took place, in 1973, I think. That was the biggest change I found in the job where they reduced the tour of duty on the rocks from eight weeks to four. At the same time the helicopters took over gradually and made a big difference. And on top of that they had a big recruiting drive because of double manning. New crowd of people came in – different type of person shall we say, different to the old hands – a lot of them were ex-university students.

This new crowd that came in, they changed the job completely. They weren't prepared to tolerate the old fuddy duddy ways of the old PKs – although discipline wasn't compromised – but they had their own ways. Even the eating habits changed, new foods came in like curries and lasagne and they ate when they felt like it [at] all hours of the day. Some of the foods, the old PKs hadn't even heard of. And this was resented…. I liked it – it was a breath of fresh air. Off duty the discipline was more relaxed but we still did our job.

From time to time there were medical emergencies. The Keepers possessed basic first aid skills, but occasionally matters grew serious.

Eddie Matthews: We had a big medical book, but they'd fly out doctors if it was really bad – and if they could. It all depends how bad it was. We had automatic access to a doctor for whatever and, of course, we'd phone him and he would ask for all the gen, but if we couldn't handle it, if we were in a storm, God help the bloke. You would have to do your best for him.

The long hours

Despite the demands of their routine duties, the Keepers had to pass the time and often developed unusual hobbies.

John Ball: People wonder how we can manage to pass away our time off here, well it is a very dull monotonous life, but we manage to get over it very well, by passing our time away after our duty is done, by fishing, carpentering, knitting and various other things, nothing coming amiss to us, so with good cheerful mates, rock life is not by any means to be despised.

Eddie Matthews: That was one of the best things about being on a lighthouse. Think about it, I'm off duty now, right? I can sit down, I can go fishing, I can paint, I can do anything, I can write poetry – as life is going nowhere. Of course, when I first started there was no television out there and nothing like that, so I would love to read. I have learnt a hell of a lot from books. There was a time when I wasn't bothered with flaming books, but out there I loved to read. Newspapers – now that's my delight. My wife used to save them all so when the mid-relief came I'd get twenty-four newspapers and I'd go through them all. It's a better way of learning. You go to school, they try to cram something into you in six months, but if you could take a couple of years, you start taking it in and we had the time to do that.

One of THV Satellite's *motor launches hauling a man off from the Eddystone in about 1950. Note the heavy coir bow lines running up to mooring points on the lighthouse landing, from where the photograph has been taken. Hidden by the suspended keeper, a warp runs astern to an anchor, dropped as the boat approached the landing.*

Assistant Keepers Richard Packer (left) and John Dobinson discuss the news.

A game of cribbage on Beachy Head.

Dermot Cronin: It was a time for hobbies basically. Ships in bottles...most people had some hobby. Even now you still have people who have hobbies. Barry Hawkins was [good at] painting, Bob Collis did ships in bottles....

Terry Johns: I remember a time when after every lunch it was either cribbage, or three handed euchre, or Scrabble every day, and in the evenings we would go on to more serious stuff like a game of chess or something like that. We used to work with the ornithological people as well. We used to go round and help them with their bird counts. That was better, you had somebody else to talk to and spend a bit of time with. That was nice – up on Coquet Island. We used to get the old terns – especially when they were nesting in the summer – thousands of puffins. And rabbits; the rabbits used to swim in the sea.

Mike O'Sullivan: Most of the keepers had hobbies; everyone had a hobby of some sort. Strange thing happened though: these hobbies that everybody had – ships in bottles, painting (some lovely painters in the job) all sorts of marquetry – as soon as the TV came all the hobbies seem to stop overnight. As a matter of fact one chap, although he had this hobby of making ships in bottles which used to keep him occupied most of the time, he couldn't have been all that interested because as soon as the TV arrived he threw everything out the window into the sea – all his bottles and his little ships models and his tools as if so say, 'now the TV is here I won't need these any more'! Wasn't that strange? It's as if...it was just a way of passing the time. It was sad really; when the telly arrived that was it: he didn't want to do anything else and in case it would interfere with the telly he threw all his tools away. Mind you he wasn't very good at it really, he wasn't an expert.

Mike Williams: The TVs weren't supplied until late, the 1970s I think. The first lighthouse to get a TV was Bishop Rock – and that was donated to them – and I think the second was on the Needles and that was in the early Sixties. The one on the Needles was donated by the Lymington Flower Club and it had an inscription on it saying [so]. Not only did they present the television but they also repaired it because it used to break down quite often. I don't know why TV wasn't supplied [sooner]; perhaps because a keeper might watch it when he was on duty. I know in the old rule book

when you had to keep a watch in the lantern in the old days they could have a table and a chair and it said something like there was to be no piece of furniture where a keeper could recline – you couldn't have a sofa up there or anything like that. Of course when they had paraffin oil lamps you to stay in the service room and watch them all the time.

And we had boxes of books and magazines from the Missions to Seamen, The British Sailors' Society, and the Marine Society. They were ordinary books, all sorts of novels – just what you would see in the library. Have them for a couple of months and then the ship would come along and replace them. Came in proper little wooden boxes. We used to look forward to those.

Fishing from the landing at The Needles. This was a fine-weather activity and, even then, courted danger from an occasional heavy swell.

With proper attention to orders, the lightsmen aboard No17 at South Goodwin demonstrate their hobbies for the benefit of a Daily Herald *photographer in 1960.*

A fine drying day. A keeper does some 'dhoby' at Beachy Head.

Dermot Cronin: I did my radio amateur's exams in 1976 and I operated [radio] stations from the [Royal] Sovereign and South Stack. I have spoken to people all over the world. I could listen in to all over Europe. It was great because you had no interference on the station. I could talk with them at home as well and if you didn't have a telephone, messages could be relayed back and forth.

Eddie Matthews: That's right. But we kept our own [official radio wave-] band in case someone had to come in with an important message. Many a time I'd be on there yapping [to the keepers on another light] and all of a sudden a damn [Trinity House] ship comes up: 'Get off the bloody air, we want to talk to someone!'

Bill Arnold: When you were offshore, there were some good island lighthouses – where you could get outside the lighthouse and have a potter about, do a bit of potting or fishing or even swimming – [and] they were good places to be. But even on towers, Wolf Rock, Bishop Rock, Eddystone wherever, providing you were with a decent crew you could have a good time. Trinity left you alone on the towers because nobody wanted to go out there. Apart from the old Superintendents who would come out, nobody would bother you. You were left to your own devices. And, although you weren't supposed to have booze – and we didn't have it to that extent, I'm not talking about spirits, I used to take three litre boxes of wine out with me – a couple of glasses of plonk at the end of each day makes life bearable. Little things like that – if any of the mechanics or electricians or whoever were coming out to do some work, they would always bring a box out with them.

We used to have a good laugh, I mean the work got done, nothing got missed. You could never really be bored out there because there was always something to do. I mean, summer times we used to get up on the top on the helipad and I even took a windbreak out with me because that was the bugbear, there was always a bit of breeze, and I used to stick this bloody windbreak on the helipad and get behind it in the nude and sunbathe.

Terry Johns: And I used to grow all our veg in the garden if it was a good one. A lot of the lighthouses used to have lovely gardens.

Eddie Matthews: That was the other thing about lighthouses, the communication. Every morning all the rocks at 8.00am [would] call each other [over the radio-telephone on the dedicated District frequency] and say what the day's events are and then at 5pm, the afternoon watchmen call each other again and just check that everybody's all right.

Bill Arnold: TV drove me bloody crackers. On the lighthouses offshore they used to religiously watch all the bloody soaps. On some lighthouses to stop any arguments they would have a rota for what they were watching.

There used to be a lot of fishing. Some of them on the towers used to do kite fishing. I was very lucky – I was on Eddystone with a chap, dead and gone now, who was the bee's-knees at kite fishing. He used to make these kites, well I'm only 5'6", but they were as big as me. He used to make them out of the old rocket sticks and old lantern curtains. He had a job to lift these bloody things, but they flew all right. He would fly the kite off the lantern gallery of the tower, drop [it] onto the water and when he had a bite, the tail of the kite would dip which automatically lifted the face up a bit so he could fly it up again.

Dermot Cronin: That's right. I read a book about kite fishing in the 1950s and I tried it. Off the tail you would have maybe six feathers with bait on them. The feathers would move with the wave and as soon as the fish took the bait the kite would rise. I didn't believe this – but we actually got it to work. Although we had some disasters – we did lose kites, and we got into many a tangled mess. It was far easier to fish with rod and line but we were just experimenting.

Terry Johns: We used to have two or three different sizes of kite because the stronger the wind the smaller the kite would be, the lighter the wind the bigger the kite. The tail could be as long as the actual tower itself. And then when you caught a fish the kite would go up in the air and the fish would come up and just bang on the gallery rail and another keeper would open the kitchen window and pick the fish off the hook!

Bill Arnold: That's right. There'd be a tap on the bloody pipe and you'd be down in the kitchen and pull the tail in with a couple of mackerel on. Then you'd be gutting and cleaning them while the kite flyer got on with catching the next one. You tell people now you used to fish on a lighthouse with a kite and they look at you unbelieving like.

Dermot Cronin: We used to catch three- or four-pound bass and pollock – sometimes bigger.

Eddie Matthews: It put me off fishing for life! Now I only catch fish to eat, I wouldn't catch it for sport – to me it's not fair. But some of us used to judge lighthouses by the fish – the Wolf,

you could get the greatest pollock. The Eddystone – the best bass. The Lundys – a variety. Mackerel, the Longships. The Bishop was no good for fishing at all. But the Royal Sovereign was great, out in the Channel, that was mixed fishing. And, of course, we used to eat a lot of the fish.

Mike Williams: A lot of keepers fished and some used a boat for that purpose – not to go anywhere in particular just to fish. On the Royal Sovereign for example there was a place where people did a lot of fishing because it is so easy. You'd put a line over the side, go and watch *Coronation Street* and go out again and pick up some pollock it was that easy.

The BBC Home Service was an important feature in the keeper's life before the advent of television offshore.

Going home

But it was for their reliefs that the Keepers most keenly waited and the subject, with its threat of being overdue, was rarely out of their minds.

Mike O'Sullivan: I could never say people used to enjoy being out there on the towers. On the way out every single time there were chaps saying this would be their last trip and then the same thing would happen the following time – they were saying this for years, so obviously they weren't happy. Yet, when you got there, unpacked and settled down to work, it was OK then. When we used to do the eight weeks, the first two weeks went OK, the middle four weeks was a terrible time – if anything was going to happen, bad humours or anything like that it always happened in the middle four weeks. When it got to the last two weeks everyone bucked up and looked forward to the relief.

During the time when we used to do the eight weeks there were four permanent keepers to each station so we had four weeks off. What happened was three of them did four weeks together. We didn't have two Principal Keepers, the senior AK would act up, plus you needed a Supernumerary for a month in every three to bring the cycle back to normal and to keep the continuity.

There were one or two lighthouses like the Wolf Rock where, if you were overdue for a day short of three weeks it was cancelled altogether and we called it a lost relief [because] you would only have been ashore for one week – if you waited you got your whole four weeks off. It didn't often happen, they usually got the people off. The ships' crews did some reliefs in very bad weather.

In my experience Smalls was the worst place for getting on and off, unlike the Wolf, Bishop Rock, and where it was done by breeches buoy. At the Smalls, because of the nature of the

Leaving a rock lighthouse sometimes required more than simply stepping into the motor launch.

reef, the boat had to go in between two rocks. The boat's crews were marvellous, [negotiating] massive seas sometimes, which used to come over the back of the lighthouse and into the landing. You could only do the relief on half tide when it was ebbing. The rule was the boat used to wait twenty minutes after the last sea came over before they would attempt to go in, but sometimes you would wait and wait, sitting in the boat freezing cold about quarter of a mile off.

Terry Johns: My first posting was on Wolf Rock. That and the Smalls are the two worst in the job I think. And one of the main things I remember is that we hardly had any dry relief.... Nine times out of ten we got wet, unless it was a really calm day. Those buggers [the boat's crew at one end and the keepers at the other, working the breeches buoy at the Rock] always dipped you in the water....

But the other thing in them days there was a lot of danger when it came to relief. Getting on and off the lighthouses at the beginning and end of your stint out there. When you think of the experiences there for God's sake. Being hauled out of that boat with the sea pounding past you, we'd be up in the old breeches buoy and the coxswain of the boat just waiting his time and as the wave rose the bowman would say 'right get him up' and as the wave went by, the boat dropped and you were away – up into the air like. And of course they had to be quick because the next wave, if you were too low, the next wave would hit you and you would be soaking wet...for about two hours until the job was finished and you could go up [into the lighthouse] and get changed. When the helicopters came in to do the relief – with helipads on most of the lights – all that changed. That was the beginning of the modern age.

Eddie Matthews: Oh, Christ! the breeches buoy. It's like a sling, you put your feet through and if you just grip it there is no way that you can come out, [even] if you go into the water. Once I got dragged under the boat for God's sake. But I'm here to tell the tale, aren't I? Then of course we got the helicopters. I've been in this game forty-two years and I could see it modernising, you know.

Dermot Cronin: In the days when there were boat reliefs your life depended on the coxswain and the crew of that launch and you put your

trust in them – and I must say over the years I depended on them entirely. Your life was in their hands....

The power of the elements

The entire life of the keepers was influenced by the weather and the sea conditions. They were close observers of these and some even relished the drama of a storm which broke the monotony and held a numinous hint.

Terry Johns: You used to have green water going up over the top of you on the Wolf Rock. Even though they had storm shutters they were only like little flaps and I've been in my bed many a time when the storm shutters have smashed in. I used to enjoy it, it was quite fun really. Admittedly when I first went on there in a bad storm it was frightening, but you soon got used

A keeper at the Longships sends a message by semaphore to his wife ashore at the cottages at Sennen, 1946.

Right: Longships Lighthouse

bloody big storm. Normally when the sea hits the bottom of the tower, the tower shudders and has time to settle back before the next one hits. But this time, a wave hit the tower and it was shuddering, and within five seconds of that one hitting it... another bugger hit it and it went loopy... bloody alarms started going off and we thought – oh hell this is it!

Mike O'Sullivan: I was on South Stack where we experienced the worst storms, the cliffs are 100 feet high and the lighthouse stands on [the top of] them. On the southwest side there are eight windows along there, three bedrooms, the engine room and the battery room, and if the weather was that bad the sea came up and smashed all the windows – eight windows all smashed in. Terrible weather, never seen anything like it; for the sea or spray to go up that far and smash all those eight windows on that side and I remember there were three keepers there, PK Charlie Warmsley, myself, and one of the Occasional Keepers [these were part-time relief keepers employed locally in times of short-manning by the District Superintendent].

Far right: A boat relief to the Eddystone Lighthouse in a near gale.

to it. Coal buckets – I've seen them jump off the floor, six inches into the air, with the force of the waves hitting the rocks below the tower.

Eddie Matthews: We used to literally sit in the lamp [structure]; we had a big optic surrounding the lamp in those days, not like we got now. The story about the seventh wave going over the top – the seventh one usually was the biggest one – it's true. It smashed up around us. It's like being in a submarine in the middle of a storm.

Bill Arnold: When the weather was really bad, I used to go up and sit in the lantern on the Wolf and watch it. It was a sight – the bloody sea roaring...and smacking across the tower and rushing up over it. On Bishop Rock, I remember once, I had just been appointed Principal Keeper, and it was just after Christmas and just before the New Year and we had a

This was a Captain Hughes, an ex-coaster skipper he was. He must have been getting on for seventy. Charlie and I were up at the time and the Captain was in bed in one of the rooms where the windows were smashed in and of course there was a hole where the window was and the wind was so strong – he got out of bed and he couldn't open the door! He couldn't pull the door against the wind. He was shouting for us and it took three of us, would you believe – him inside pulling and Charlie and me shoving with our shoulders – to open the door

everybody except for one chap, and that was on an island so that didn't make any difference to me. So, in thirty-six years I only came up against one really awkward customer and that was over a stupid thing – not worth talking about. I got along with most people and there was always someone else coming out every month, a change, so I wasn't stuck with the same faces all the time.

Eddie Matthews: We used to have some wonderful nights out [ashore] because all the reliefs were roughly done at the same time [the Trinity House Vessel proceeding around all the stations in turn] so, in the South West here, you may get five crews ashore at the same time. So you would all go down the night before, or the day before, to grub-up at the grocers, to make your order and pack it and everything else. And of course you had the whole evening together and the comradeship was fantastic – the stories we could tell – it was lovely. Any outsider listening in would fall over laughing; we had a wonderful time.

Left: Smalls Lighthouse

Below: Delivering supplies to Smalls Lighthouse on a blustery day.

against the wind. When we got in, the place was flooded, there was about three inches of water lying on the floor. The old bloke's pyjamas were soaked and he picked a long piece of glass out of his pocket. Of course, he was saying afterwards that he went to get a pair of dry socks out of the drawer and the socks were floating in the drawer! He said he had spent all his life at sea on coasters and in fifty years at sea this was the first time he had ever got wet in his bunk. He had to go to a lighthouse to get wet in his bunk!

Getting along together

Maintaining a good relationship with their colleagues was imperative if three souls were to co-exist in a confined space for weeks on end.

Terry Johns: Only a certain type of chap makes a good keeper. You have to be able to mix and get on well with people. Which is strange if you think about what most people think about lighthouse keepers. If you are fiery or something like that...I don't know, Trinity seem to realise what people are like and I got on with

Sometimes, of course, it wasn't all sweetness and light.... You had a Principal Keeper, now he was God – he ruled the place, but it really was his job, if there was any trouble or any friction, he would tell the Depot when he came ashore, when he reported to the Superintendent. And then, if somebody didn't get on with somebody, they would swap him over with someone else.

The Principal Keeper didn't try and sort it out. No, you couldn't do that. Too close and it would lead to a lot of pressure and problems out there and you didn't need that friction on station. There was no way you could get away from the lads, you know. Being that close you begin very quickly to understand people. Somebody comes from Manchester and somebody comes from Birmingham…we are all English, if you know what I mean, but you could have completely different ideals of life. I suppose that was the trickiest bit of all. It wasn't personal habits or anything, I think it was what we believed in. Say, for argument's sake, somebody was a true blue bloody Tory and you were a Labour man right down to the grass roots, and you were stuck on that place with him – you had to learn to take the other man's views. You really had to learn to live with these people. And if you only had these two blokes together, you certainly had a chance to talk it out. I can tell you I learnt to read and the whole world came open to me.

Dermot Cronin: For me there were various things not spoken about on lighthouses – politics and religion were two of them. I'm not saying we didn't discuss the odd thing about the general election or anything like that, but we didn't go into things too much.

It was just easier not to bring some things up. I am Irish – and very few people, keepers and all, would even mention Northern Ireland. So the conversation would be about whether you caught any fish last night – that sort of thing. And you would find that, yes, you would talk about children and families, but you wouldn't go into the intimate personal details. No, nothing like that, just general chat. If somebody at home was sick – you'd enquire how she is today, or how are the kids? How are they doing in exams? That sort of thing. You'd show an interest more than anything else.

Eddie Matthews: All I have really seen about keepers, I suppose, is they love each other; if somebody was short of something there's no way you could nip ashore and get it – you'd borrow it, and things like that, and cook for each other – it was nice. No, I didn't see much friction at all. It was there but I never saw it. There were certain guys I disliked in the job, but the good ones out-weighed the bad ones.

Bill Arnold: Well yes. I was on the Bishop and we had this young lad come out there, he was only

about twenty and if I told him once I must have told him twenty bloody times that you try and go up and down the stairs in the tower quietly because usually there is somebody in bed trying to have a kip. They were metal stairs and those Trinity issue shoes were noisy as hell on them. Usually you wore your uniform going out to the tower and then as soon as you got there you put your old working clothes on and trainers; not this fella – clump, clump, clump, clump, clump – he didn't mean it, he just didn't have the common sense to realise what he was doing. In the end Pete Dobson, who was with me, said – I can't stand this anymore. So when the lad was in bed he took his bloody shoes and hid them!

Then there was the time when I was on this lighthouse – I won't say which one – and we had this new chap. It was the middle of the afternoon and I couldn't find him nowhere. I

started to get a bit worried and I happened to look up and notice that the lens was going round and in those days during the day the lens was still and the curtains [hung] up [to protect everything from the sunlight which otherwise heated the lantern up through the outer glazings]. So I thought, Oh, he must be up in the lantern. So I went up in the lantern and he was sat in the middle of the [prismatic] lens with the lens turning – smoking a spliff. I said, 'what the bloody hell are you doing?' And he's sat there, and he just says: 'The colours, man! The colours!' Needless to say he didn't stay long. He was right though, you sit in the middle of the lens and turn [it] and if the sun is shining you get all the colours of the rainbow – all enhanced. God knows what colours he was seeing!

Facing: Beachy Head in the 1950s. Assistant Keeper John Dobinson occupies his off-duty time with some rug-making, while his colleague, Richard Packer, looks to see how he is getting on.

Above: The last team on The Needles. From left to right, Gerry Douglas-Sherwood, Principal Keeper Gordon Medlicott, and Tony Elvers.

The keepers at South Lundy, 1991.

Loneliness

But, despite these ways of tolerating and getting along with each other, there was one thing the keepers could not avoid, even the more robust and phlegmatic of them.

Eddie Matthews: But the main shock, the thing to get used to, is, well, the loneliness. That is a terrible word…loneliness means depression and I was never depressed except a couple of times at Christmas maybe. But let me explain this. Monday to Friday, I think it is in every Englishman's mind…that's the time for work, but come Friday night, Saturday, and Sunday, stuck in there, you are wondering where the pub is! But then you were months ashore, you had all the money in the world – you could spend it – you were a single man for God's sake, when you came ashore you had a wild time.

I loved being on my own, mind. And that is what my family couldn't understand. Because I wasn't like that at all and yet I was too. You wouldn't believe it to see me in a pub. My partner she says you're a chicken and egg, you are – when you're on station you're like a bloody hermit, when you get up here you're the

life and soul of the town. She said she didn't understand it.

I don't really, either. I mean sometimes I'm sitting in that pub and I'm thinking what the hell am I doing here? I heard this same conversation yesterday. They all argue amongst themselves, same old thing – why don't they read about it – but of course these people haven't time. They do their day's work, they're knackered, a bit of telly, tea, *Coronation Street*, then bed. I've had time to read, as a lighthouse keeper.

I was married, but that's a bit personal. My marriage went up the creek – like anybody else's, I suppose. And I now have a partner and I've got no problems on that side. But Christmas was a bitch. It was always difficult – especially if you had young children.

Bill Arnold: Some Christmases were OK. We used to arrange it all beforehand – you knew who you were going to be out there with for Christmas, so you would arrange who was getting the turkey, who was getting this and that – you'd have a proper Christmas dinner and all that. We've had some bloody good Christmases on the Wolf – I had three Christmases there and they were all good. Christmas Day when you are on the tower, certainly in the last ten years or so, the bloody phone was red hot all bloody day. You'd be phoning people and people would be phoning you. It was good in that way.

Eddie Matthews: I remember one nightmarish Christmas. Well, Christmas came and we were still waiting for our grub and of course nothing came to the Wolf Rock 'cos the weather was too bad. We had a couple of tins of corned beef, couple of tins of bangers. And of course on the radio they were saying on the other stations in the group, 'my turkey was smashing today' and 'we had a bottle of wine' – bastards, they were, kept rubbing it in. And it was four days after Christmas when we got the grub – that was a hell of a long time. Another hard one was when I had to leave for the light on Christmas Eve. There's a lovely picture of me by the helicopter with the kids on Christmas Eve. Now that nearly crippled me. But that was the way the days fell and it couldn't be helped.

Terry Johns: Being away from your family for long periods, especially if you were overdue, if you were on places like the Wolf Rock, that was always difficult. We used to have a shortwave radio so you could have a one-way conversation and you could talk to them and tell them you weren't going to be home on time. Of course there weren't any telephones back in the early days. When I was on the Longships you could do the old semaphore and Morse from the lighthouse to the cottage [within sight on the mainland at Sennen]. We could send messages straight back home. I know some people who get really uptight about being out on a lighthouse when their homes ashore are so close that they can see people walking around and things like that. We used to have a telescope on one lighthouse and it was directed on the cottages. Some of the blokes used to get quite irate, they used to say – 'You're not looking at my missus!' Fat lot of good it would do you anyway!

Eddie Matthews: People get upset over things, don't they? The simplest of things, I mean. I have seen people when their wives have rung up and said something very simple like, 'I went up and saw so and so', and the keeper would start to think, why is she up there talking to him? And

Next to an experimental wind generator, a keeper keeps an eye on something along the coast. The keepers at Beachy Head grew used to reporting incidents, from cars to suicides coming over the cliffs to the north of the lighthouse.

before you know it your head's in a spin, you know. And you can't sort things out 'cos you know damn well if you go ashore you might get it all sorted out, but you know you've got to go back to the light again as well. And in the end I think the best wives have enough sense not to say anything. Instead of saying little Johnny's not been well, and he might be the apple of the man's eye, next thing the bloke starts sitting thinking…. Little things can get blown out of proportion. So some things are best not said really.

Dermot Cronin: Being a father was difficult. I suppose I've seen my kids for about half of their lives. I have missed a lot of the growing up. But I tried to make up for it when I went home. Then you have a lot more time. You take the average man working, when he comes home the kids are probably in bed. The only question they asked was, 'when are you going back?' My wife will tell you that after a month away they would

come down, especially when they were younger, they would have everything ready to tell me that was wrong, before she could tell me anything. And there was that whole thing about being a parent in authority and if you are away for a month and then come back, that's very difficult for the kids to get used to. You had to be fair or seem to be fair anyway. I think that as they got older they respected that I was away and they had to make the most of the time when I was there.

The first few days home there was a lot to say to each other and then it settled down. Just like when you went back on the station, the first couple of days took a bit of getting used to. Likewise when you went ashore you had what were called 'the Channels'. That was really a seaman's term for a funny feeling when you were just getting home and you were getting into the English Channel. It was 'the Channels' in seaman's language and it rubbed over onto lighthouse keeper's talk.

I only heard of one particular fellow, I never met him, but he was on the Bishop Rock, who preferred being on station to being at home. Generally, I think, they enjoyed their time out there, but they also wanted to go ashore.

Bill Arnold: My first wife, she used to say that in the month that I was away she would be her own boss. And she used to say for the first two or three days that I was home, she used to resent me being there because it altered her routine. Lighthouse keeping was all right if you were young and single, and not too bad if you were over thirty and married and your kids were getting on, but in between times – early twenties with a young family – it was very difficult. Especially in the old days when you were relying on radio-telephone calls and you were only allowed so many of them. The best way for your missus to get hold of you, instead of trying to get hold of you themselves, was to contact the depot and ask them to get hold of you. Not that you could do anything anyway.

It's an unusual job, but in a way I enjoy a bit of attention – everyone has this romantic idea of lighthouse keeping and I am a bit of an extrovert anyway. I try and tell people what it was actually like. I don't make up fairy stories. I tell 'em about bucket and chuck it.

What's that? Now don't be daft. Use your imagination. People have this romantic bloody nonsense about lighthouses, I mean, Christ! It's not that many years ago, when we were on the Wolf, we didn't have a bloody flush

Principal Keeper William James, a stopwatch in his left hand, checks the oil-powered light at Beachy Head.

loo, mate – we had a Porta-potti. The morning watchman's job every morning was to empty it over the side. There's nothing romantic about that, mate, I can tell you.

Dermot Cronin: No, there's nothing romantic, that's one of the myths…I suppose if you have an artistic attitude of mind you could be up on a lighthouse like the Bishop Rock, the Smalls or the Eddystone on a very stormy night and things would be cradling in your mind. There have been some fantastic sunsets and some even better sunrises. And some spectacular seas – particularly at the Bishop.

Eddie Matthews: Yes, I have seen rare sights that no townie or anybody ashore has ever seen and Billy will tell you the same thing. There's one thing called the green flash and I saw it twice in my life. I was on the Eddystone, it was a beautiful clear night, everything sharp and clear and just as the sun, the last of the sun, goes below the horizon it reflects through the top of the sea, the very top and there's just a brief flash – it goes over the sky green, pure green. That is a beautiful sight and I saw that twice, and not many people ever see that….

Some of the sunsets are fantastic – and the other beautiful thing I suppose is something to do with the reflection off the clouds. I was on Wolf Rock and there is no way you can see the Bishop Rock in the Isles of Scilly from the Wolf Rock – but I have seen it three or four times. Somehow the image is projected from off the cloud and you see the rocks at the base of the Bishop on top of the Bishop – it is all an image, like a mirage. That was a marvellous sight. But you sit there sometimes and look, and it is perfectly calm and a beautiful sky one way, and you look the other way – complete opposite. You see it both ways and I don't know what it means, but I think it means something. You have got to have faith in something and this is a chance to think and learn about it.

Not all the optics were massive, this small but powerful electric-driven unit had a nominal range of fifteen nautical miles and was not difficult to keep immaculate.

Dermot Cronin: What is the best thing about being a lighthouse keeper? I've never really thought about it, but I think the freedom. Especially when I was made PK and I was my own boss. When you're a PK, the station is yours.

Eddie Matthews: As I said, to be a lighthouse keeper you have to learn to live with yourself, your inner thoughts, and also right opposite, 'cos you have to learn to mix with people in the same environment, and you either do it or you don't. They gave me the perfect start: stuck me on the Wolf for three and a half months. I could have come ashore a raving lunatic, but I took to it. And all my family couldn't believe it.

Bill Arnold: I went back to the [unmanned and automatic] Bishop [Rock] recently with a Dutch film crew hoping to do a series on lighthouses of the world. It felt weird going back there. I came off there in Christmas 1992 when it was automated. I never thought I would ever be back there again, I'd said my goodbyes to the place, and yet it felt as though I had not been away. I came down the stairs inside the place and walked into the kitchen and I half expected to see Pete Robson and Julian sat there with the tea in the pot. You know, it was funny not seeing them.

Eddie Matthews: I couldn't go back to the lighthouses now, not at my age. I did nine years on the Wolf Rock as trainee, AK and Principal Keeper. So I did the whole lot. I've done the worst and just the thought of climbing up and down those steel stairs…I've seen a lot of accidents on those stairs. I saw a man fall two flights with two buckets of coal in his hands, he crunched down, he took the skin off the backs of his legs, from his heel to the bottom of his backside. Blood everywhere. But he never spilt a piece of bloody coal!

Terry Johns: They kept saying to me, 'there's another world over the other side of the Tamar Bridge', and I kept saying 'I'm not interested in that. Cornwall will do me'. I have lived here all my life. They sent me from here right up to Northumberland. I had twelve years up there, but otherwise I've always been down here.

Eddie Matthews: What it did for me was what I've read and seen on the telly. Now I want to go and have a look at it. I know it's a bit late but I'm doing it. I've been to the Nile, I've been to

Kenya. This year I am going to India. I'm taking one trip a year and I am beginning to enjoy it. Even though I am sixty this year I dearly want to see it all – different cultures.

Bill Arnold: I know I've said about not getting any time off or anything but probably one of the best aspects of the job, once you were an Assistant Keeper or a Principal Keeper, is that Trinity do – or certainly did – look after their workforce. I remember when they found themselves short of men. My son was seventeen at the time, and they phoned me up and said, 'you know, we are short of keepers', and I said, 'well, my lad is sitting around doing nothing, why don't you give him a job?'. So my lad joined and, as it turned out, he was one of the last keepers to be employed by Trinity. That was a bit of a tradition in years gone by and it turned out that we were the last father and son to be employed by Trinity!

Dermot Cronin: You asked if it means anything to us that we are among the very last lighthouse keepers. When I joined in 1965 somebody said to me, 'you will probably be one of the last lighthouse keepers in this job'. I am privileged in a way to be one of the last; as you say it, is part of British maritime history. It is sad. The other thing is that now a lot of these lighthouses are going to be opened up to the public. It is part of the British heritage and people want to visit and see what it was like 100 years ago.

Bill Arnold: I actually wrote a bit of an ode when we left the Bishop, but I ain't kept a copy of it. Called it Requiem for a Prince because I always looked upon the Bishop Rock as being the prince of tower rocks as it was the biggest and there was more room on it. I left the copy in the order book that stays with the station. Well the order book is now in Penzance Depot so it might still be in the order book there.

But that time I went back. One thing that I had forgotten, surprisingly: we went down and opened the bottom entrance door, and while I was stood there looking out I heard the sound of the sea lapping up against the tower. And I thought, Shit! I'd forgotten about that – because that is with you all the time, even in your bunk, you can always hear the sea lapping. And I had completely forgotten about that. It did feel good, remembering that.

Eddie Matthews: And…the Wolf Rock man: there was a bloke [a young Supernumerary

Facing: Preparing a detonator for the explosive fog signal at Beachy Head in the late 1950s.

Assistant Keeper who] went fishing from the door and they never saw him again…the weird thing was they found a book on black magic on his bunk and they just wondered. Another guy on the Wolf went for a swim for Christ's sake, never saw him again. Go for a swim off the Wolf Rock! Some crazy stories.

Terry Johns: I've had thirty-six years full-time and nearly three years part-time. But it wasn't the same as it was once. I used to enjoy the companionship. I used to love the old rough weather too. Not when you're ready to go ashore admittedly, but lightning storms and things like that – I used to love watching those. Oh yes, a good storm lasts for days. It is quite spectacular.

Bill Arnold: I have been lucky, I'm staying on as an Attendant. But there's a few people that I know, since redundancy, that don't fit in anywhere. Because, I mean, the life that they were used to, what can you compare it to? There isn't any comparison.

Eddie Matthews: Well, I'm finished now, with the lighthouse keeping. It's the end of an era, but there've been some times….

Despite the passing of the keepers' era, Trinity House staff continue to 'keep' the lights. Ashore, at the Operational Control Centre, they monitor and control from a distance; afloat, the task of maintaining, fuelling and repairing aids to navigation goes on.

The Lighthouses

The Northeast of England

Heugh Hill
OcRWG6s24m5M

Guile Point
OcRWG6s9m4M

Bamburgh
Oc(2)WRG8s12.5m14/11M

Farne Islands

Longstone
F20s23m26M
Horn(2)60s

Farne
Fl(2)WR15s10/7M

Coquet
Fl(3)WR30s25m21/16M
Horn(1)30s

Northern Hill

Cresswell Skerries

NEWCASTLE-
UPON-TYNE

SOUTH SHIELDS

SUNDERLAND

HARTLEPOOL

MIDDLESBROUGH

Whitby
IsoWR10s73m18/16M

WHITBY

Filey Bay

Flamborough
Fl(4)15s65m25M
Horn(2)90s
DGPS290.5KHz150M

BRIDLINGTON

Bridlington Bay

KINGSTON-
UPON-HULL

River Humber

GRIMSBY

Haile Sand

Rosse Spit

Dowsing BD1
Fl(2)10s28m23M
Horn(2)60s

Inner Dowsing
Fl10s12m15M
Horn(1)60s

Inner Dowsing Overfalls

The coal trade between the mines of County Durham and London increased in the Eighteenth Century as 'sea-cole' superseded wood in the capital's kitchens and a slowly increasing industrialisation took place. There was also a busy coastal passenger trade, especially between Edinburgh and London, carried in fast sailing packets and later by small steamships. The East Coast of England remains a busy shipping route, and, with the short-sea trade to Europe and the Baltic, demands modern navigational aids to support it.

Previous pages: Hartland Point was known to the Romans as 'the Promontory of Hercules'.

Facing: The BD1 production platform lies in the Amethyst gas field off the Humber. It also marks the Dowsing shoal, thus replacing a lightvessel, displaying a navigational light as well as its own standard warning lights.

Abbreviations for Light Characteristics	
F.	Fixed
Fl	Flashing
Fl(n)	Group Flashing
Iso	Isophase
Oc	Occulting
Oc(n)	Group Occulting
G	Green
R	Red
W	White
m	Metres
Nm or M (chart)	Nautical Miles
s	Seconds
MHWS	Mean High Water Springs

Heugh Hill Light Beacon

Latitude	55° 40.09'N
Longitude	001° 47.89'W
Established	1875
Height of tower	8m
Height of light above MHWS	24m
Character	OcRWG(6)
Range	5Nm

Combined with Guile Point, Heugh Hill Light Beacon provides a visual reference to small craft entering Holy Island harbour. Trinity House assumed responsibility for the beacon from the Trinity House of Newcastle-upon-Tyne on 1 November 1995. The steel structure provides a light at night and in conditions of poor visibility, and a conspicuous red triangular daymark; it is known locally as the 'Black Beacon'.

Guile Point Light Beacon

Latitude	55° 39.49'N
Longitude	001° 47.50'W
Established	1826
Height of tower	21m
Height of light above MHWS	9m
Character	OcRWG(6)
Range	4Nm

The original beacon, with a brick-and-stone-clad wooden framework, was built in 1826 by the ancient Trinity House of Newcastle-upon-Tyne. It is one of a pair raised to guide small vessels into the harbour at Holy Island, or Lindisfarne. A solar-powered light was fitted to the front beacon about one third of the way up the obelisk, for which Trinity House assumed responsibility in November 1995 along with Heugh Hill.

Longstone Lighthouse

Latitude	55° 38.64'N
Longitude	001° 36.56'W
Established	1826
Height of tower	26m
Height of light above MHWS	23m
Character	Fl20s
Range	26Nm
Fog Signal	Horn(2) 60s

Sir John Clayton, an early advocate of lighthouses on the East Coast of England, proposed and, in 1673, built a tower on the Inner Farne, one of a group of islands, islets and rocks off the Northumbrian coast owned by the Diocese of Durham. It was never lit, since it failed to obtain approval from Trinity House who, in turn, were unable to guarantee financial support from its likely beneficiaries, or to conclude agreement with the leaseholders. In 1727 a second application was made by coastal traders and a third in 1755 by Captain J. Blackett, a member of the family that held the lease to the islands. Financial difficulties bedevilled progress but, in July 1776, the pressing need to warn shipping off the shore the islands and the dangers of the strong tides that swirled about them prompted Trinity House the Blacketts a lease for the construction of two lighthouses. One was set upon the Inner Farne coasting vessels through the inshore passage, the other was on Staple Island; both September 1778. In 1784 the Staples Island light was damaged by bad weather; rebuilt in 1800. In 1796 Robert Darling had become keeper and he and his family were most lighthouse built on Brownsman's Island that same year, though the fixed light on Brownsman satisfy local shipmasters. (In 1786 Trinity House had taken over the lease of the lights and Blacketts, as beneficiaries of the light dues, to fit Argand lamps and reflectors to improve Then, in 1810, all the interested parties met to renegotiate terms and, as a consequence, appointed Daniel Alexander to organise the building of two new lighthouses, one on Island and another on the Outer Farne, or Longstone. Alexander's new light on the which Darling was transferred, bore one of the first revolving, flashing optics in the world. In 1822 an Act of Parliament empowered Trinity House to buy the site for £36,446 and four years later extensive works were undertaken by Alexander's successor, Joseph Nelson. Nelson enlarged the red-and-white painted tower on the Longstone at a cost of £4,771. Longstone was now crowned with a light produced by twelve Argand lamps in parabolic reflectors and encompassed by a catadioptric lens, a prodigious apparatus costing £1,441. Additional modifications were made over the years, including the installation of a fog signal, but, most notably in 1952, when electric generators were fitted, a unique 'spectacle' optic was also fitted and the station housed a radio beacon.

Robert Darling's granddaughter Grace achieved worldwide fame when, in September 1838, she and her father, William, rescued survivors from the wreck of the coastal passenger steamer *Forfarshire*. Bound from Hull to Dundee, the *Forfarshire* was caught in a gale and driven on to rocks a mile from the lighthouse. Seeing people clinging to the broken hull in the aftermath of the gale, Grace persuaded her father to take the lighthouse boat across to the wreck. Making two trips they took off nine people, caring for them in the lighthouse for two days until the weather moderated.

Longstone lighthouse was automated in 1990 and, in 1997, monitoring and control was assumed by the new Operational Control Centre at Trinity House's principal depot at Harwich in Essex.

Left: The Victorian heroine: on the morning of 7 September 1838 Grace Darling and her father row their coble from the Longstone Lighthouse towards the wreck of the steamer Forfarshire *on the Harcar Rocks, a mile away.*

Bamburgh Lighthouse

Latitude	55° 37.00'N
Longitude	001° 43.35'W
Established	1910
Height of tower	9m
Height of light above MHWS	12.5m
Character	Oc(2)WRG8s
Range	14/11Nm

A number of castles exist along the coast of Northumberland, remnants of the border country's turbulent history. One of these is Bamburgh which, in the Eighteenth Century, had fallen into disrepair and was occupied as a charity school by a Dr Sharp. Sharp's philanthropic instincts, apparently funded by the Trustees of Lord Crewe's estate, also prompted him to take an interest in the plight of seamen. Shipwreck was a common event around the British coast, as was the washed-up bodies of drowned sailors, the burden of whose burial fell upon the parish. Sharp instituted a lifeboat station at Bamburgh and established a warning and lookout system on the castle ramparts where a bell was rung and a large swivel gun was discharged in fog. During gales two riders were employed to patrol the extensive beaches and report ships in distress; one was to render assistance while the other summoned aid. Salvage equipment was stored at Bamburgh Castle and Sharp offered rewards for those advising the castle of any shipwrecks along the coast.

It is a measure of the commonplace nature of the hazard and incidence of shipwreck that Nineteenth Century sailing directions contain the advice that on this coast 'dead bodies cast on shore are decently buried *gratis*' and that mariners washed up alive would be reclothed and given a week's free lodgings. It was in this culture, rather than surrounded by the opportunist prayers for 'a good wreck' that were prevalent elsewhere, that Grace Darling was brought up, and she lies buried in Bamburgh churchyard.

It is not known when Sharp's fog signals were discontinued, but Bamburgh lighthouse, a small secondary station, was not built until 1910. With its automatic, acetylene-powered coloured sector light, and in conjunction with the lighthouse on Inner Farne, it guides coastal craft through the inshore passage between the Farne Islands and the Northumbrian coast. It was extensively modernised in 1975; mains electricity was installed in the 1980s, supported by stand-by diesel generators. The station is now 'kept' by a local attendant and monitored from Harwich.

Farne Lighthouse

Latitude	55° 36.92'N
Longitude	001° 39.22'W
Established	1673
Height of tower	13m
Height of light above MHWS	27m
Character	Fl(2)WR15s
Range	10/7Nm

Right: Seen from seaward, the Farne Lighthouse marks the inner passage between the Farne Islands and the Northumbrian coast beyond.

As already noted, a tower was first built on Inner Farne by Sir John Clayton but the refusal of Newcastle merchants to pay any toll dissuaded the good Sir John from lighting it. As a consequence of the renegotiations of 1810, Daniel Alexander built a new circular tower and dwellings on Inner Farne in 1811, equipping the tower with Argand lamps and reflectors. Another small tower, exhibiting a fixed white light, was built on the northwest point of the island to aid inshore traffic.

In 1825 the leasehold for the site, like that of the Longstone, was acquired from the Blacketts. Upon the building of Bamburgh lighthouse in 1910 the small fixed light was demolished and the main Inner

Farne lighthouse was converted to acetylene operation, the gas being generated on station. The keepers were withdrawn and the station remained thus until the installation of solar power in late 1996, when monitoring was assumed by Harwich through a telemetry link.

Coquet Lighthouse

Coquet is a small island off the Northumberland coast near Amble. Inhabited from early times, St Cuthbert, Bishop of Lindisfarne, visited a small religious community on the island in 684. But it was not until 1841, as part of a general improvement in aids to navigation following the Act of 1836, that Trinity House laid out £3,268 for the building of a square, sandstone tower here. It was built on the ruins of a Fifteenth Century structure, part of a Benedictine monastery, and even earlier ecclesiastical remains. The lighthouse, a massive tower with a crenellated parapet, which confers a fortress-like aspect, was designed by James Walker. Its first keeper was William Darling, elder brother to Grace, and it is said that it was on a visit to William in the summer of 1842, that Grace contracted a chill that turned into a fatal consumption.

Home to many species of birds, Coquet supports a colony of eider ducks and seals. The station was converted to automatic operation in December 1990 and the keepers were withdrawn. Today Coquet is controlled from Harwich.

Latitude	*55° 20.03'N*
Longitude	*001° 32.28'W*
Established	*1841*
Height of tower	*22m*
Height of light above MHWS	*25m*
Character	*Fl(3)WR30s*
Range	*21/16Nm*
Fog Signal	*Horn(1)30s*

Whitby Lighthouse

Latitude	*54° 28.56'N*
Longitude	*000° 33.99'W*
Established	*1858*
Height of tower	*13m*
Height of light above MHWS	*73m*
Character	*IsoWR10s*
Range	*18/16Nm*

The high cliffs of the North Yorkshire coast hide a number of small ports, the most significant of which is Whitby. Captain James Cook was apprenticed to a Whitby shipowner, and made the first of his epochal voyages of discovery (1768-1771) in a converted Whitby-built 'cat' – a small, ship-rigged collier renamed *Endeavour*.

Trinity House built the Whitby Lighthouse to James Walker's design in 1858. Originally one of a pair which, when aligned in transit, marked the position of the off-lying Whitby Rock, the station was altered in 1890. A more effective light with a red sector covering the rock was sited in the higher tower and the lower was closed down. The station was fully automated in 1992.

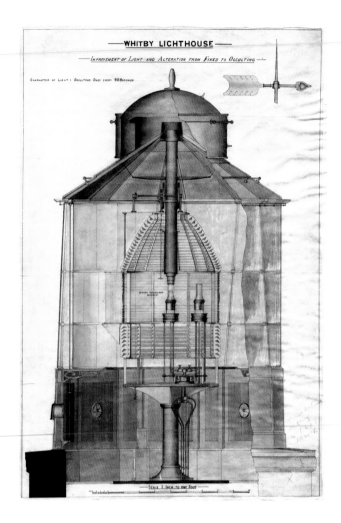

Flamborough Lighthouse

Latitude	*54° 06.98'N*
Longitude	*000° 04.96'W*
Established	*1669*
Height of tower	*25m*
Height of light above MHWS	*65m*
Character	*Fl(4)15s*
Range	*24Nm*
Fog Signal	*Horn(2)90s*
DGPS	*290.5KHz 150M*

Contrary to early assumptions of it being the place of 'a flame', Flamborough's name is derived from the Saxon word for dart, 'flaen', which it resembles in shape; in the Domesday Book it is referred to as 'Flaneberg' and was the site of another of Sir John Clayton's abortive schemes. The first tower on Flamborough Head was built by Clayton in 1669 and, though never lit, it was marked on charts as a 'lighthouse'. This prompted Thomas Hood's caustic comment on the cartographers of the day: 'As for myself, I will not give a fart for all their cosmography, for I can tell you more about it than all the cosmographers in the world'. Nevertheless Clayton's tower provided a daymark and later charts bore legends such as: 'a lighthouse but no fire kept in it', or the more hopeful: 'a high lighthouse but doth not burn as yet'. Clayton gave up the enterprise in 1678, despairing of obtaining either official permission or the means of establishing his lighthouse.

The modern Flamborough Head lighthouse was designed by Samuel Wyatt, architect of the Trinity House that stands on Tower Hill in the City of London, the foundation stone of which was laid by the then Master, William Pitt, in 1793. Wyatt contracted John Matson of Bridlington to erect the lighthouse at Flamborough Head in 1806 at a cost of £8,000. The light was first shown on 1 December from an optic designed by George Robinson; this consisted of a rotating vertical shaft upon which was mounted a triangular frame, each face of which bore seven parabolic reflectors and Argand lamps. Red glazings covered two of these facets so that the then unique characteristic of one white and two red flashes was produced. The light's power was equivalent to that of 13,860 candles. An early fog signal was initiated from Flamborough Head consisting of rockets fired at five-minute intervals and said to soar to a height of 300 metres. How helpful these were to the mariner offshore is hard to judge.

Following pages: Longstone Lighthouse.

In 1940 electric power was laid on and in 1975 the compressed-air-driven diaphone fog signal was superseded by an electric apparatus. Following the full automation of Flamborough, the keepers left on 1 May 1996. Fitted with a local fog detector to control the signal, the station is today monitored at Harwich.

Dowsing B1D Light

The proliferation of platforms in the North Sea gas fields enabled Trinity House to fit a powerful aid to navigation on one such structure, thereby rendering redundant the Dowsing lightvessel that was stationed nearby. The lightvessel's position had been established in 1861 and was withdrawn on the lighting of the Dowsing Light on Platform B1D in 1991. The B1D Platform is part of the Amethyst Field, from which natural gas is extracted.

Latitude	*53° 33.66'N*
Longitude	*000° 52.77'E*
Established	*1991*
Height of light above MHWS	*28m*
Character	*Fl(2)10s*
Range	*23Nm*
Fog Signal	*Horn(2)60s*

The East Anglian Coast

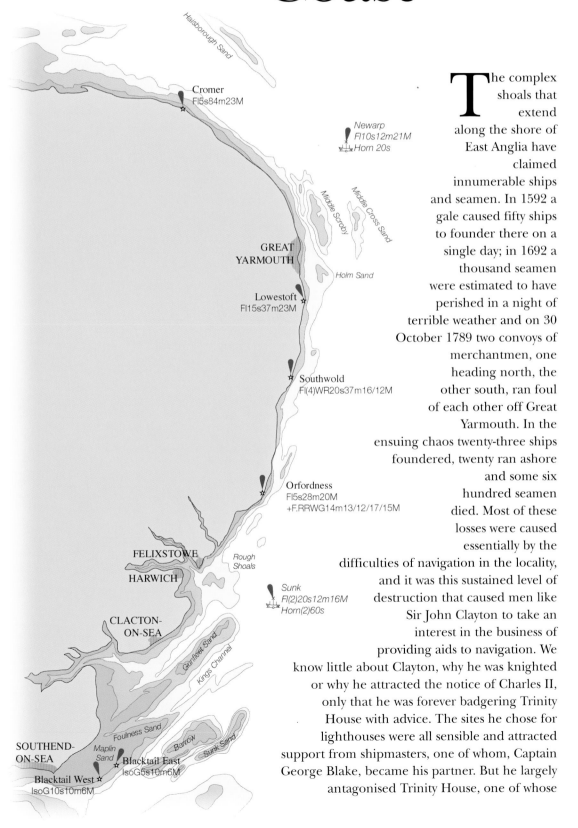

Cromer
Fl5s84m23M

Haisborough Sand

Newarp
Fl10s12m21M
Horn 20s

Middle Scroby

Middle Cross Sand

GREAT
YARMOUTH

Holm Sand

Lowestoft
Fl15s37m23M

Southwold
Fl(4)WR20s37m16/12M

Orfordness
Fl5s28m20M
+F.RRWG14m13/12/17/15M

FELIXSTOWE

Rough
Shoals

HARWICH

Sunk
Fl(2)20s12m16M
Horn(2)60s

CLACTON-
ON-SEA

Gunfleet Sand

Kings Channel

Foulness Sand

Barrow

Sunk Sand

SOUTHEND-
ON-SEA

Maplin
Sand

Blacktail East
IsoG5s10m6M

Blacktail West
IsoG10s10m6M

The complex shoals that extend along the shore of East Anglia have claimed innumerable ships and seamen. In 1592 a gale caused fifty ships to founder there on a single day; in 1692 a thousand seamen were estimated to have perished in a night of terrible weather and on 30 October 1789 two convoys of merchantmen, one heading north, the other south, ran foul of each other off Great Yarmouth. In the ensuing chaos twenty-three ships foundered, twenty ran ashore and some six hundred seamen died. Most of these losses were caused essentially by the difficulties of navigation in the locality, and it was this sustained level of destruction that caused men like Sir John Clayton to take an interest in the business of providing aids to navigation. We know little about Clayton, why he was knighted or why he attracted the notice of Charles II, only that he was forever badgering Trinity House with advice. The sites he chose for lighthouses were all sensible and attracted support from shipmasters, one of whom, Captain George Blake, became his partner. But he largely antagonised Trinity House, one of whose

Facing: Dominating the heart of a pretty Suffolk town, Southwold Lighthouse was commissioned in 1890.

105

Secretaries smugly claimed the Corporation had succeeded in damning every scheme Clayton had put forward. Such an attitude is scarcely consonant with the present attitude of the Corporation, but in 1675 Clayton had lit a lighthouse at Corton, and so infuriated the Master of Trinity House, Samuel Pepys, that he promptly ordered immediate improvements in the Corporation's lighthouse at Lowestoft, declaring it would henceforth operate free of dues.

Cromer Lighthouse

Latitude	*52° 55.45'N*
Longitude	*001° 19.10'E*
Established	*1676 (present location and tower 1833)*
Height of tower	*18m*
Height of light above MHWS	*84m*
Character	*Fl5s*
Range	*23Nm*
Racon fitted	

Another site chosen by Clayton was Foulness, a headland just east of Cromer on the Norfolk coast; it has long since been washed away by the North Sea. Clayton's tower of 1676 was never lit, since he again failed to obtain permission to raise dues for its maintenance. In 1719 George I issued letters patent to the owner of land on Foulness to maintain a lighthouse. These men, Nathaniel Life, a merchant, ship-master and Younger Brother of Trinity House, and Edward Bowell, constructed an octagonal brick tower well inland of Clayton's. Life and Bowell were empowered to raise dues at one farthing per ton on general cargo, and one half-penny per chauldron (a coal measure of 36 bushels, 1.25 imperial tons) on Newcastle coal. The rent was set at £100 per annum and the tower and a surrounding acre of land were to go to Trinity House at the expiry of the sixty-one-year lease. The coal-fired light was enclosed by glazings and was first lit on 29 September.

By 1792 the tower had duly passed to Trinity House who installed a revolving optic similar to that at Flamborough, the three-sided optic having fifteen reflectors and lamps, though with no red glazings. Mariners, being a conservative race and suspicious of innovation, at first condemned the quickness of the flash; they might perhaps have been even more disapproving had they known, as one authority claims, that the first keepers were 'two young women who together received a pound a week for wages with certain perquisites'. Sadly the nature of the perquisites is even more obscure than the identity of the young women.

Successive landslips in 1799, 1825 and 1832 endangered the building. In June 1833 the encroachment of the sea led to the tower's abandonment and the swift erection of a new one 400 yards

inland. The new tower was unusual on the East Coast of England in being masonry-built and it has been suggested that its speedy construction was because the stones were already being prepared for a West Coast lighthouse. It is this tower that forms the basis for Cromer's present lighthouse which, despite standing on England's generally low East Coast is, at 84 metres, one of the highest Trinity House lights and an indication of Foulness's former prominence. In 1852 further erosion occurred and after heavy rainfall in 1866 the old tower fell into the sea.

In 1905 a spur was taken from the town's gas supply and provided a brilliant new light. Thirty years later the station's main light was converted to electricity, with an acetylene stand-by. In 1958 full electrification took place and in June 1990 the keepers left Cromer lighthouse, which thereupon became fully automated and controlled from Harwich.

Lowestoft Lighthouse

Latitude	*52° 29.19'N*
Longitude	*001° 45.46'E*
Established	*1609*
Height of tower	*16m*
Height of light above MHWS	*37m*
Character	*Fl15s*
Range	*23Nm*

The first of Trinity House's lighthouses at Lowestoft was established in 1609 as a result of the continued loss of life and property in the area.

Two candle-lit towers had been built on Lowestoft Ness to lead vessels into Lowestoft and through the inner passage along the coast by way of the Stanford Channel (variously also the *Standford* or *Stamford* Channel deriving, it is thought, from the original 'Stand-forth' Channel). These lighthouses were rebuilt in 1628 and again in 1676 when the rear light was moved back from the headland onto higher ground where it could better serve as a much needed passage light. This new high lighthouse, which cost £300, was a substantial building topped by a coal fire. Erosion put paid to the old low light in 1706, but a new leading light was built in 1730. A moveable device, so that it could keep pace with shifts in the Stanford Channel, this was illuminated by whale oil burning in an open-cupped lamp.

In 1777 the coal fire in the high light was replaced by a new light 2 metres high. This consisted

of a central column around which were glued 4,000 tiny mirrors reflecting the ring of oil lamps set about it. This 'spangle' light was visible 20 miles offshore, thus providing a valuable landfall and passage aid. In 1796 it was replaced by what was then becoming the state-of-the-art lighthouse optic, Argand lamps set in silvered parabolic reflectors, costing some £1,000.

In 1870, following experiments elsewhere, electrical power was planned for Lowestoft and the old tower was replaced by a stronger structure at a cost of £2,350. But the new paraffin burners were proving so efficient and economical that the plan for electrification was dropped and oil was substituted. Combined with a revolving lens, this ended Lowestoft's fixed light status by providing a white flash every thirty seconds. By 1923 the Stanford Channel had closed up, so that in August the lower light was discontinued.

Lowestoft Lighthouse was finally electrified and automated in 1975. In 1997 further modifications were made and the station was linked to Harwich.

Southwold Lighthouse

Built as part of Trinity House's general improvement in passage lights undertaken in the late Nineteenth Century, Southwold Lighthouse was begun in 1888. Construction was supervised by James Douglass, Engineer-in-Chief to the Corporation, and its completion enabled operation of the low light at Orfordness to be discontinued.

During the building work in 1889 a temporary light was exhibited from a wooden structure close by. The new tower was first lit by an Argand burner on 3 September 1890 and in 1906 this was replaced by one of Matthews's incandescent oil lamps. In 1923 a Hood paraffin vapour burner with a 100mm mantle was installed and, with its supporting lens, remained in service until electrification and automation in 1938, when the keepers were withdrawn and an attendant was appointed.

In May 2001 an improved optic came into service to provide a main light of white with red sector lights shining out over shoals to the north and south.

Latitude	*52° 19.60'N*
Longitude	*001° 41.00'E*
Established	*1889*
Height of tower	*31m*
Height of light above MHWS	*37m*
Character	*Fl(4)WR20s*
Range	*16/12Nm*

Orfordness Lighthouse

Latitude	*52° 05.01'N*
Longitude	*001° 34.59'E*
Established	*1634*
Height of tower	*30m*
Height of main light above MHWS	*28m*
Character	*Fl5s +F.RRWG*
Range	*20Nm +13/12/17/15Nm*
Racon fitted	

The bleak Suffolk headland of Orfordness is a featureless shingle promontory, almost cut off from its hinterland by the River Ore. Like Dungeness, it is difficult to see and is beset by strong tides that cause overfalls offshore and, also like Dungeness, it was a notorious grave for ships and men. On one night of bad weather in 1627, thirty-two vessels were cast ashore on Orfordness, with scarcely a survivor among their companies. Other ships were lost on the Aldeburgh Napes and the Shipwash Bank nearby.

In February 1634 Sir John Meldrum, a courtier who had built lighthouses further north at Winterton in the teeth of opposition from Trinity House, took up the cause of a light on Orfordness. Declaring he would free fishermen and colliers from light dues, he petitioned Charles I and was granted leave to build 'two temporary lighthouses to lead between Sizewell Bank and Aldeburgh Napes to the north'. For a while Meldrum was the greatest proprietor of lighthouses in England, owning both the Winterton lights and, briefly, those on the Kentish forelands. However, in favour of the latter, he sold his interest in Orfordness to Alderman Gore.

Gore built two timber towers, the high rear light to burn a coal fire, the lower front to exhibit a candle lantern. In 1648 one of the keepers died and Gore was persuaded to approve the man's widow as successor. She was from a 'lighthouse family', but it was a decision he was afterwards to regret. 'I have had more complaints in this half-year than ever I had in your father or your husband's time. I did not think you would have been so careless,' he wrote to the Widow Bradshaw, adding, with what effect we do not know, 'but I excuse you because you are a woman'.

Ironically, it was Gore's daughter, Sarah, who inherited the lights, proprietorship passing to her husband, a lawyer named Edward Turnour, on her marriage. Sarah died young, leaving a large family, but Turnour did well, as lawyers are wont to do, earning a knighthood at the Restoration. In 1661 he was elected MP for Hertford and afterwards Speaker of the House of Commons, obtaining an extension of his lighthouse lease as 'a personal reward for services to the Crown'. Sir Edward strengthened his own position by buying the land upon which the lighthouses stood and a large area of Lantern Marsh to secure rights of access. Turnour went on to become Solicitor-General and Lord Chief Baron of the Exchequer – a man of high office who did not disdain the ownership of a lighthouse, but whose proprietorship tended to create an unfavourable political link in the public imagination.

Despite his personal high achievement, under Turnour and his wastrel heir supervision of the remote Orfordness lights was less effective. Moreover, a long and complex legal wrangle over ownership of Orfordness now began, while complaints made to Trinity House about the lights were ignored by the owners and stimulated only imaginative excuses from the keepers: 'the east wind doth darken the light' one whined. One hardly sympathises when learning that in 1690 one keeper was carried off by the naval press, while the encroachment of the sea carried away the low light the next year. At this time the coasting trade refused to pay dues and a damning report was submitted by Samuel Hunter, a clerk sent by Trinity House to investigate. In 1702 a party of Elder Brethren arrived to inspect improvements put in hand after Hunter's visit.

Then, on 23 June 1707, the lighthouses were raided by a French corsair. The privateersmen damaged the lantern and stole various items, including the keepers' bedding; why is not quite clear. This sorry tale continues the following year when, disdaining such paltry pickings, a second corsair 'have…Shoote at the Lithouse and have Broke all the glass'.

Two years later the sea carried away the replaced low light and little seems to have been done about it until 1720 when a Henry Grey was finally confirmed as owner. Visiting the lighthouse, which was still manned by Turnour's men, Grey was at first refused access, but towards evening returned with his local agent and his new keepers. There was a scuffle before Turnour's wretched keepers were evicted. Grey promptly built two brick towers at a cost of £1,180, but in 1724 the front light was again demolished by erosion and he replaced it with a moveable structure. However, the opportunist Grey was now in financial trouble and, leaving a suicide note, he disappeared. Just as the Commons formally pronounced him dead some years later, Grey reappeared. This curious man not only took up his duties again but, in 1731, obtained an extension of his lease.

Meanwhile the sea continued to scour the ness and a further lighthouse had to be built, although this time Grey boldly introduced oil as the illuminant. Alas, the keepers proved incompetent and the light set fire to the wooden tower. Incredibly its successor also burned down, and its replacement was the fifth tower to have been erected here since 1720. It stood until 1792, by which time Lord Braybrooke had inherited ownership through Grey's steadfast wife, who after Grey's death, remarried and became Countess of Portsmouth. Braybrooke ordered a new 'great light' to be built much further inland from the distal point of the headland. It was designed by William Wilkins, the son of a Norwich plasterer and stucco-maker, and still stands today, high above the remote shingle headland. It became the new high light, the old high light taking over the duty of the lower front leading light. The former low light, teetering again on the water's edge, was abandoned and soon fell.

Under the powers of the 1836 Act, Trinity House bought out the third Lord Braybrooke at a cost of £13,414. By coincidence it was Braybrooke who had deciphered the diaries of Samuel Pepys and edited them for their first publication. He omitted Pepys's condemnation of the private ownership of lighthouses, which the diarist had sedulously opposed when Master of Trinity House, losing his seat as MP for Harwich as a consequence.

By 1888 Trinity House had become the public body that Pepys had envisaged two centuries earlier, when it undertook major works as part of a rationalisation policy. A new light was then building at Southwold and the old low light at Orfordness, once the higher of the two and itself now on the very shoreline, could be abandoned. Braybrooke's great light was made occulting and fitted with red and green shades to form guiding sectors. In 1914 a revolving lens was installed to give a white flash every five seconds and the green and red sector lights were set lower, to provide clearing marks over shoals lying north and south of the lighthouse.

In 1959 electrical power was supplied to the lighthouse, backed up by stand-by generating facilities, and the keepers' dwellings either side of the lighthouse were demolished. From its shaky start, the red-banded Orfordness is not only the most powerful light now exhibited on the East Coast of England but, on 6 July 1964, was the first to be remotely controlled from Harwich.

Above: In former times, selected lighthouses and lightvessels displayed storm warnings for the benefit of coastal shipping. Alerted by a telephone call, a keeper at Orfordness hoists a black cone – apex up signifies an expected gale from the north, apex down would have meant a southerly blow.

Blacktail East and West Light Beacons

These two steel starboard-hand light beacons mark the southern edge of the Maplin Sands in the Thames Estuary. Established in 1968 they were originally battery powered with photo-electric cell control, then powered by experimental wind generators until 1996, when they were converted to solar power.

Blacktail East	
Latitude	*51° 31.77'N*
Longitude	*000° 56.57'E*
Blacktail West	
Latitude	*51° 31.43'N*
Longitude	*000° 55.30'E*
Established	*1968*
Height of towers	*13m*
Height of light above MHWS	*10m*
Character	
Blacktail East	*IsoG5s*
Blacktail West	*IsoG10s*
Range	*6Nm*

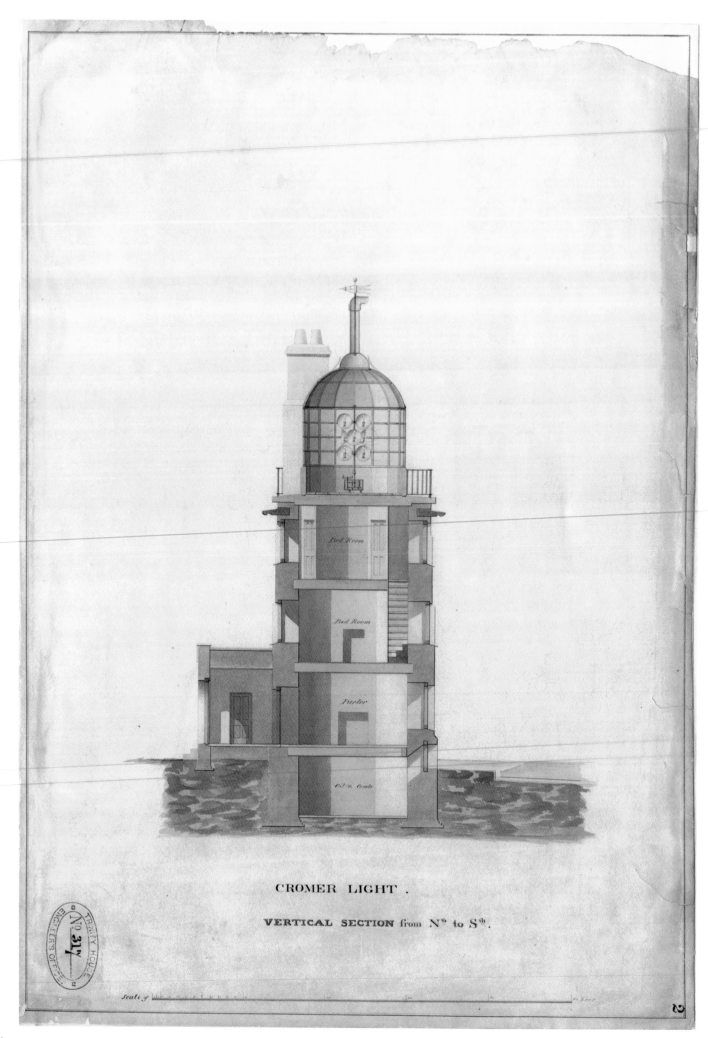

CROMER LIGHT .

VERTICAL SECTION from N⁰ᵗ to Sᵗʰ.

CROMER LIGHT (FOULNESS)

ELEVATION looking N.N.W!

scale of |⊢⊢⊢⊢⊢⊢⊢⊢⊢⊢| | feet

The Strait of Dover

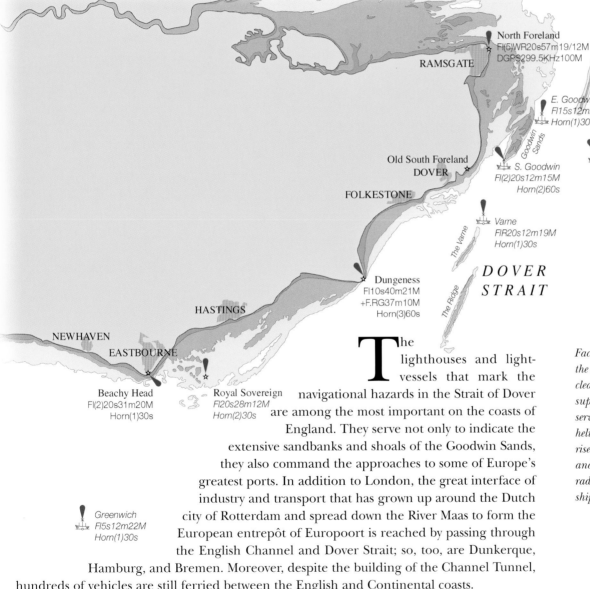

North Foreland
Fl(5)WR20s57m19/12M
DGPS299.5KHz100M

RAMSGATE

F3
Fl10s12m15M
Horn(1)10s

South Falls

E. Goodwin
Fl15s12m23M
Horn(1)30s

Goodwin Sands

Sandettié Bank

Old South Foreland
DOVER

S. Goodwin
Fl(2)20s12m15M
Horn(2)60s

Sandettié
Fl5s12m15M
Horn(1)30s

FOLKESTONE

Varne
FlR20s12m19M
Horn(1)30s

The Varne

DOVER
STRAIT

Dungeness
Fl10s40m21M
+F.RG37m10M
Horn(3)60s

The Ridge

HASTINGS

NEWHAVEN
EASTBOURNE

Beachy Head
Fl(2)20s31m20M
Horn(1)30s

Royal Sovereign
Fl20s28m12M
Horn(2)30s

Greenwich
Fl5s12m22M
Horn(1)30s

The lighthouses and light-vessels that mark the navigational hazards in the Strait of Dover are among the most important on the coasts of England. They serve not only to indicate the extensive sandbanks and shoals of the Goodwin Sands, they also command the approaches to some of Europe's greatest ports. In addition to London, the great interface of industry and transport that has grown up around the Dutch city of Rotterdam and spread down the River Maas to form the European entrepôt of Europoort is reached by passing through the English Channel and Dover Strait; so, too, are Dunkerque, Hamburg, and Bremen. Moreover, despite the building of the Channel Tunnel, hundreds of vehicles are still ferried between the English and Continental coasts.

The fundamental importance of the safety of shipping in this area, to both British trade and defence, is reflected in the early establishment of the lighthouses at North and South Foreland and at Dungeness. The fickle Goodwin Sands resisted all attempts to erect even simple beacons upon them, though in due course the sandbanks were marked by lightvessels and buoys, allowing the great anchorage of The Downs to be reached by inner channels. In the prevailing southwesterly winds this area is in the lee of the Kent coast and has ever been a safe refuge for small vessels in bad weather.

Facing: The 'telescopic' construction of the base of the Royal Sovereign tower is clearly seen from sea level. This supports the accommodation and services block which in turn forms a helicopter landing area. In one corner rises the tower with its light, fog signal, and an array of aerials including a radar link for the surveillance of shipping in the Strait of Dover.

The Goodwin Sands are extensive. Concealed at high tide, it is only at low water that they reveal something of their full extent, although even then much remains beneath the shallows. In the great storm of the night of 26/27 November 1703, when the first Eddystone lighthouse was destroyed and terrible damage was done throughout the whole of southern England, a squadron of Royal Navy men-of-war, under the command of Rear Admiral Basil Beaumont, was at anchor in The Downs. Torn from their cables, the ships were driven ashore and wrecked upon the sands to leeward of the anchorage. Along with Beaumont's ships, numerous merchantmen were also destroyed and thousands of seamen perished in this appalling disaster.

Over the years literally hundreds of privately-owned merchant ships and several men-of-war have been lost on these banks. While little could be done to mitigate the violence of such 'Acts of God' as the great storm of 1703, the more common reason for shipwreck was poor navigation. In times past a ship was safer in the open waters of the ocean than when approaching a coast where a prejudice held that helping a mariner deprived the local pilots of their living, and where, too, a fear of invasion often existed. This latter was particularly acute on the historically vulnerable coast of Kent that had suffered the incursions of Romans, Angles, Saxons, and Jutes. Later it was similarly exposed to the French and Spanish while, in our modern age, it was the focus of German attentions in both World Wars. In due course, and in the face of indefensible losses of ships and seamen, common sense prevailed and the lighthouses and lightvessels marking the Goodwin Sands were established, not only giving mariners a physical indication of the limits of the danger, but also providing them with static points from which to calculate their positions by cross-bearings.

Nothing, of course, can protect us from the extreme violence of great meteorological convulsions and, curiously, exactly 251 years after the great gale of 1703 another terrible storm took its toll when, on the night of 26/27 November 1954, the South Goodwin Lightvessel was herself torn from her moorings and cast upon the very sands that she marked. When located next day her wreck was half full of sand and within a week she had vanished.

North Foreland Lighthouse

Latitude	*51° 22.50'N*
Longitude	*001° 26.83'E*
Established	*by 1499*
Height of tower	*26m*
Height of light above MHWS	*57m*
Character	*Fl(5)WR20s*
Range	*19/12Nm*
DGPS	*299.5KHz 100M*

At the southeast corner of the Thames Estuary, North Foreland Lighthouse looms majestically over cabbage fields on the suburban fringe of Broadstairs. It holds a unique place in the history of Trinity House lighthouses as one of the earliest to be placed under the management of the Corporation and as the very last to be a manned station.

North Foreland provides a point of reference for vessels entering or leaving the Thames, for those making a passage through the Dover Strait, and for vessels coming into Ramsgate. In addition to its powerful flashing main light, a red light is shown over a narrow arc, or sector, indicating off-lying dangers near the anchorage of Margate Roads.

The local historian, W.H. Lapthorne, gives the earliest reference to a light on North Foreland, in a deed dated 1499, to 'ye beacon that lyith at ye hedd of ye cliffe at Beecon Hill'. At that time it was almost certain that the beacon was used to warn of attack or piracy rather than as an aid to navigation and it was from such fears that local xenophobia arose. Lapthorne describes the beacon as an iron basket containing a wood fire that was hoisted up and down using a lever, or 'swape', a medieval technique common in wells and early cargo hoists as well as for elevating lights. The swape was later replaced by a small tower of chalk blocks topped with a brazier. The chalk eroded and was in turn replaced by a lantern with twenty-four candles on a long pole. This apparatus was probably lit when needed rather than kept continuously alight, and quite how it was protected from being blown out remains something of a mystery.

In 1634 merchant shipmasters petitioned for a light at South Foreland near Dover to mark the southern end of the Goodwin Sands and to help guide ships into the safety of the Downs between the shore and the Goodwins. Sir John Meldrum was the guiding force behind the petition. Meldrum had already crossed swords with Trinity House and the Privy Council over lights on the East Anglian coast. Again at his own expense Meldrum had quickly built two towers on the Forelands in response to the wishes of shipmasters. On 9 February 1635 Charles I approved a grant for Sir John, but the matter was stalled on account of a protest from Trinity House, which argued that there would be an unacceptable expense laid upon shipping. Moreover, the light would attract enemy privateers or men-of-war that would attack ships at anchor in The Downs.

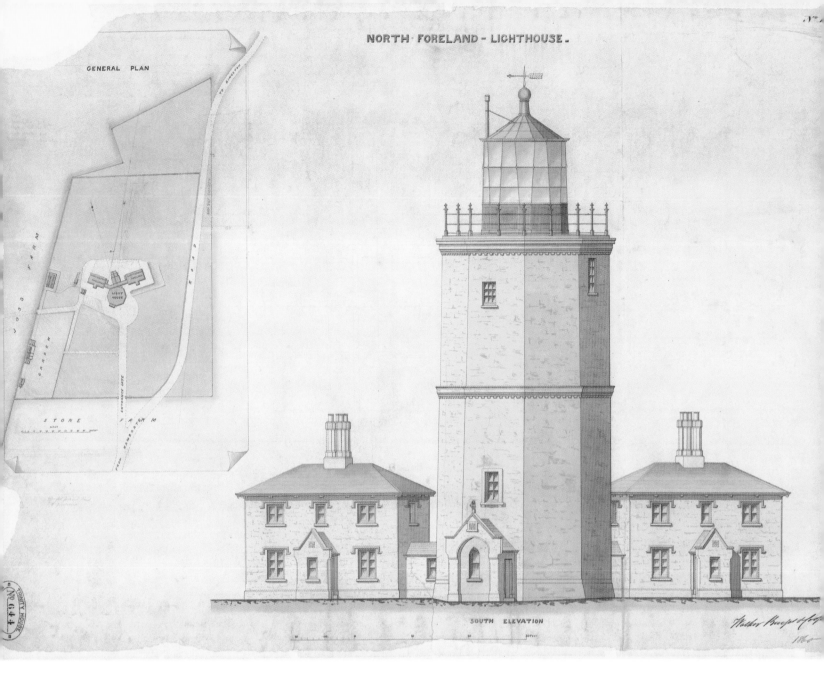

GENERAL PLAN

SOUTH ELEVATION

Above: Walker's modifications of the old octagonal tower at North Foreland were carried out in 1866. They included the provision of two fine dwellings for the keepers and their families.

This protest was clear evidence that Trinity House was reacting to the lobbying of local pilots, or Lodesmen (named after the magnetised lodestone from which the mariner's compass had derived). Their Court of Lodemanage at Dover had long argued that lighthouses were no more than 'costly follies' and stated dismissively that 'We at sea have always marks more certain and sure than lights, high land and soundings [the known depth of water at certain known locations] that we trust more than lights…the Goodwins are no more dangerous now than time out of mind they were, and lighthouses would never lull tempests, the real cause of shipwreck'. The Lodesmen had a point: there was no doubt that contemporary light sources were uncertain; they concluded with a fine, sophisticated flourish, 'If lighthouses had been of any service at the Forelands the Trinity House, as guardians of shipping, would have put them there'.

There was an impasse and the matter was referred to the Lords Commissioners of the Admiralty who discussed it on 25 March 1635. They decided against Meldrum who, knowing his lights were welcomed by mariners and that they were in the majority and came armed with the support of their profit-making owners, remained undaunted. He repeated his petition for a patent. As well as describing the benefits of the lights at North and South Foreland he claimed that he was £7,000 in debt over Winterton Lighthouse, which he had built on the coast of Norfolk. His persistence paid off and Sir John was issued with his patent on 13 February 1637. This allowed him to maintain fires at North and South Forelands for fifty years at a rent of £20 a year to the Crown. To recoup his expenses he could levy a due of one penny a ton upon passing ships.

This somewhat cynical granting of a patent to Meldrum partially addressed the problem of the light source, stipulating that Meldrum's lights exhibited 'fires'. Meldrum rebuilt his towers, erecting two at South Foreland, one higher than the other, with their transit leading vessels clear of the southern limit of the Goodwins. His single wooden tower at North Foreland was destroyed by fire in 1683 and its temporary replacement, which consisted of a candle in a lantern hoisted on a pole, predictably drew

Above: North Foreland in the Eighteenth Century when owned by the Trustees of Greenwich Hospital.

complaints. In 1691 a 12-metre high octagonal tower was constructed of flint and brick and topped with a fire basket. An internal shaft was provided, fitted with a gin block and whip, for hoisting fuel.

Letters of instruction dating from the late Seventeenth Century survive. Written by the owner of the lighthouse to his agent at Deal, one includes the order to: 'Pray give all my servants at the lighthouses a strict charge to be diligent in keeping good fires this rumbustious weather that no damage may come by their defaults'. On windless nights the wretched keepers had not only to haul the coal to the open grate – 100 tons during a typical year – but to work bellows to keep the blaze conspicuous.

In 1690, during the war against the French, the keepers worried about being seized by the press-gang to serve in the Royal Navy. They feared that their trips offshore to fish exposed them to the risk of impressment. Fishermen were fair game to naval officers anxious to man their ships and they were used to impressed men pleading all manner of excuses to avoid service – that of 'lighthouse keeper' probably seemed as ridiculous as all the others. Equally indifferent to the feeding of the keepers' families, the owner of the light wrote of 'The dangers yt [that] ye lighthouse men apprehend themselves to be in from ye Press-masters proceeds I find from themselves and therefore you did very well in charging them to mind ye lights which is their proper business and leave off their fishing. Otherwise I shall suspect my concern to be neglected and thereby their disadvantage may be greater than their gains by fishing. Besides, I don't know how they can be sufficiently watchfull after sayling all ye day."

In 1719 the North and South Foreland lights passed by will to the Trustees of the Royal Naval Hospital at Greenwich and thus, not without a certain irony, came under the indirect management of the Royal Navy itself. The brick foundations were extended to form a fine, octagonal tower. In about 1728 the open grate was enclosed with a glass lantern fitted with large sash windows, in an attempt to save coal and induce an efficient draught to produce a light rather than a mere source of heat. Despite this and the continuing use of bellows, smoke and soot obscured the light so that in 1730, following complaints from shipping, the lantern was removed.

By 1792 the benefits of lighthouses were well understood and the Admiralty, anxious about the safety of the anchorage at The Downs, persuaded the Trustees to raise the height of the tower. Under the direction of the Surveyor to Greenwich Hospital, John Yenn, another two storeys were added, raising the tower to its present height. In addition a glass lantern was again fitted in which an oil light was now installed. The apparatus was made by Thomas Rogers. He used a circular lamp, three inches in diameter, which was fitted with polished reflectors of silvered glass. Rogers also fitted convex lenses in front of the lamps, forming part of the glazing. These were of solid glass, five-and-a-half inches thick at its maximum. They were intended to collect and horizontally concentrate the light but their thickness tended to diminish it. In the first use of such lenses in the world, Rogers had supplied similar equipment at Portland in Dorset in 1788/9 and at a number of lighthouses in Ireland. These were all removed in around 1812. However, at North Foreland the Trustees of Greenwich Hospital kept the system in place and the lenses were not removed until 1834, two years after Trinity House took over the management of both the North and South Foreland lighthouses. The Corporation paid the Trustees of the hospital £8,366 for both lights and the dues were reduced.

In the mid Nineteenth Century North Foreland was modernised to the design of James Walker, Trinity House Engineer-in-Chief. When the work was completed in 1866 the lighthouse looked much as it does today. The intermediate floors within the tower were removed and two keepers' cottages were built at its base. Most of the windows in the tower were blocked up and the exterior was rendered and painted white. A new lantern was installed with a multi-wick burner and a first-order catadioptric fixed lens was fitted. This is still in use.

In 1880 the light character was changed to occulting – the opposite of flashing where it is the period of darkness which is short. (A number of Trinity House lighthouses were similarly altered around this time as it was an effective way to increase the number of characters available, whilst keeping them distinctive and easy to recognise.) In 1905 the light at North Foreland was changed to an incandescent oil burner and it was electrified in 1930, when the character was changed to its present flashing character.

A radio beacon was established at North Foreland in 1930. This enabled ships to take a bearing by radio, addressing the great dilemma of how to navigate through fog; it was useful, but not as accurate as a visual bearing. In the last years of the Twentieth Century the Global Positioning System – by which ships fitted with a special receiver are able to determine their position with astonishing accuracy from a constellation of artificial satellites high above the earth – has reduced all other systems of navigation to secondary status. To refine this data to centimetric accuracy for use by hydrographic surveyors, fossil-fuel prospectors and so forth, Trinity House provides a number of 'Differential Stations', one of which is North Foreland. By monitoring its own apparent, satellite-derived position and comparing this with its actual global location, a Differential Station is able to eliminate any error induced, deliberately or accidentally, in the Global Positioning System. This 'differential correction' provides the surveyor-cum-prospector with the highly accurate location he or she requires.

Moreover, by the late 1980s the relentless march of technology had added another responsibility beyond the mere keeping of the light and fog signal when North Foreland became an area control station. From their tower on the northeast corner of Kent, the keepers now became responsible for the lightvessels in the Dover Strait, along with the lighthouses at Dungeness and Beachy Head. In total they monitored eleven major aids to navigation in addition to their own; they had come a long way from their wretched predecessors, driven to sea to fish for their families.

While this augmentation of responsibility meant added work and an increase in the manning of North Foreland, it meant redundancy elsewhere. Moreover, it was but a coda to the finale, for it was only a matter of time before technology rendered even local monitoring redundant. By the autumn of 1998 the Operational Control Centre at the main Trinity House depot at Harwich in Essex had taken over from all such stations.

The final service day of the six lighthouse keepers at North Foreland was one redolent of ineluctable change and of the passing of time. It was the anniversary of the destruction of Beaumont's squadron on the Goodwins and the loss of the first Eddystone lighthouse in 1703, and of the tragic loss of the South Goodwin lightvessel in 1954. On 26 November 1998, HRH The Prince Philip, Duke of Edinburgh and Master of Trinity House, attended North Foreland lighthouse in the company of Rear Admiral, now Sir, Patrick Rowe, the Deputy Master and a group of Elder Brethren and senior officers of the Trinity House Service. Prince Philip unveiled a large slate plaque commemorating the occasion and honouring the memory of the keepers. In this emotional atmosphere the defaced red ensign of Trinity House was lowered for the last time under a grey, wintry sky.

After the rush of work to get the lighthouse absolutely spotless for the closing ceremony, to make the final adjustments of the new equipment, and to hold the interviews with television and radio worldwide, there was only the road home for the six men. Principal Keepers Dermot Cronin and Tony Homewood, Assistant Keepers Dave Appleby, Tristan Sturley, Colin Bale, and Barry Simmons went on their way. Their departure was eloquent of the triumph of mankind's intellect in the production of electronic technology, but it also marked the passing of an age of personal service. In their departure, most of the human element of lighthouse keeping disappeared. What modernity substituted in its place may prove as efficient and more cost-effective, but it detaches men and their families from an ancient and valuable tradition – a tradition upon which those to whom it was a way of life can look back with pride and pleasure.

After a year of quiet during which the lighthouse was visited only by the part-time attendant, former keeper, John Farmery, North Foreland was opened to the public in 2000 in partnership with the East Kent Maritime Trust. Close to the seaside resorts of Broadstairs and Margate, it had already become a popular place for holiday-makers to visit.

South Goodwin Lightvessel

Latitude	51° 07.95'N
Longitude	001° 28.60'E
Established	1832
Height of light	12m
Character	Fl(2)20s
Range	15Nm
Fog Signal	Horn(2)60s

To the south of North Foreland lie the notorious Goodwin Sands. As early as 1580 a proposal was made to mark them with a beacon that would also provide a refuge for sailors cast ashore there. A petition from Gawen Smith to Queen Elizabeth I laid down the dues that would be charged and described the construction of the proposed structure. It would stand well above high water with room for thirty or more people and it would burn a fire visible for twenty or thirty miles at night. Somewhat presumptuously Smith proposed that the Crown should reward him with £1,000 'when he shall delyver her Majestie grasse, hearbes or flowers growinge naturally in that place', and £2,000 if he managed to set up a piece of ordnance at the beacon. Alas, there is no record of this bold proposal being put into action.

In the late Seventeenth Century Trinity House investigated the sands with the idea of building a beacon, but they found no solid ground under the sand, so again nothing was done. Finally, in the early Nineteenth Century, a warning beacon was established in the Swatchway, a narrow channel between the drying banks on the eastern side of the sands. This utilised a vessel filled with stones, which was towed into position and then sunk. A flag pole was mounted on the hull with a large spherical 'daymark' on top. Alas, the vessel was washed away by the force of the sea and, in 1841, required replacement by a larger craft. Despite being laden with sixty-four tons of ballast this second beacon disappeared in 1843.

Following this, six further beacons were built to warn of the dangers of the Goodwins. The first was constructed in the autumn of 1840 by a naval officer, Captain Bullock. It consisted of a heavy timber mast with a platform to act as a refuge and bearing a flagpole on top. It was anchored by an oak frame in the shape of a cross, which the sand covered and buried. This simple but effective design lasted for four years until it was run down by a ship.

Meanwhile, in 1841, William Bush, a civil engineer, had begun work on a lighthouse. His design was based on a great iron caisson sunk into the sands as a foundation. After many trials the basic structure of the lighthouse was nearing completion in January 1845 when 'on the 19th instant Mr Bush and a party celebrated the raising of the Lighthouse Beacon by partaking of roast beef and plum-pudding on a platform laid on its summit'. For this celebratory feast Mr Bush and his workmen were accommodated in a makeshift roundhouse on the platform. At the time they were completing the living quarters that consisted of octagonal chambers for cooking, living, and sleeping, above which the lantern was situated.

Facing: The final phase of lighthouse keeping before centralisation: the control room at North Foreland when the station acted as a monitoring station for the lightvessels in the Strait of Dover. The duty keeper is at the electronic desk, calling up the station reports from the remote, automated 'out-stations'.

Left: Bearing spherical daymarks at her three mastheads, the Goodwin Lightvessel, later renamed the South Goodwin, has a hoisting lantern, lowered to the deckhouse during daylight. To the left of this is the emitting trumpet of her diaphone fog signal. The ensign is worn from a jigger mast to which a boom is triced up. A steadying sail was spread from this in bad weather. Some of the lightvessels also displayed storm warnings when instructed to do so.

Work was so far advanced by July that Mr Bush's wife and son joined him to live on the beacon. Unfortunately for Mr Bush that same month Trinity House ordered the whole structure removed. Despite all the care taken in building the beacon it was so badly placed – right in the centre of the sands (apparently on the orders of the Admiralty) – that when lighted, it was thought that it would lead ships into disaster rather than warn them of it. Such muddled thinking and dislocated enterprise benighted similar initiatives during the period and were a remnant of the *laissez faire* attitude that still prevailed, despite the great Act of Parliament of 1836.

However, despite its apparent success it was unlikely that Bush's structure would have lasted for very long. In 1844 James Walker designed a beacon similar to Captain Bullock's but more massive and made of iron. This structure withstood the storms but the shifting sands overwhelmed it, so that it was barely visible by 1850. Another more elaborate construction designed by Walker in 1847 lasted only two months. The last attempt was made in 1849 by Captain Vinten of Trinity House. He constructed his beacon at the eastern edge of the sands where it remained until being swept away in December 1879. Since then the Goodwins have been marked only by navigational aids floating along its margins: buoys and lightvessels.

A handful of lightvessels had been established around the coast of England during the Eighteenth Century following the success of the first at the Nore in the Thames Estuary in 1732. In 1791 a petition was made to Trinity House for a vessel to be placed at the northern end of the Goodwin Sands. The petitioners argued that 'the bare interest of the property lost on the Goodwin Sands in one year would maintain a floating light as long as this world endures'. Trinity House was reluctant to establish a vessel due to the exposed position, stating that 'in the event of a hard gale of wind breaking her adrift,

there is not the smallest chance of the vessel or any of her crew being saved'. The Board of Trinity House were also mindful of the complications and obligations of her manning and management.

However, in 1793 Trinity House bowed to the strong wishes of the trade and obtained a patent. In October 1794 it was resolved that: 'three distinct lights be exhibited in this vessel, to distinguish them from the North and South Foreland Light[house]s, and that a large bell be fix'd in the vessel, to be constantly rung in hazy and thick weather to warn ships as they approach the Goodwin Sands'. Named the North Sand Head the new lightvessel was established in 1795.

She was purpose-built by Messrs Randall and Brent who had, in 1788, constructed a new buoy-yacht for Trinity House at their Rotherhithe yard at a cost of 12 guineas per ton. The new lightvessel was 150 tons and was fitted with Argand oil lamps obtained from a Mr Robinson, who supplied copper lanterns, lamps, oil cisterns, plate glass, and an iron hearth. On completion, ten seamen, a mate, and Mr Grice, formerly Master of the Owers Lightvessel, were appointed to the North Sand Head. To distinguish her, she bore three lanterns, each of which was hoisted to the head of a mast at sunset every night. By day each mast carried a wicker-work sphere. In September 1795, with the country once again at war with a now fervently republican France, the Board of Trinity House grew concerned about the safety of the crew in their exposed position. They requested that the Admiralty direct the commanders of cruisers to assist and protect the North Sand Head Lightvessel and also ordered arms for the crew in case they were molested. They consisted of two light 4-pounder carriage guns, a dozen muskets, six brace of pistols and a dozen long boarding pikes. It seems to have deterred the enemy, for there are no records of interference.

During and after the Napoleonic Wars the number of lightvessels deployed at sea increased as their usefulness and reliability was demonstrated. The Gull Lightvessel was placed on the western side of the Goodwins in 1809 to mark the inside passage of the Gull Stream. At first this was a wooden vessel with two fixed lights but in 1860 a revolving light was fitted.

In 1832 a lightvessel was established at the southern edge of the sands. Named the South Sand Head, this was again a purpose-built wooden craft of 184 tons. In 1875 she was fitted with a fog siren, and received a flashing light in 1884.

At about this time the old North Sand Head Lightvessel was replaced by a 184-ton iron ship built at Blackwall in London. In 1877 the station's light was changed from three separate lanterns to a single flashing light. Finally, in 1874, the east side of the sands was marked by the East Goodwin Lightvessel bearing a revolving light giving one flash every 15 seconds and, unusually, coloured green.

Thus, by the 1880s these four lightvessel stations, supplemented by buoys, stood guard over the Goodwin Sands. However, apart from the South Sand Head which had a siren, they all still relied on the limited benefit of large gongs that were beaten in fog. Lightvessels are always vulnerable to collisions, in the past often because ships' officers misjudged the set of strong tides. The danger increased in conditions of low visibility, and sound signals were necessary to warn approaching shipping of a lightvessel's presence. During the next twenty years the East Goodwin and Gull Lightvessels were equipped with reed horns whilst sirens were installed on the North Sand Head and South Sand Head Lightvessels, which were at this time renamed North Goodwin and South Goodwin.

Despite the increased effectiveness of the light and fog signals, collisions continued to occur. In the early morning of 17 March 1929 the Gull Lightvessel was struck down in thick fog by the steamship *City of York*. Badly holed, she sank before the startled crew even had time to launch a lifeboat. Apart from the Master, Mr Williams, who must have been trapped in his cabin close to the point of collision and whose body was later recovered from the sunken lightvessel, the crew were rescued by the *City of York*, which had anchored nearby and lowered a lifeboat to assist.

The wreck of the lightvessel (No 38, built in 1860) was raised and, after a refit, placed back on station in 1930. However, due to changes in the position of the sandbanks she was relocated to the western side of the Gull Stream rather than the eastern as before, and the name of the station was changed to Brake.

During the early part of the Second World War the Brake was only manned part-time and lit only when required by passing coastal convoys. On the freezing night of the 16 January 1940 a gale was blowing and snow flurries reduced visibility. An Italian steamer, the *Ernani*, broke adrift from her anchor in The Downs and drifted into the Brake, holing her just above the waterline. The crew abandoned ship and, after rowing for an hour in the icy conditions, managed to find help. The Master, Mr J. Beet, and two others were suffering from exposure and frostbite.

However, the lightvessel, then eighty-years old, remained afloat and those of the crew who were sufficiently fit were returned to her by a Trinity House Vessel the next day. Under the direction of the tender's officers the hole was patched and, in due course, the damage was permanently repaired at Harwich. Lightvessel No 38 went on to serve at the Mouse station in the Thames Estuary and was finally sold to the Thurrock Yacht Club in 1947, serving as their headquarters for some years. Now she sits sadly derelict on the bank of the River Thames whose once busy traffic she so faithfully served.

The South Goodwin Disaster

The accidents at Gull and Brake are overshadowed by a far more serious incident alluded to earlier – the loss of the South Goodwin Lightvessel on the night of 26/27 November 1954.

At that time Lightvessel No 90 a modern steel vessel built in 1937 by Phillip and Son of Dartmouth, was on the South Goodwin station. Onboard was an experienced crew: the Master, Horace (known as 'Tom') Skipp, had served with Trinity House for twenty-four years. With him were the Lamplighters, Kenneth Lanham and Sidney Philpott; Fog-Signal Drivers, Walter Viney and George Cox; Seaman Henry Lynn and Extra Seaman Ben Porter.

Also onboard was twenty-two-year-old Ronald Murton, who was working for the Ministry of Agriculture and Fisheries and monitoring bird numbers on an 'infestation control' project. He had boarded the South Goodwin on 1 November and was to be its sole survivor. After the loss of the vessel Murton was interviewed by the Trinity House Board of Enquiry and his answers provide us with the only record of the tragedy.

On the night of 26 November 1954 there was a high southerly wind, Force 10 to 11 on the Beaufort scale. This was strong enough to generate a swell of 10-12' within the shelter of Dover Harbour. Around midnight, at the height of the storm, the tide was running at its swiftest, flowing to the north. In these conditions the strain on the lightvessel's anchor cable was enormous, but the cable was heavy and had a breaking strain of over 90 tons. Owing to the subsequent disappearance of the lightvessel, the exact reason for the failure of the mooring was never established, but it is generally supposed to have occurred at one of the swivels set between the links. Be that as it may, in these extreme conditions, the cable suddenly broke and the lightvessel was cast adrift, broaching-to broadside to wind and sea and rolling most horribly.

Through his fitful sleep that evening Ronald Murton became conscious that the ship was moving more than usual. Around midnight, after a particularly bad roll, he put a sweater on over his pyjamas and went up to the wheelhouse. Here Henry Lynn and Sidney Philpott were on watch, Tom Skipp was also there and, before long, Ken Lanham joined them.

The position of the vessel, her head to the southwest, was worrying everyone. Tom Skipp, went forward to inspect the mooring. He put his hand on the cable and, from the wheelhouse windows, the others saw that he was able to move it – they realised that it had parted. After this Murton's recollections are of a rush of events:

'Philpott went to the door…and exclaimed "The East Goodwin Light is on top of us". I looked out myself and saw the beam of the East Goodwin which brightly illuminated the inside of the wheelhouse.' At this time the lightvessel must have been passing to the west of the East Goodwin, over the sands that were to claim her in the following minutes.

Murton rushed below to fetch the rest of the crew. They were all awake and Cox was following behind as Murton ran back up to the galley. Just as they got there the lightvessel hit the sands with a juddering impact. Murton recalled: 'The ship lurched. She had a heavy list.... The next instant we went over completely right on to her side.... Water was coming in through the hatch, filling [everything] up in seconds. In consequence we were out of our depth in water. As water came in everyone was knocked about but I cannot visualise this very clearly.... The water was rising rapidly...I realised I had to get out and made for the skylight. There was a heavy swell. Water gushing in the galley door and absolutely fantastic conditions, it took me about ten minutes to get to the skylight.'

Murton managed to climb out, trying to help George Cox: 'I was clinging on the outside and reached for his hands. I got hold of him but a wave came and hit me and I went under and was nearly washed off and lost Cox. After that there was no noise or anything from inside the galley.'

Murton realised that it was too dangerous to stay where he was. In complete darkness, the waves lashing over him, he worked his way up to the handrails of the boat deck and wedged himself there. He heard someone calling from the wheelhouse but after a time the cries stopped. Dressed only in his pyjamas the hypothermic young man clung to the rails, concentrating hard to maintain his insecure position through the rest of the night. As day broke he heard aircraft passing overhead bringing hope of rescue. The tide had receded and Murton heard a knocking from a skylight; inside he could see Tom Porter:

'I asked him how he was. He replied that he was hungry. I assumed that he could not be too bad. I asked if anyone else was with him and he said, "Viney and the Skipper". Neither of these two men spoke but Porter said they were in a bad way. Porter wanted me to get the window open or to break the glass. I could not lever it open with my hands. It was impossible to break [the armoured] glass with my hands. I told him this and that I had heard planes overhead and that rescue would not be long. I could not do anything for him and I sat down.'

The alarm had been raised by the crew of the East Goodwin Lightvessel through the Coastguard station at Deal through whom the group of Goodwin lightvessels maintained routine contact with Harwich. The Ramsgate, Dover, and Walmer Lifeboats were launched but they could not get near to the wreck due to the violent sea conditions. Meanwhile at Harwich the Chief Superintendent had ordered THV *Vestal* to sea; she had sailed at 0520.

Since the South Goodwin Lightvessel had struck the sands the tide had been falling but as the morning drew on the tide turned and began to flood again. The wind, which had lulled, was also increasing. An American Air/Sea Rescue plane, which took off at 0730 from RAF Manston, near Ramsgate, made several passes over the wreck but the pilot reported no sign of life. However, a helicopter crew volunteered to take another look. The helicopter's pilot, Captain Curtiss Parkins, reported reaching the wreck around 0915 and saw Ronald Murton still clinging to the railings despite the seas that were again washing over the wreck. Parkins took his aircraft perilously low and managed to winch up the half-blinded and frozen Murton – an act for which Parkins was awarded the Silver Medal of the Royal National Lifeboat Institution, the first airman ever to receive the award.

As soon as he was in the helicopter, Murton told the crew that there were men still alive inside the South Goodwin Lightvessel but conditions were too dangerous for boats to land. At 1030 THV *Vestal* arrived at the wreck and put her motor launches in the water but, due to the heavy surf, they were unable to land a rescue party on the sands. Another attempt in the afternoon proved fruitless and it was only at dawn the following day, when THV *Patricia* had arrived to relieve *Vestal*, that her first officer, Mr Claude Parsons, together with Royal Navy divers which had arrived in HMS *Romola*, at last landed and searched the capsized lightvessel. The hull was already filling with sand and they found no sign of Skipp or his crew, despite returning at dawn, 29 November, with oxy-acetylene cutting equipment. The dead men's bodies were never recovered and No 90 lightvessel was left sinking in the sands. Parsons, afterwards a District Superintendent with the rank of Captain, was awarded an MBE for his tenacious efforts to find the crew.

This vulnerability to collision, combined with their relative helplessness in the face of adversity (for they possess no independent propulsion and have to be towed to and from station), made lightvessels early candidates for replacement by unmanned and automatic substitutes. Today, as a result of the navigational review of 1987, many former lightvessel stations, like the North Goodwin, have been discontinued or down-graded to increasingly sophisticated, solar-powered buoys. The most important stations, including the South and East Goodwin, are now occupied by unmanned lightvessels, monitored and controlled by the Operational Control Centre at Harwich.

Latitude	*50° 54.77'N*
Longitude	*000° 58.67'E*
Established	*1615*
Height of tower	*43/37m*
Height of light above MHWS	*40m*
Character	*Fl10s* *+F.RG*
Range	*21Nm* *+10Nm*
Fog Signal	*Horn(3)60s*

Dungeness Lighthouse

The flat headland of Dungeness is surrounded on its seaward side by deep water. Giving no warning of the proximity of land, for there is hardly any indication of shoaling. Moreover, at no point does the great ness reach any serious elevation, and landmarks inland may only confuse the hapless mariner. The dangers of rounding Dungeness and the effectiveness of its lighthouse were broadcast in an early navigational direction: 'a shipp may be in 10 or 12 faddome water and in a quarter of an houres sale may runne uppon land…. Besides experience showes that the steeple of Lyd (Lydd), a towne neere by, doth unhappily present unto straungers uppon those seas the forme of a sale of some tall shipp which hath binn a meanes oftentimes towards night to incourage marriners to steere their course confidently that way…whereby many shipps have…runn on ground and perished, which dangerous mistake this light doth prevent.'

The shingle mass moves under the impetus of the tidal scour, its inexorable eastward migration a problem for builders of lighthouses and nuclear power stations alike. A focal point for shipping, Dungeness once provided shelter for the French corsairs who infested this coast during the American War of Independence and the French Revolutionary and Napoleonic Wars, waiting to pounce on homeward-bound British merchantmen. More recently the large cruising pilot-cutters of Trinity House lay here, awaiting ships inbound for London, or ready to disembark pilots bringing outward-bound vessels down Channel, bound for the four corners of the earth.

The first lighthouse at Dungeness was established in 1615 to warn of the extended danger of the obstructing headland after claims that more than a thousand seamen were lost annually on it 'for want of a light'. A burgess of Rye named John Allen proposed the building of a lighthouse, but could not obtain a grant because he had no influence at court. William Bullock, a Customs official, then tried and failed for the same reason. Bullock approached William Bing who, in turn, tried William Lamplugh who held a royal sinecure as a Clerk of the Kitchen. It was Lamplugh who persuaded Sir Edward Howard to petition for a light, since Howard stood a good chance of success, being both a cup-bearer to the King and also the nephew of the Earl of Nottingham, then the Lord High Admiral. After duly consulting Trinity House as to the need for such a lighthouse and receiving a positive response, James I granted a patent to Howard in August 1615.

In November 1616 a formal agreement was made for sharing the profits of the lighthouse. Howard would get one half, Lamplugh and Bing would share the other. William Bullock (who claimed to have built the lighthouse) was not included in the agreement but Lamplugh and Bing agreed that he could have a third of their share. A few years later, in 1620, Sir Edward Howard died. His executor assigned his half share to William Bullock who then claimed a controlling interest and initiated a train of contentious debate over the lighthouse. However, Lamplugh did not give up and the argument over ownership continued for the next fifteen years. Such legal wranglings, which were commonplace during the age of private lighthouses, did little to promote lighthouse management as a disinterested service to the mariner. It was perhaps not surprising therefore that, during Lamplugh's time at Dungeness, Trinity House made an attempt to oust all private owners of lighthouses by having a Parliamentary Bill passed, supplementing an Act of 1566, to give them complete control of lighthouses. They did not succeed due to the opposition of the King for whom the patronage of patent-granting was politically useful. However, the debates of 1621 revealed the condition of Dungeness Lighthouse at that time. It was alleged that the light was badly kept and that instead of a stone tower lit by an open fire there was in fact a timber tower lit by candles.

Discontent about the lighthouse continued and in 1623 a Commission, set up to look into the question of dues for the light, submitted its report to the Lord High Admiral. The original patent allowed for the collection of a penny every time a ship passed the light, both on their inward and outward passages. Mariners had protested that the shipowners should pay half the dues but the owners had refused. The Commission concluded that the dues being charged were more than the seamen had agreed to pay at the time of establishing the light, and attributed this to a mistake by the Lord High Admiral of the time (who was of course the original patentee's uncle).

The commission criticized Lamplugh for falsifying accounts and keeping the light badly. (On another occasion Lamplugh was also found to be obtaining dues by falsehood; the East India Company had agreed to pay a lump sum for their own vessels' contribution, and then found that Lamplugh was levying the full dues on their individual ships as well.) Despite all this Lamplugh remained in possession and in 1627 the King actually ordered customs officers to assist him in collecting his dues.

As the lighthouse was such a good source of income, various local bodies also tried to gain possession. During the debate in 1621 the Dover Court of Lodemanage proposed that they take over the running of the lighthouse, a cynically different attitude to the expressed view when they had debated the establishment of lighthouses on the Kentish Forelands. Next the ancient Cinque Ports made a claim and, in 1624, the townsmen of Rye joined the fray, proposing to use the profits to repair their harbour.

In 1635 the argument over ownership, which had rumbled on even after Lamplugh's death, was finally resolved when the patent was re-issued in the name of William Bullock. The Privy Council also settled the dispute over dues, the toll remained a penny each way but was to be payable on the return voyage, and the merchants were ordered to pay their half.

In natural defiance of this bickering, Dungeness itself steadily migrated towards the southeast, so that Bullock was obliged to build a new lighthouse closer to the extremity of the point, following complaints from mariners that the light was too far from the sea. This new tower was lit by a coal fire and was to continue in service until 1792. A representation of the Dungeness Lighthouse survives on a light-dues receipt dated 10 December 1703. It shows a circular tower with dwellings surrounding its base in a hexagonal or octagonal form. The dwellings appear to be wooden or at least weather-boarded, as does the lower part of the tower. The top is surrounded by an open parapet and a keeper stands between this and a huge fire contained in an iron basket-grate. A winch is being used to hoist up the coal. A later drawing at Trinity House shows the same building but with some modifications: it now seems to be a rendered stone or brick structure and the coal is hoisted up the centre of the tower.

The drawing on the light-dues receipt gives an insight into the difficulty of maintaining a satisfactory open fire on top of a tall tower. Stoking the fire, drawing up the coals, and disposing of the cinders required continual hard labour. If the ash was not treated with care it could create a hazard: in

Facing: The second lighthouse at Dungeness with its open coal fire and after the addition of surrounding dwellings. The amount of smoke gives a good idea of the relative ineffectiveness of this form of light, and of the difficulties the keepers had in maintaining it. This tower was in service until 1792.

Below: Thomas William Coke's new Dungeness Lighthouse, designed by Samuel Wyatt and built in 1792.

1791 George Anderson, the keeper at the Isle of May Lighthouse in Scotland, his wife and five of his eight children were suffocated by fumes from the cinders piled up by the tower.

By the mid Eighteenth Century the patent to maintain the Dungeness Lighthouse and to collect tolls was held by the Earl of Leicester. His descendant, Thomas William Coke, the famous agriculturalist of Holkham Hall in Norfolk, rebuilt the lighthouse in 1792 to the design of Samuel Wyatt, the architect of Trinity House itself. It was a tall tower – 38 metres to the top of the lantern – and was a generous 13 metres wide at the base to provide both stability and accommodation for the keepers.

Robert Stevenson, the pioneering Scottish lighthouse engineer, visited the place in 1818 on one of his three famous 'lighthouse tours'. He recorded that the building had been in danger of falling but that four buttresses had been built to support it. In the lantern were eighteen reflectors which had been made in 1802 by Mr Howard of Old Street in London. Stevenson also cannily observed that the owner must be receiving a great deal of money from the lighthouse.

Despite opposition from Trinity House, which was by then taking an increasing responsibility for the practical management of lighthouses, the lease was renewed in 1828 for twenty-one years. However, part of the dues, which had averaged over £7,000 a year, were transferred to the Crown, reducing Mr Coke's income to around £2,000 a year. Under powers granted to Trinity House by the 1836 Act of Parliament, the Corporation finally purchased the lighthouse in 1837 paying £20,954 for the remaining portion of the lease. A few years later, in 1843, keepers' dwellings were built encircling the base of the tower.

Facing: The modern elegant concrete lighthouse paid for by the Central Electricity Generating Board and commissioned in 1961.

Below: The replacement tower brought into service in March 1904 still stands. Here it appears to rise from the dwellings that were added to Wyatt's lighthouse and which remained after the demolition of his old tower.

In the 1850s the Board of Trinity House, prompted by their scientific adviser Michael Faraday, 'the father of electricity', experimented with electric light at South Foreland Lighthouse. Encouraged they decided on a permanent installation at Dungeness. The steam generators and 'magneto-electric' machines were placed in a room at the base of the tower and the boilers for these went into a corrugated-iron shed nearby. Provided by a Holmes generator, the electric light was first shown on 1 February 1862, but it was then shut down and its use postponed for four months on the grounds that the keepers were not capable of running the generating machinery. However, the new form of lighting

served its purpose. It was only required for short periods – sometimes five minutes when word would come via the signal station – "OK they have gone over".'

Mr Simon and the other wartime keepers had a narrow escape at Beachy Head when 'a mine was observed drifting towards the station, we passed the word to the naval authorities and were told that if it was over 200 yards away to attempt to sink it by gun fire. We told whoever it was at the other end that we had no guns, and after a slight hesitation he said, "Well, just standby". It continued to drift towards us and in a few minutes it passed with no more than three feet to spare, heading for the shore where it struck a rock and exploded, blackening the cliff to the very top. I sometimes wonder what would have happened to the tower – and to us – if it had struck.'

The paraffin vapour burner and explosive fog signal remained in operation until 1975 when mains electricity was provided via a cable from the cliff top. Before that the keepers cooked with solid fuel and, just as Simon and his colleagues had, used paraffin for domestic lighting. The only electricity on the station was a battery charged by a windmill generator on the gallery and used to run a television.

Following and below: Beachy Head Lighthouse.

The smell of paraffin dominated the cramped living spaces of the tower and clung to the keepers' clothes when they went home. Less than a decade after electricity was installed at Beachy Head the lighthouse was automated and on 28 July 1983 the last three keepers left the station for the final time.

Meanwhile the Belle Tout Lighthouse enjoyed mixed fortunes. After abandonment in 1899 it was left until 1923 when it was restored and lived in as a private house. During the Second World War the building was used for target practice by the British and Canadian artillery and almost destroyed. In 1956 it became a home again but was missing a lantern until it was used by the BBC in 1988 for filming the programme *Life and Loves of a She-Devil*. The BBC restored the building and erected a replacement lantern. Thereafter the old light became a private dwelling again. Further drama came in March 1999 when the whole building was moved 15 metres back from the crumbling cliff edge. The owners now offer bed-and-breakfast accommodation in the tower which, of course, has wonderful sea views.

Beachy Head Lighthouse was further modified in 1999. This was complicated by a massive chalk fall above the lighthouse knocking out the mains cables. A generator was placed on a scaffolding platform outside the tower to provide power during the work. New cables were put in place by mid July, enabling the installation of the new lamps, fog signal and emergency light to go ahead.

The South of England

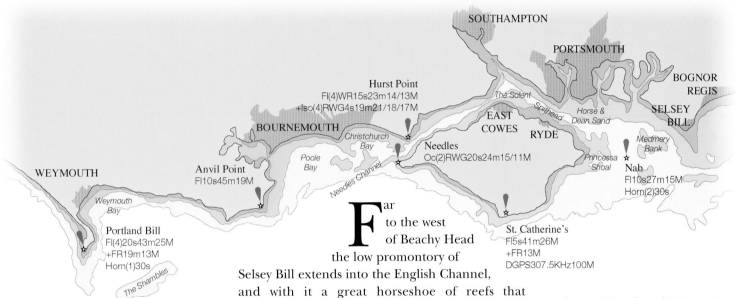

Facing: Hurst Point Lighthouse from the north, seen across the tranquil saltings of Keyhaven.

Far to the west of Beachy Head the low promontory of Selsey Bill extends into the English Channel, and with it a great horseshoe of reefs that terminate in the Owers Bank. For many years the extremity of the Owers was marked by a lightvessel but today buoys guard the dangerous crescent of shoals that lie in the eastern approaches to the busiest area on England's beautiful South Coast, for beyond Selsey Bill lies the Isle of Wight, The Solent, and the ports of Portsmouth and Southampton.

The eastern portion of the strait that separates the Isle of Wight from the mainland is known as Spithead, the traditional fleet anchorage of the Royal Navy since Tudor times lying, as it does, on the doorstep of Britain's principal naval base of Portsmouth. In addition to the royal dockyard, Portsmouth provides marinas for yachtsmen, a ferry terminus connecting with France, and commercial berths for small merchant vessels.

Beyond Spithead the narrow channel becomes The Solent, a strait upon which, at almost any time of the year, yachts may be seen. Its western entrance is narrow and terminates at The Needles. At the confluence of the rivers Itchen and Test lies the commercial port of Southampton. Once the terminus of the great transatlantic ocean liners, today Southampton supports a container trade in general goods as well as providing facilities for handling bulk cargoes and serving as a terminus for cruise-ships. Upon the western shore of the conjoined estuary lies the huge oil refinery of Fawley and, to the west again, another river, the Hamble, drains into Southampton Water.

The Hamble, like Langstone and Chichester Harbours to the east of Portsmouth, and the Beaulieu and Lymington Rivers to the west of Southampton Water, provides moorings, marinas, and extensive cruising grounds for sailors of all ages, ability and means. This is, of course, mirrored on the offshore side of the Solent where, along the coast of the Isle of Wight, from Bembridge in the east to Yarmouth in the west, with Fishbourne, Cowes, and Newtown Creek in between, yachts proliferate during the long sailing season.

The eastern entrance to this crossroads of maritime life is guarded by a singular lighthouse, the Nab Tower.

The Nab Tower

Latitude	*50° 40.04'N*
Longitude	*000° 57.07'W*
Established	*1920*
Height of tower	*27m*
Height of light above MHWS	*27m*
Character	*Fl10s*
Range	*15Nm*
Fog Signal	*Horn(2)30s*
Racon fitted	

The channels leading into Spithead from the east were once marked by several lightvessels, the Owers, the Warner and, most notably, the Nab, around which the first *America*'s Cup was raced for in 1851. As might be expected, the Admiralty shared the business of marking the shoals and navigational dangers that encumber the entrance to Spithead, taking upon itself the duty of buoyage within the limits of the Dockyard Port of Portsmouth, a duty now supervised by the Ministry of Defence. Beyond this, however, it was Trinity House to whom the matter was entrusted... except that there was the curious anomaly of the Nab Tower.

During the First World War the German submarine offensive against enemy merchant shipping proved near catastrophic to the survival of Great Britain. It was decided to deny enemy access to the Strait of Dover and thus to compel marauding U-boats leaving their bases in Germany to waste fuel by having to pass to the north of Scotland in order to reach the Atlantic. The plan would also protect the supply route across the Strait of Dover to the British armies fighting on the Western Front. In order to accomplish this, steel-wire nets were extended across the Channel, handled by 'boom-defence vessels' and suspended from buoys. As the war dragged on more efficient means were sought and it was decided to establish a number of prefabricated concrete-and-steel structures, between which the nets would be more effectively suspended. These nets would also carry mines, designed to destroy any enemy submarine attempting to force a passage.

Designed by the principal assistant to the Admiralty's Engineer-in-Chief, Mr G. Menzies, construction of the first of these towers was put in hand at Southwick near Shoreham in Sussex. Three thousand labourers were drafted in and, under conditions of official secrecy, formed a reinforced concrete, irregular-shaped octagon, 60 metres long with a depth of 24 metres. It contained four tiers of hexagonal cells, each 1.8 metres across, the total concrete in the structure amounting to 9,000 tons. From this rose a steel tower, 17 metres in diameter, supported by an exterior steel lattice, the whole weighing some 1,000 tons.

Unfortunately the war ended before the first tower could be towed and sunk in position and, faced with an embarrassing expenditure of £1.25 millions, an alternative use was sought for the dominating structure. It was decided that the tower should replace the Nab Lightvessel, acting also as a naval signal station and later, during the Second World War when its twin Bofors guns were credited with a couple of enemy aeroplanes, as an anti-aircraft gun-platform.

On 12 September 1920 the tower was floated out of Shoreham, towed by two naval paddle tugs. The design allowed slow flooding of the cells, but these filled more rapidly than planned and the bottom of the caisson struck the seabed prematurely. As a consequence the tower settled with a 1.5° list to the southwest, a mile from the old lightvessel's position.

The tower was a great improvement on the old lightvessel, a better aid to navigation, being a fixed point and exhibiting a superior array of aids – a main navigation light, a fog signal and sector lights to cover the deepwater channel into Spithead. In due course the contraction of the Royal Navy resulted in the removal of the naval personnel and only the Trinity House lighthouse keepers remained until, in 1983, the tower was fitted with an automatic acetylene light, and was fitted with a concrete helipad to enable access for maintenance staff by air, and a new, prefabricated lantern-tower was air-lifted in. Experiments in wind generation to maintain charge in batteries intended as a reserve power source were undertaken on the Nab, but the results were considered unsatisfactory when compared with the potential of solar power. Accordingly, in 1995, a new electric main light was installed, powered by solar cells deployed on the upper deck. Two years later the Nab was transferred to the Operational Control Centre at Harwich.

The Nab Tower provides a waypoint for coastal shipping passing up or down the English Channel, a landfall mark for vessels making for Spithead, Portsmouth or Southampton, and a guide through the shoals inshore of its location. An ugly, uninspiring structure, it was never dignified by the name of 'lighthouse' remaining always a 'tower', its light called colloquially 'the Nab Tower light'. Although its inelegance might be considered a monument to the ugly imperatives of war, the Nab has nevertheless provided a useful guide for the mariner, be he admiral or amateur, for almost a century. Moreover, its size and unorthodox shape, originally designed to accommodate ninety naval personnel, provided its keepers with living quarters of a capacity and relative comfort not found in many other offshore stations.

The immense strength of the structure was illustrated seventy-nine years after its establishment when, in November 1999, the banana-laden *Dole America* of 10,500 tonnes collided with it. Some slight damage was suffered by the tower, whereas substantial injury was caused to the hull of the vessel.

Hurst Point Lighthouse

The western approaches to The Solent are much narrower and more dangerous than the eastern. The south coast of the mainland extends in an area of tidal saltings and sand spits, to terminate in Hurst Point. To guard this western entrance to the Royal Navy's main base, Henry VIII built one of a series of defensive castles. Hurst Castle is low, a platform for cannon, and acted briefly as a prison for Charles I when the unfortunate monarch was on his way from confinement at Carisbrooke Castle on the Isle of Wight to his trial and subsequent execution in London.

Hurst Castle was modernised in the mid Nineteenth Century when a string of forts, including Fort Albert across the water on the Isle of Wight, were built to improve the outer defences of Portsmouth itself. Hurst Castle now squats on the littoral, its row of embrasures closed by great iron shutters. To the west of Hurst Point an extensive shoal known as The Shingles confines navigation to the Needles Channel. On the Isle of Wight shore the western extremity terminates in a series of narrow and

Latitude	*50° 42.44'N*
Longtitude	*001° 32.94'W*
Established	*1786*
Height of tower	*26m*
Height of light above MHWS	*23m*
Character	*Fl(4)WR15s +Iso(4)RWG*
Range	*14/13Nm +21/18/17Nm*

precipitous chalk stacks known as The Needles.

In the days of sailing ships the favoured approach to Portsmouth and Southampton was the safer, eastern passage, but it took longer and often necessitated a beat to windward in the prevailing westerlies, to fetch Southampton. Small craft took advantage of local knowledge and carried the wind and tide through the narrow western Needles Channel, an expertise that others envied. It was a passage bedevilled by strong tides and, though the conspicuous chalk 'Needles' were included in instructions for navigating as early as 1621, it could realistically only be attempted in favourable, daylight conditions. In 1781, therefore, a meeting of shipmasters and merchants, headed by two of the latter, William Tatnall and Stephen Mignon, requested Trinity House to provide lights to mark the Isle of Wight from seaward and to assist shipping to safely pass through the Needles Channel. They deposed that 'ships and vessels have been lost...and the lives, ships and goods of his Majesty's subjects as well as the King's Royal Navy continue to be exposed to the like calamities more especially in the night time and in hard southerly gales...'. A patent was obtained in January 1782 and negotiations were opened with Tatnall, but these were first delayed by war with France and then fell through after three years of arguing. Tatnall had been granted £960 per annum for a twenty-one year lease from which he would pay for the building of the lights. Setting about his task, Tatnall engaged Richard Jupp to design and oversee the construction of the towers 'at the Needles and Hurst Beach, and also the lighthouse

Above: Hurst Point Lighthouse with the original castle in the centre foreground and the later embrasures spreading to the west and northeast aound the point itself. Along the rear of the rampart to the left of the old castle can be seen the former lower leading light, and on its left, the red-painted iron replacement that was added to conform to the shifting of the Shingles Bank.

on St Catherine's Point', which Trinity House had decided should be built at the same time. Jupp was a surveyor to the Honourable East India Company and had been recommended to Tatnall by Captain John Travers who, in addition to holding office as an Elder Brother, had been an East India Company Commander and was shortly afterwards elected a Director of the Company.

Keen to start deriving an income from light dues, Tatnall advertised illumination of the lights on midsummer's day 1784 and had purchased lamp-oil and engaged his keepers. At this point an alternative proposal was put to Trinity House by a Lieutenant Mackenzie. Ordering Tatnall to delay the illumination, the Corporation sent Mackenzie to substantiate his claims and, on 7 October, Mackenzie reported the findings of his survey to Trinity House. The assembled Court listened to Mackenzie and also considered a report that Jupp, 'having delivered an Account of the charges of building them amounting to £2,364 whereof the sum of £1,750 had been advanced him, which leaves a balance due thereon of £614...'.

There can be no doubt that this sparked off a row that rumbled on for months. No doubt Samuel Wyatt, Trinity House's own architect, had been critical of Jupp but, on 3 November 1795, Travers claimed that while he had put up Tatnall and Mignon to petition for the lights, the whole concept originated from him. He renounced any claim to the light dues, which had doubtless been his private intention, but the revelation ended in the declaration that Tatnall's lease was void. Thereafter Trinity House accepted that the task would fall directly on itself and proceeded with Jupp's design. Finally, by the autumn of 1786, three lighthouses had been completed, one at Hurst Castle, another at St Catherine's Point and the third high on the cliffs above the Needles.

The first light at Hurst was situated to the southwest of the castle, and consisted of a tower 17.5 metres tall with a small adjoining cottage for the keeper. Rainwater was collected to provide fresh water and vegetables were grown. Fish were caught and wildfowl shot, but fuel and other foodstuffs had to be carried in by boat or along a track over the shingle. The garrison of the castle proved uneasy neighbours for, in July 1792, the keeper, John Howell, and his wife, Ann, were assaulted by a soldier who was afterwards bound over to keep the peace. By the census of 1851 three keepers and their families manned the station and they had been joined by coastguards and fishermen.

The location of this light soon proved unsatisfactory, being 'masked from certain directions' by the Needles. In 1812 a tower light was built some few hundred yards beyond the castle, the light of which shone out over the narrow channel entrance from a greater elevation and, by combining this higher light and forming a transit with the lower, provided a leading mark both by day and night for safely entering the Needles Channel. Designed by Daniel Alexander, Wyatt's successor at Trinity House, this High Light, as it became known, was first lit on 27 August 1812. By the time the stations were visited by Stevenson on his tour of 1818 each tower was fitted with reflectors and Argand lamps.

In 1860, the development of the ironclad warship led to the rebuilding of Hurst Castle during the next thirteen years. The original low light was in the way of the reconstruction and both towers had to be taken down and rebuilt during the undertaking of these extensive works. The new low light was erected as part of the curtain wall of the new defences, reached by a staircase on the outside of the fort where a cottage was erected for the keeper. The rebuilt lighthouse was illuminated in September 1865. To maintain the transit through the narrows the high light was shifted 15 metres to the eastward, furnished with cottages and relit in September 1867.

Unfortunately the southwest extremity of the Shingles Bank was unstable and the transit did not hold good for long. After fifty years the situation had become acute. The low light was abandoned and a red-painted iron lantern was set up on the castle's rampart. This could be moved laterally to conform with any subsequent shifting of the channel and was lit on 30 November 1911.

The keepers were withdrawn in 1923 when both lights became early examples of automation using acetylene. The gas was generated on station in a gas-house from rainwater and calcium carbide, and kept in gas-holders. In 1968 this system was replaced by banks of accumulators supplied from a Trinity House Vessel. By July 1997 however, the provision of a high-intensity electric light situated below the main light in the higher tower but visible in daylight, rendered the upkeep of any lower light superfluous. This new light is directional and capable of adjustment for any subsequent shifting of the channel, thus the tower now exhibits two lights providing the mariner with a warning if straying off the line of safe approach into the dangerous sector, as well as a conspicuous passage light for general navigation. Today the channel is used by ships of most sizes, including cruise ships, although very large tankers, constrained by their size and slow manoeuvrability, approach Fawley refinery by way of the Nab.

The Needles Lighthouse

If Jupp's tower at Hurst proved something of a failure it was not an irredeemable one. The same could not be said of his provision for the lights to mark The Needles, or the additional light on St Catherine's Point. Quite what contribution Mackenzie had made to the final outcome, beyond delineating the extent of the Shingles Bank is not clear, unless the prevarication he caused served solely to bring

Latitude	50° 39.7'N
Longitude	001° 35.43'W
Established	1786
Height of tower	31m
Height of light above MHWS	24m
Character	Oc(2)WRG20s
Range	15/11Nm
Fog Signal	Horn(2)30s

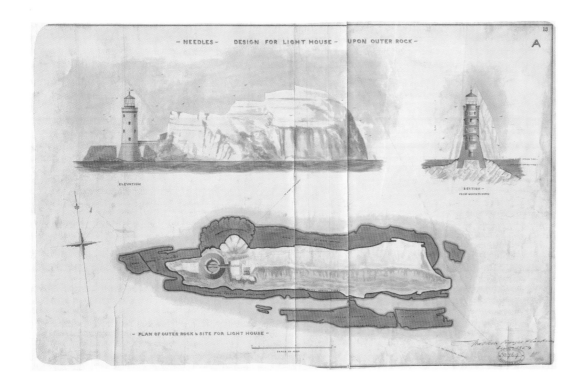

139

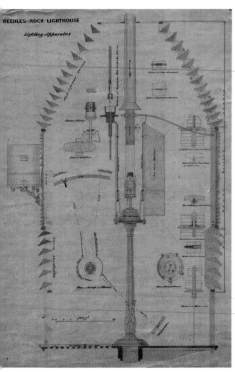

Top: Sectional drawing of Walker's design for the Needles Lighthouse. The vertical structure and stepped base are clearly seen; the arched vault in the base formed the fresh-water reservoir.

Above: The lighting apparatus showing how, from a relatively small light-source, the optic concentrated the rays into a broad horizontal plane.

Travers's misdeeds to light. Be that as it may, both the Needles and St Catherine's lights were set so high above sea level that they were frequently shrouded by cloud. This orographic nightmare was to dog the establishment of numerous lighthouse stations and it is difficult to see why the lesson, learned once, was not applied universally.

It appears both were soon abandoned, circumstances which gravely disappointed the expectations of mariners and merchants alike and did little to enhance the popularity of the Elder Brethren whose collective professional reputation was at that time at its nadir. In fact the Brethren, who had not themselves supervised the actual building of a lighthouse since 1680, were acquiring an increasing knowledge of the business as leases reverted to the Corporation, and they were less inclined to farm out the business. Concurrently with this change of attitude came the improved lighting technology of parabolic reflectors and Argand lamps. But neither of these expedients solved the problem of the high elevations of The Needles or St Catherine's lighthouses, and it was 1858 before the matter was addressed by James Walker. The Corporation's architect, Walker designed and oversaw the erection of a lighthouse situated on the most seaward 'needle'. He did not follow Smeaton's example of forming an upward curve from the base to the tapering diameter of the rising tower (see the Eddystone Lighthouse), but built his base in a series of stepped, annular courses of granite blocks. Walker's idea was to break up the kinetic energy in the waves as they hammered at the base of the tower and it has proved a successful modification. Extensive excavations in the rock formed the foundations and enabled Walker to locate water-tanks deep below the tower, while a cave, used for the storage of tools during construction, afterwards served as a store.

Walker's tower cost £20,000 and, in order to make it conspicuous against the white of the chalk to the east, was banded in red. Inside, to provide greater living space for the keepers, he reduced the thickness of the walls as they went up. It was illuminated on 1 January 1859. The powerful occulting light exhibits a series of coloured sectors to assist navigation: red over the Shingles and Dolphin Banks, green over the Warden Bank, white through the narrows past Hurst Castle and white to seaward.

The relative ease by which visitors may reach the Needles lighthouse resulted in it becoming an attraction for many people, including the Prince and Princess of Wales in 1863 and Charles Lutwidge Dodgson, alias Lewis Carrol, author of *Alice in Wonderland*. The Needles has also been used as a staging post for yacht and air-races, the keepers frequently benefiting from the generosity of local yacht clubs.

For some years after keepers elsewhere were relieved by helicopter, the Needles was thought unsuitable for such transport and the men continued to be transferred by boat from Yarmouth but, in 1987, a helipad was erected on top of the lighthouse, its supports conforming with the astragals of Walker's lantern. On 8 December 1994 the keepers were withdrawn for the last time and today the fully automated station is controlled at Harwich.

St Catherine's Lighthouse

Latitude	*50° 34.5'N*
Longitude	*001° 17.8'W*
Established	*c1323*
Height of tower	*25m*
Height of light above MHWS	*41m*
Character	*Fl5s +F.R*
Range	*26Nm +13Nm*
DGPS	*307.5KHz 100M*

Like The Needles high above Scratchell's Bay, Jupp's tower at St Catherine's was, at 228 metres, frequently lost in cloud during southwesterly airstreams. Yet it was in these very conditions that an efficient lighthouse was most wanted on the southern headland of the Isle of Wight, a need articulated centuries earlier.

The matter had come to a head in 1314 when a wine-laden vessel, owned by a monastery in Picardy, ran aground and broke up on the Atherfield Ledge, to the northwest of the headland. The cargo 'disappeared' and was believed to have been sold by the destitute crew, an argument not appealing to the charity of the distant monks, who charged a local landowner with receiving stolen goods. A legal wrangle ensued, ending in an appeal to the Pope in Rome who, in 1323, instructed the local gentleman, one Walter de Godyton, to erect an oratory and a light tower. De Godyton had perforce to obey, for he was threatened with excommunication, and by 1328 he had built his chapel, paid a priest to say masses for the souls of those lost at sea, and erected a tower on Chale Down to maintain a light to warn shipping to keep their offing. De Godyton's light was, like its successor, too high to have done much good, but his endowment existed until it was abolished at the Reformation around 1530. The 11 metre high octagonal structure remains and, with its pointed tower, is known locally as 'the Pepper Pot'. Not far away, Jupp's never-completed conical tower complements it as 'the Salt Cellar'.

Two years after the Act of 1836, Trinity House finally addressed the problem of a lighthouse at St Catherine's Point, ordering the construction of an elegant, crenellated octagonal tower not far from the Pepper Pot. Designed by James Walker and built of ashlar stone it rose in a series of diminishing tiers and was lit in March 1840. Alas, although Walker had surveyed his site well and selected a natural terrace on the Down, the tower, too, proved too tall and the top two tiers were removed in 1875 to reduce the height by some 13 metres. This was satisfactory for all practical purposes and forms the structure we see today though, like all lights, a dense surface sea fog will still obscure it. Even before the drastic modification of lowering the tower, a reed fog signal, to the design of the American sonic engineer C.L. Daboll, was installed in 1868, situated in a purpose-built house on the cliff edge. An additional keeper was assigned to the station to assist with the maintenance of this expensive addition, which was driven by a coke-fired caloric hot-air engine. In 1888 the lighthouse was converted to electric operation and Daboll's fog signal was replaced by a siren emitting two blasts every minute, one high pitched, the second lower. By 1932 the fog-signal house was seriously under-mined by erosion and had to be replaced. A smaller copy of the main lighthouse was built in front of it to accommodate the new fog-signal apparatus. With their propensity for nicknames, the locals christened the twin towers the 'Cow and Calf'.

On 1 June 1943, during the Second World War, German aircraft attacked the lighthouse, dropping incendiary bombs that set fire to the engine house in which the three keepers, Richard Grenfell, Charles Tomkins, and William Jones had taken shelter. Their incinerated bodies were later dug from the debris and laid to rest in Niton churchyard and a commemorative plaque is situated in the light tower.

In the post-war period the powerful, 5.25 million candela light was visible on a clear, dark night for thirty miles, with a red sector shining over Atherfield Ledge. From 'the Calf' a powerful super-Tyfon fog signal boomed out into poor visibility until its removal in 1987 from which time a radio-beacon transmitted its locational signal.

In 1991 the Trinity House Development Department established a light range and experimental station at the lighthouse, but its days as a fully manned establishment were numbered. Having served for many years as a weather reporting station and briefly as a local area control station, St Catherine's was fully automated and on 30 July 1997 the keepers left, handing over control to Harwich. St Catherine's remains an automatic weather reporting station and, like North Foreland, provides differential corrections to the Global Positioning System.

Anvil Point Lighthouse

Beyond the bights of Christchurch, Poole, Studland, and Swanage Bays lies the chalk headland of Anvil Point. Once joined to the Needles, a number of chalk stacks encumber the coast before the soft white rock retreats inland and the coast to the west is composed of limestone. Off Anvil Point and St Alban's Head, close by, heavy overfalls and swirling tide-rips can prove dangerous to small ships and yachts.

Built by Trinity House in 1881, to a design by James Douglass, as part of the rolling programme to provide a series of passage lights, Anvil Point avoids being veiled in orographic cloud by being a squat tower. Originally supported by a fog signal and with its keepers' dwellings inshore of the lighthouse, Anvil Point was one of those pleasant land stations where the keepers lived with their families, a small community and, for the older men, was a haven after years served offshore.

In 1960 the station was converted to electric power, the large optic was removed and donated to the Science Museum in London. A smaller optic was fitted and the fog signal, an ancient five-minute carronade, was replaced by an electric emitter. This was discontinued in 1988 and full automation followed, the keepers leaving on 31 May 1991.

Latitude	*50° 35.48'N*
Longitude	*001° 57.52'W*
Established	*1881*
Height of tower	*12m*
Height of light above MHWS	*45m*
Character	*Fl10s*
Range	*19Nm*

Portland Bill Lighthouse

Connected to the mainland by the long shingle spit of Chesil Beach, Portland is geologically an island. Its southern extremity, the Bill itself, extends into the English Channel to cause both the flood and ebb tides to swirl in its shadow with an enormous ferocity, causing the notorious Portland Race. In strong gales the area may be torn with high and unpredictable breaking seas, causing extensive damage to yachts and ships alike. Just to the east of the headland lies the dangerous shoal known appropriately enough, for the term once referred to the blood of butchery, as The Shambles.

Behind Portland Bill and Chesil Beach lies Portland Harbour, enclosed to the east by long stone breakwaters constructed by prisoners awaiting transportation to Australia during the 1840s. Accommodated in a mist-shrouded prison, The Verne, on the summit of this 'island', these wretches quarried the stone which became famous as Portland stone and Portland cement. Once a great naval base, Portland, together with neighbouring Weymouth, is now a commercially operated port. Thus, with the offshore danger of the Portland Race a threat to the safe passage of ships, the necessity of providing a landfall and a passage seamark makes the lighthouse at Portland Bill important.

The area was greatly feared in the days of sail when ships were frequently unsure of their

Latitude	*50° 30.82'N*
Longitude	*002° 27.3'W*
Established	*1716*
Height of tower	*41m*
Height of light above MHWS	*43m*
Character	*Fl(4)20s +F.R*
Range	*25Nm +13Nm*
Fog Signal	*Horn(1)30s*

143

position as they entered the Channel and often found themselves unable to weather the Bill; embayed, they became wrecked on Chesil Beach. Portland Bill was another location for which, in 1669, Sir John Clayton obtained a patent for a lighthouse, but once again the scheme foundered. It was not until the merchants and shipowners of Weymouth, led by a Captain William Holman, petitioned George I that, on 26 May 1716, after much vacillating, Trinity House issued a lease for the erection of a lighthouse. The lease was for sixty-one years at a rent of £100 per annum and the dues were set at one farthing per ton for English vessels, a half-penny for foreigners.

William Borrett, Francis Browne and a number of others employed a builder named Charles Langridge to build two towers, each of which was to bear a coal-fired chauffer, or grate, behind glazed lanterns. These were lit on 29 September 1716. The lower, seaward tower provided a transit to clear The Shambles but this proved ineffective. Furthermore, in 1752, two of the Elder Brethren, inspecting the lights from the Corporation's yacht, complained that 'it was nigh two hours after sunset before any light appeared in either of the lighthouses'. At the expiry of the lease in 1767, Trinity House assumed management of the lights. In 1788-9 £2,000 was spent on rebuilding them, a William Johns of Weymouth being engaged to undertake the work. On completion the then brand-new Argand lamps were installed, along with square reflectors and, in the case of the lower light, another innovation: glass lenses. The new lamps were reckoned to produce 1,500 candle-power, quite an achievement for the period and one that induced the Elder Brethren to take a rather high moral tone – above the door of the tower they suffered an inscription to be made: 'For the Direction and Comfort of NAVIGATORS; For the Benefit and Security of COMMERCE and for a lasting memorial of BRITISH HOSPITALITY to ALL Nations this lighthouse was erected by the Worshipful Brethren of Trinity House of Deptford Strond. Anno 1789.'

During wartime the remote location of the lights attracted the attentions of French men-of-war and privateers. In order to deter the enemy from landing and damaging the lighthouses, in 1798 two 18-pound cannon were mounted on the Bill.

Johns's towers were replaced in 1869 but, by the end of the century, the maintenance of two leading lights was being discouraged. In 1906 the dwellings were sold off into private hands and a new lighthouse was constructed on the very extremity of the Bill, a fine tapered white tower girded by a bright-red band. Powered by electricity the modern, now-automatic lighthouse is open to the public. In the former keepers' accommodation a visitors' centre provides information about the lighthouse, local shipwrecks and the area's wildlife.

The keepers were withdrawn on 18 March 1996, leaving record of some extraordinary predecessors. In 1721 a man named Comben was appointed keeper at Portland and in 1721 his wife

presented him with a son named Christopher. The younger Comben succeeded his father as keeper in 1771 and was, in turn, followed by his own son and grandson, Richard. Richard became Principal Keeper in 1836, the year of the great Act of Parliament effectively 'nationalising' English lighthouses. Members of the Comben family continued in the Corporation's service and, from 1902 to 1911, one R.J. Comben served as Assistant Keeper at Portland Low Light, transferring to the new single tower on its completion in 1906. The family became known as 'the lighthouse Combens' and possessed so distinctive a facial characteristic that they were said to posses the 'lighthouse nose'.

Below Left: Construction work on the new lighthouse at Portland Bill in 1906.

Following: Racing fleets often pass close to Portland Bill in order to avoid its tide race; the lighthouse is then a vital pilotage tool.

The Channel Islands

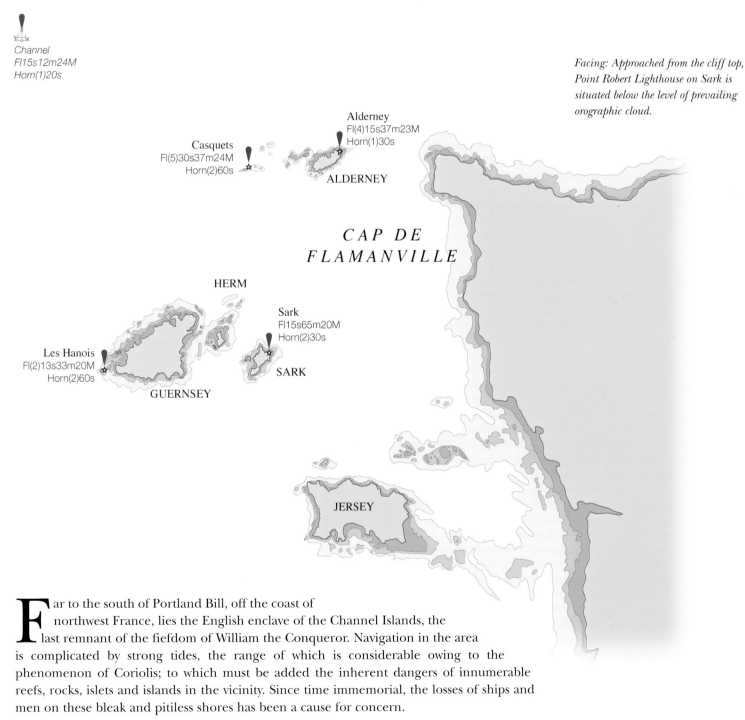

Channel
Fl15s12m24M
Horn(1)20s

Facing: Approached from the cliff top, Point Robert Lighthouse on Sark is situated below the level of prevailing orographic cloud.

Alderney
Fl(4)15s37m23M
Horn(1)30s

Casquets
Fl(5)30s37m24M
Horn(2)60s

ALDERNEY

CAP DE FLAMANVILLE

HERM

Sark
Fl15s65m20M
Horn(2)30s

Les Hanois
Fl(2)13s33m20M
Horn(2)60s

SARK

GUERNSEY

JERSEY

Far to the south of Portland Bill, off the coast of northwest France, lies the English enclave of the Channel Islands, the last remnant of the fiefdom of William the Conqueror. Navigation in the area is complicated by strong tides, the range of which is considerable owing to the phenomenon of Coriolis; to which must be added the inherent dangers of innumerable reefs, rocks, islets and islands in the vicinity. Since time immemorial, the losses of ships and men on these bleak and pitiless shores has been a cause for concern.

The Casquets Lighthouses

Latitude	*49° 43.37'N*
Longitude	*002° 22.53'W*
Established	*1724*
Height of tower	*23m*
Height of light above MHWS	*37m*
Character	*Fl 5)30s*
Range	*24Nm*
Fog Signal	*Horn(2)60s*
Racon fitted	

Roughly contemporaneous with interest in a light at Portland, it became clear that a light on the largest of a group of rocky islets northwest of Alderney would prove of great benefit. This little archipelago was known as the Casquets from the peaked rocks being thought to resemble casques, or helmets.

In the early hours of 8 January 1701, the small merchantman *Michael*, bound from London to Lisbon, drove ashore on the rocks. Nine of her sixteen-strong company managed to clamber onto the largest outcrop before the ship began to break up under the pounding seas. The survivors had only what they stood up in but managed to construct crude shelters from the wreckage of the *Michael*. More important, they had no food apart from the limpets and seaweed they found on the rocks. Nearly a week into their ordeal they were forced to desperate measures: 'After the first five days we killed and ate with relish our dog, for he was miraculously saved on a little rock near by, and so he preserved our lives'.

After seventeen days the marooned survivors had given up hope of leaving the barren rocks alive; then they were seen by a vessel trading to the islands. All nine were taken off alive and nursed back to health, but they were little more than a lucky minority of the hundreds of unrecorded seamen lost on the Casquets.

It seems to have been Thomas Le Cocq, a magistrate of Alderney to whom the corpses of washed-up seamen were reported, who conceived the idea of building a light on the Casquets. He approached another Channel Islands man, Admiral Hardy, an Elder Brother of Trinity House, and together they prepared a petition to submit to the Court of Trinity House. Hardy advised Le Cocq that they would need the backing of merchants and shipowners and the two men set about collecting 800 signatures.

On 7 November 1722 the proposal was laid before Trinity House as being due solely to Le Cocq's initiative – Hardy taking no obvious part in the proceedings, but also failing to declare an interest. By February 1723 it was agreed that Le Cocq would apply for a patent in the name of Trinity House and then build and maintain the lights. His lease was for sixty-one years from first lighting at a rent of £50 per annum. The dues would be one half-penny for outward and homeward English vessels and double for foreigners.

The three 6 metre tall towers were roughly built of rock quarried from the reef itself. They were named St Peter, St Thomas and Dungeon and were surmounted by iron grates enclosed in glass lanterns, The Casquets were first lit on 30 October 1724. Almost immediately the soot forming on the small glass panes obscured the lights, but the provision of the lanterns reduced coal consumption and controlled the rate of burning, particularly in gales when exposed fires were apt to get out of control.

In 1729 Admiral Sir Thomas Hardy was elected Master of Trinity House but died the following year. It was then discovered that he had been secretly receiving a quarter of the income for the lighthouse. Trinity House challenged the bequest of the light-dues to Hardy's children and, after eighteen years, won the case, receiving the arrears and the Admiral's quarter share from then on.

As with other coal lights of the period complaints were frequent and the matter came to a head in 1744 when, on the night of 4 October, HMS *Victory* (the predecessor of Nelson's flagship) ran ashore and was lost with all hands, including Admiral Balchen. The death toll was about 1,100 men and, although this was due more to the tempestuous weather than to the obscurity of the lights, the fact that *Victory* was the largest ship in the world and a man-of-war of enormous prestige, meant that her loss in

British waters was an immense blow. The event therefore focused attention on the question of the efficiency of lights exhibited from lighthouses and gave impetus to the quest for improved equipment.

Continuing bad reports on the Casquets light compelled Le Cocq to request Trinity House to recommend a new keeper to be put in charge. They sent a Mr Norris who reported that many of the small panes of glass in the three lanterns, having broken in the intense heat, had been replaced by wood rather than glass. Norris also found that larger grates, supplied by Trinity House in an attempt to improve the light, had not been installed. Le Cocq, not wishing to compromise his profits, had not wanted to burn more coal than was necessary. In 1760 Thomas Le Cocq died and his share of the lighthouse was divided between his four grandchildren, but they proved even less assiduous proprietors than their grandfather. The expiry of their lease was approaching and they were reluctant to spend money – consequently the lighthouses fell further into disrepair. The family was content to leave matters to their agent, a Mr Anley, who procured supplies of coal, and recruited and victualled the keepers.

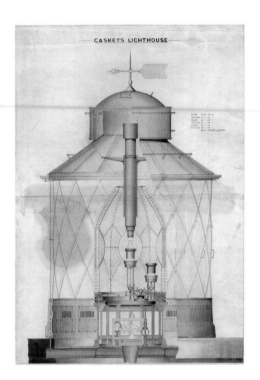

CASKETS LIGHTHOUSE

Above: A section through the lantern, showing the lower murette, pierced for ventilation, the glass section with its diamond-shaped glass panes and astragal framework, together with the chimney to draw off the heat of the burner. This has a secondary stand-by unit and the lens was rotated by a clockwork motor in the entablature, driven by a weight descending through the tower. The large wind vane had an indicator fitted inside the lantern.

After the inevitable dispute the owners agreed to pay three quarters of the cost for Trinity House to rebuild the lighthouses. Norris must have reported favourably upon Anley, for it was he who supervised the rebuilding of each tower. Anley installed new copper lanterns with plate glass within which the coal fires were replaced with new oil lamps and reflectors. On 30 October 1779 Anley reported to Trinity House that the work was complete and that, 'The lamps and reflectors have a very surprising effect compared with what the coal had, and that at Alderney the Caskets seemed all on fire every night'. Pleased with this improvement and the reduction in labour, Trinity House ordered Anley to reduce the number of keepers from seven to four.

Anley's duties were onerous, the task of landing stores and coal, let alone people, on the rocks was hazardous. It was also difficult to recruit keepers. Local men were scared of the press gang and, later, of a disease which struck keepers at the lighthouse. It broke out in early 1780s and lasted for some years; initially blamed on the oil fumes, it was probably dysentery caused by water polluted by bird droppings and other organic decay. By January 1785 matters had so far deteriorated that keepers had to be engaged in London and Trinity House decided to order and ship provisions and stores to the station themselves, rather than through an agent. They sent the following items in the sloop *Glatney*, a vessel trading between London and the Channel Islands:

2 cwt Beef	1 cwt Cheese
2 cwt Port	2 firkins Butter
Some pickled tripe	2 bushels Salt (for preserving fish)
Some suet	$1/2$ ton of good Malt Liquor
5 cwt Biscuit	4 half-hogsheads Porter
2 cwt Potatoes	$1/2$ cwt Rice
2 cwt Flour	1 firkin Oatmeal
4 bushels Pease	2 firkins Barley
4 cwt Currants	$1/2$ cwt Soap
1 cwt Sugar	

But this early experiment in self-supply ended disastrously when the *Glatney* foundered off Guernsey and the stores had to be replaced. After this abortive attempt, responsibility was passed back to the local agent until, in 1849, the wages of the keepers were raised to include the cost of their providing their own victuals.

In 1790 the newly developed parabolic reflectors were installed at Casquets along with Argand lamps. The three lights were all revolved by a mechanism similar to that of a grandfather clock. The machine was linked by ropes and sheaves to the three sets of reflectors and lamps which were installed in their towers at the angles of the triangular walled compound.

The Elder Brethren visited the Casquets in their splendid new buoy yacht, which had been commissioned in 1788, escorted by a naval sloop-of-war, an event commemorated in a painting by the celebrated contemporary marine artist Thomas Whitcombe. Another visitor was the famous Scots lighthouse engineer, Robert Stevenson, who made his third inspection of English lighthouses in 1818 from the yacht of the Commissioners of Northern Lights. Stevenson formed a low opinion of the Casquets, describing the lights as 'unsatisfactory and most rudely got up…little attended to either in keeping or putting up'. Each lantern was fitted with eight lamps and reflectors of silvered copper but these had not been kept clean and were, as Stevenson put it, 'quite furred with sea-gum'. In attendance was the keeper Louis Hougre and his family, along with a young woman who had been out at the light acting as a servant for five years in an attempt to redeem her character: she had formerly been a 'very bad girl'. To be fair to Hougre, he had only taken up his post a few weeks earlier and was to stay for many years on the reef. Sadly, there is no record of the fate of his scarlet servant. Stevenson added that Hougre signalled to Alderney when he was running low on stores, and that he received £52 a year and his victuals.

Local historian John Jacob gives a detailed description of the lighthouse around 1830, recording a complex of buildings within the triangular wall surrounding the three towers – a dwelling for the keeper, another for the agent during his visits, plus accommodation for visiting workmen. In addition there was a bakehouse and a small vegetable garden, maintained with great difficulty for many years. In 1793 a violent storm destroyed the vegetables and swept away the soil, so two tons of earth had to be despatched from Alderney. Various shipments of soil are recorded in the Trinity House minutes over the years, but the meagre produce grown in this small garden was essential and considerable effort was expended in landing and handling the soil necessary to its growth.

Soil, victuals, firewood, and oil all had to be supplied during the summer months when a landing could be effected and two of the towers provided storage for the provisions. To supplement their diet and the produce from their garden the inhabitants kept chickens, plundered sea-birds' nests, and caught great quantities of fish that was eaten fresh or salted away in casks.

Louis Hougre was still serving on the rock when Jacob wrote his description and the story he tells of the keeper's daughter has passed into folklore. Apparently she went out to the Casquets as a small child and did not leave it again until she was eighteen when she set out to visit relatives on the neighbouring island of Alderney. However, she returned home after a few days in a distraught state, claiming that 'the world was full of trouble and noise'. Notwithstanding this delicacy, love prevailed, for the young woman is said to have married a young carpenter who visited the lighthouse to carry out repairs; she went to live with him on Alderney.

We have another glimpse of Hougre, by way of a party of Elder Brethren who inspected the Casquets in 1833 in what was to become an annual event. 'Louis Hougre who had his wife and eight children living there, was a steady man'. A few years later the agent describes the method of keeping watch during Hougre's time: 'he and his son go to bed immediately after lighting up; his wife and his two elder daughters then remain on watch until midnight in summer, and in winter until one o'clock, when himself and his son leave their beds and watch for the remainder of the night'.

In 1847 a large bell driven by a clockwork mechanism was installed at the Casquets as a fog signal, this sounded every five minutes in thick weather. Two years later, after thirty-one years service, Louis Hougre applied for a pension due to ill health, said to be rheumatism. He was allowed a pension of his full pay, £52 per year, and he and his family moved to Alderney.

Instead of a family three keepers were now appointed to the lighthouse, working a roster of two at a time out on the rock. The Principal Keeper was paid £5 a month and the assistants £4 each; they were also to have one shilling and sixpence a day to buy their own food.

In 1853 James Walker proposed substantial alterations to Casquets: the towers would be raised to increase the range of the light; new and larger lanterns would be fitted, each containing twelve lamps with reflectors. The renovation was completed by summer of 1855 at a cost of £4,748. During the work it was suggested that the three lights be synchronised, for they all revolved at the same speed but started at different points of the compass so that they did not show at the same time. Strangely this adjustment was not made. However, the ageing clockwork mechanism for driving the rotation was finally found to be beyond repair in 1858 and the decision was made to have the lights altered to rotate simultaneously. At James Douglass's recommendation a pendulum was fitted to each of the three lights and two more clocks were supplied so that there would be one in each tower. This machinery continued in use for twelve years, but breakdowns were so frequent that the agent suggested that no new keepers should be appointed to Casquets as the existing ones had learned from long experience how best to keep the apparatus working.

In 1877 the lights were finally reduced to one which exhibited a new group character of three

flashes every 30 seconds. This light was built on the St Peter tower. The other two towers were reduced in height and a fog siren, powered by a 'caloric engine', was installed in the Dungeon. Because of the quantity of coke needed to run this, the landing-place was rebuilt and a special store constructed at Braye Harbour on Alderney. The siren was replaced by a diaphone in 1922. In 1928 a radio beacon was installed in the St Thomas tower and in 1939 a radio telephone was installed and experimental communications made with Hanois Lighthouse and Guernsey lifeboat station. By this time, although an agent continued to be used for local liaison, management of the lighthouses in the Channel Islands, as on the English mainland opposite, was vested in the District Superintendent at East Cowes.

With the Fall of France in June 1940, the Casquets was shut down and the men evacuated along with all the Trinity House keepers in the Channel Islands. It was not long before the Germans occupied the Casquets, which they converted into a small fortress armed with anti-aircraft guns. Barbed wire was fixed all around the rocks along the water's edge. The Germans used the light and radio beacon to assist their own ships and aircraft, installing powerful radio equipment to monitor allied communications in the Channel.

On the night of 2/3 September 1942 an attack by a dozen British commandos on the island caught the German garrison unaware and all seven men were captured. During the raid the commandos destroyed the radio equipment and picked up code books whilst British aircraft attacks damaged the lantern glazing and optic, putting the light out of action. Reoccupied by thirty-six men, the German garrison of the Casquets surrendered on 19 May 1945. The buildings were intact but the light could only be operated on reduced power and the allies retained six Germans to repair some of the damage.

New electrically powered equipment was installed in 1952 with the present character of five flashes every 30 seconds and peacetime routine re-established itself until automation came in 1990. Maintained by the visits of its attendant from Alderney, Casquets is again uninhabited, though technology enables Trinity House to maintain the powerful light and fog signal from the distant Operational Control Centre.

Alderney Lighthouse

Latitude	49° 43.8'N
Longitude	002° 09.78W
Established	1912
Height of tower	32m
Height of light above MHWS	37m
Character	Fl(4)15s
Range	23Nm
Fog Signal	Horn(1)30s

Alderney Lighthouse was built on Quénard Point on the northeast corner of the island in 1912 as part of a scheme to improve the lighting of the Channel Islands for general navigation. The tower rises 32 metres and is painted white with a central black band to make it more visible in daylight. Offshore to the eastward is the Alderney Race, a notorious strait of water between the island and Cap de la Hague in France in which the tidal rate can reach speeds of six knots. An uneven sea bed adds to the turbulence and a number of hazardous rocks are located within a few feet of the surface.

During the occupation of the Channel Islands in the Second World War the Alderney light was taken over by the Germans and operated in the same way as British lighthouses during the conflict, being lit only on the orders of the local military commander to guide convoys and aircraft. In June 1940, the order came from mainland Britain to discontinue the Channel Island lighthouses and to evacuate the keepers, their families 'and anyone else who wished to come'.

The Trinity House Vessel *Vestal* left Cowes on 21 June, first calling at Portsmouth in an attempt to obtain a naval escort. There were simply no ships

available and she set off towards the islands alone, to anchor off Alderney just after midnight. *Vestal* entered the harbour at first light to collect the keepers from Alderney and Sark Lighthouses, three Trinity House pensioners and their families, along with several civilian refugees. The ship's commander, Captain McCarthy, had been given discretion to take refugees, but only a tiny fraction of the population of the islands could be taken onboard.

Next *Vestal* proceeded to Guernsey to collect the keepers from Casquets and Hanois. Here she also embarked a number of civilians, eventually carrying 121 passengers on top of her normal complement of forty. Emergency rafts were rigged up in case the ship had to be abandoned, food was shared out and the officers and crew gave up their accommodation. Six children slept in the best cabin, three at each end of the grand double bed, with their mothers on the floor beside them. At midnight they passed into safety beyond the Spithead defences and finally landed at Southampton on the morning of 23 June.

Alderney lighthouse was occupied by German troops until all the Channel Island Lights were regained after VE Day. Life at Alderney returned to normal for the keepers until their successors finally left the lighthouse on automation in 1997.

Sark Lighthouse

Sark Lighthouse was built in 1913, around the same time as Alderney Lighthouse, in an effort to improve the aids to navigation in the Channel Islands. In addition to providing a passage light, Sark lighthouse warns mariners passing through the Channel Islands of the presence of Blanchard Rock several miles to the east of Point Robert.

The white, octagonal tower of the lighthouse rises from the flat-roofed service rooms and dwellings, which are all perched on the rugged slope of the cliffs at the northeast corner of the tiny island. The only access to the station is by way of a precipitous flight of steps from the top of the cliff. Such isolation meant that Sark Lighthouse was manned from the beginning as a rock lighthouse.

The keepers from Sark were evacuated in June 1940 and the lighthouse was manned by the Germans until 1945. The first post-war entry in the station order book describes the situation after the surrender:

> *20th May 1945*
>
> *Station has been well kept but is denuded of stores. There are two gaps in surrounding wall used for gun emplacements, they will require repair. Coal-store has been used as a prison. One panel of door requires renewal. The Island has been heavily mined and these mines and booby traps extend round and close to the lighthouse, they are being cleared up by German prisoners but personnel are warned that danger may exist for a very long time from mines and booby traps that may have been overlooked.*

Latitude	*49° 26.24'N*
Longitude	*002° 20.68'W*
Established	*1913*
Height of tower	*16m*
Height of light above MHWS	*65m*
Character	*Fl 15s*
Range	*20Nm*
Fog Signal	*Horn(2)30s*

On 27 October 1945 the light and fog signal came into operation once more, under the charge of Principal Keeper, Mr L.J.E. Tucker, and two local assistant keepers who were trained on the spot. The lighthouse was automated in 1993.

Les Hanois Lighthouse

Latitude	*49° 26.16'N*
Longitude	*002° 42.07'W*
Established	*1862*
Height of tower	*33m*
Height of light above MHWS	*33m*
Character	*Fl(2)13s*
Range	*20Nm*
Fog Signal	*Horn(2)60s*

Rising from the jagged reef of Les Hanois off the southwest extreme of Guernsey, the granite tower marks the western edge of the Channel Islands, warning of the dangers of the shoals and reefs off Guernsey and providing a guide for vessels running up towards the English Channel.

Les Hanois Lighthouse is remarkable for two technical innovations. Completed in 1862 it was the first tower in which the blocks of granite were fully integrated both horizontally *and* vertically. Taking Smeaton's methods, pioneered a century earlier on the Eddystone, a stage further, Nicholas Douglass achieved the vertical connection by cutting a tapered dovetail extending upwards from the top of each block, with a tapered aperture on the underside of the next above. Slotted into one another, the blocks were then sealed together with cement, forming the strongest possible joints and unifying the tower into one solid block. This method became standard for subsequent rock towers, including the magnificent Eddystone, built in 1882 by Nicholas's son James, who succeeded his father as Engineer-in-Chief to Trinity House.

Like the other Channel Island lights, Les Hanois was occupied during the Second World War. The structure was used for solitary confinement by the military and an apocryphal story relates that a

hole in the ceiling of one of the rooms is said to have been made by a bullet fired by a suicidal prisoner; how he obtained the weapon is not revealed.

The large optic was damaged by gunfire during the war and was replaced in 1964 by a much smaller optic with electric light replacing the paraffin vapour burner and, in 1979, a helicopter landing pad was fitted above the lantern. Les Hanois's second claim to a place in lighthouse history occurred in 1996 when, following its automation, it became the first solar-powered rock tower, solar panels being mounted vertically around the lantern. Like its sister stations, Les Hanois is today controlled from Harwich.

Following: Channel Lightvessel.

Devon and Cornwall

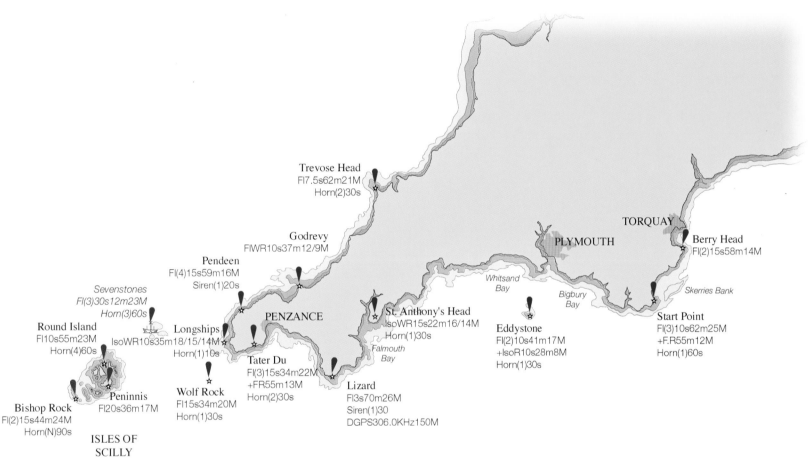

Trevose Head
Fl7.5s62m21M
Horn(2)30s

TORQUAY

PLYMOUTH

Berry Head
Fl(2)15s58m14M

Godrevy
FlWR10s37m12/9M

Whitsand
Bay

Pendeen
Fl(4)15s59m16M
Siren(1)20s

Bigbury
Bay

Skerries Bank

Sevenstones
Fl(3)30s12m23M
Horn(3)60s

PENZANCE

St. Anthony's Head
IsoWR15s22m16/14M
Horn(1)30s

Eddystone
Fl(2)10s41m17M
+IsoR10s28m8M
Horn(1)30s

Start Point
Fl(3)10s62m25M
+F.R55m12M
Horn(1)60s

Round Island
Fl10s55m23M
Horn(4)60s

Longships
IsoWR10s35m18/15/14M
Horn(1)10s

Falmouth
Bay

Tater Du
Fl(3)15s34m22M
+FR55m13M
Horn(2)30s

Bishop Rock
Fl(2)15s44m24M
Horn(N)90s

Peninnis
Fl20s36m17M

Wolf Rock
Fl15s34m20M
Horn(1)30s

Lizard
Fl3s70m26M
Siren(1)30
DGPS306.0KHz150M

ISLES OF
SCILLY

The great arc of Lyme Bay, that starts in the east at Portland, culminates in the south Devon headland of Start Point, to the west of which lies Plymouth, Britain's second great naval port. In times past the anchorage of Torbay was also of significance to sailing men-of-war, and its terminating headland, Berry Head, like Start Point, warranted a lighthouse. The approach to the magnificent natural harbour of Plymouth, the flooded confluence of two rivers, was marred by a jagged reef of red rocks, around which the tides eddied and which proved the gravestone of many a ship. This 'Eddystone' was eventually rendered less hazardous by a lighthouse, the first great rock tower in the world, an achievement that was not without its dramas.

Facing: Approaching Wolf Rock by air on a quiet day; note the ceaseless swirl of the sea over and around this isolated and dangerous steeple rock.

Berry Head Lighthouse

Latitude	*50° 23.94'N*
Longitude	*003° 28.94'W*
Established	*1906*
Height of tower	*5m*
Height of light above MHWS	*58m*
Character	*Fl(2)15s*
Range	*14Nm*

Berry Head is a massive limestone headland at the southern tip of Torbay. Rising almost 60 metres above sea-level, no further elevation is required of the light structure, or it would be lost in cloud, so the lighthouse is a squat building – a lantern set on the ground. Berry Head is an area of outstanding natural beauty; upon the grassland and broken cliffs grow the rare white rock-rose, rock sea-lavender, goldilocks aster and honeywort. Kittiwakes, herring gulls, fulmars and guillemots nest annually on the rock ledges of the cliffs while far below, under the beetling headland, the relentless action of the sea has hollowed out deep caves.

The headland commands wide views of the Channel and its western coastal approaches as well as the sheltered anchorages of Torbay and Brixham Roads. Its strategic position led to the building of fortifications during the American War of Independence when American and French privateers attacked British shipping lying in the bay. This structure was incorporated into the fort built to guard

against further French attacks during the Revolutionary War at the end of the Eighteenth Century. The remains of these defences still dominate Berry Head. The lighthouse, built at their eastern end in 1906 is one of a handful of Twentieth Century structures within the fort, others being built when the stern imperatives of war demanded a Royal Observer Corps post during the Second World War. There is also an underground Cold War monitoring station dating from 1959-60. Berry Head Lighthouse remains an important passage and local mark, for many merchant ships enter the bay to the north, seeking a pilot from Brixham.

The original oil-powered optic was turned by the action of a weight descending a 45 metre deep shaft. The light was converted to an automatic acetylene apparatus in 1921, then further modernised and converted to mains electricity in 1994.

Start Point Lighthouse

The exposed headland of Start Point runs almost a mile out to sea on the south side of Start Bay and it was on its extremity that James Walker's tall tower was constructed in 1836. Bearing the crenellated parapet characteristic of Walker's lighthouses and echoing the 'gothic' style of the day, the ground and first floors accommodated the keepers.

The lighthouse came into operation on 1 July 1836, exhibiting two white lights, the main optic revolving to provide a passage light, a lower fixed light shining in a narrow sector over the Skerries Bank to the northeast of the Point. The main unit was the first of its kind in the Trinity House Service, an improved form of dioptric apparatus designed by the Scottish engineer, Alan Stevenson. The tower was painted white to be conspicuous against the surrounding land.

A one-and-a-half ton fog bell was installed in 1862. Housed in a small building on the cliff face, it was operated by a weight that fell in a tube running down the sheer cliff. This cumbrous apparatus was replaced by a siren after only fifteen years.

Latitude	*50° 13.31'N*
Longitude	*003° 38.46'W*
Established	*1836*
Height of tower	*28m*
Height of light above MHWS	*62m*
Character	*Fl(3)10s +F.R*
Range	*25/12Nm*
Fog Signal	*Horn(1)60s*

Top and above: Start Point Lighthouse stands guard over the Channel coast.

Top: When revolving, the optic produces three flashes in quick succession.

In 1871, the intermediate floors of the tower were removed and James Douglass built two houses adjoining the tower to accommodate the keepers more comfortably. These, known as the north and south dwellings, were rebuilt in the mid 1950s. A third substantial east dwelling, again of Douglass's design, was built in 1882 and still stands.

An insight into the Lighthouse and the life of its keepers in the Nineteenth Century is given in a travelogue by Walter White: 'A substantial house, connected with the tall circular tower, in a walled enclosure, all nicely whitened, is the residence of the light-keepers. The buildings stand within a few yards of the verge of the cliff, the wall serving as a parapet, from which you look down on the craggy slope outside and the jutting rocks beyond – the outermost point. You may descend by the narrow path, protected also by a low white wall, and stride and scramble from rock to rock with but little risk of slipping, so rough are the surfaces with minute shells. A rude steep stair, chipped in the rock, leads down still lower to a little cove and a narrow strip of beach at the foot of the cliffs. It is the landing place for the lighthouse keepers when they go fishing, but can only be used in calm weather.'

In December 1989 the fog-signal house collapsed, undermined by coastal erosion of the under-cliff. Since then the site has been levelled, a new retaining wall built, the fog signal fitted to the lantern gallery wall and the south dwelling demolished. Work began on the automation of Start Point Lighthouse in August 1992 and was completed in early 1993 when the keepers and their families were withdrawn. Like Anvil Point to the east, 'the Start' had become a popular station for long-serving keepers, retaining a sense of remote location, yet possessing access to the comforts of civilisation.

Eddystone Lighthouse

One of the most famous lighthouses in the British Isles, if not the world, the present Eddystone is the fourth tower erected on an extensive reef consisting of slanting red granitoid gneiss some 14 miles south of Plymouth Sound. Much of the reef is underwater, with complex and variable tidal streams swirling about it. In strong winds, these eddies compound the height and period of the breaking waves and produce dangerous and sometimes extraordinarily high seas, which break high over the rocks and, upon occasion, over the lighthouse itself. In about 1620 Captain Christopher Jones, master of the *Mayflower*, described the reef as: 'Twenty-three rust red…ragged stones around which the sea constantly eddies, a great danger…for if any vessel makes too far to the south…she will be caught in the prevailing strong current and swept to her doom on these evil rocks'.

Latitude	*50° 10.81'N*
Longitude	*004° 15.87'W*
Established	*1698*
Height of tower	*49m*
Height of light above MHWS	*41/28m*
Character	*Fl(2)10s +IsoR10s*
Range	*17/8Nm*
Fog Signal	*Horn(1)30s*
Racon fitted	

Following the *Mayflower*'s epochal voyage, trade with America increased during the Seventeenth Century and a growing number of ships approaching the English Channel from the west found themselves cast upon the Eddystone. Even in bad weather with waves breaking over it, the reef was difficult to see until it was too late. While eastbound ships could try and keep an offing, those bound for Plymouth inevitably ran the risk of setting onto the reef. The port was then growing in importance for both naval and commercial vessels. Shipmasters, owners and merchants maintained a steady stream of petitions to the Crown, pleading that something should be done about marking the infamous rocks. In 1655 Trinity House was consulted on a proposal for a light on the reef, but the Court concluded, with justification, that while it would undoubtedly be beneficial, it was an impossible task. The Brethren could not undertake so risky an enterprise, nor coerce others to do so, even with the inducement of light-dues. It would take an extraordinary visionary, a man of faith or foolhardiness to attempt the thing.

In response to their petitioners, William III and Queen Mary decreed that 'having regard for the many gallant seamen who have perished round these dangerous rocks, these said captains, shipowners and merchants are agreed and willing to pay to the Corporation of Trinity House one penny a ton outward and…inward for the benefit of a warning light'. Still the Brethren demurred until, in 1692, a Devon man named William Whitfield came forward and, in 1694, Trinity House obtained a patent. Empowering Whitfield to build a lighthouse and receive half the dues achieved nothing more than calling Whitfield's bluff; the project foundered.

But, cometh the hour, cometh the man and this particular hour was to throw up the most flamboyant character in the long history of lighthouses. On 10 June 1696 a certain Henry Winstanley signed an agreement to build a lighthouse on the Eddystone. In return Winstanley would receive the full dues of one penny per ton for five years, then half that amount for the succeeding fifty.

Henry Winstanley was born in 1644 at Saffron Walden. His father was the bailiff at Audley End, the Earl of Suffolk's palace, and Henry worked there as an assistant in the estate office. He soon showed a talent for mechanical invention and imaginative drawing; he also possessed a desire to prove that jack was as good as his master, for he affected the manners and dress of a moneyed gentleman. Audley End was sold to Charles II and, in the dissolute court of the Restoration, Winstanley's lively character and ingenuity were appreciated. He became Clerk of Works for Audley End and, presumably by quietly mulcting his master, built a house for himself and his new bride at nearby Littlebury. This became a curiosity in its own right, for Winstanley filled it with trick devices, mechanical contrivances useful for playing practical jokes on his guests. In attempting to sit upon a chair, they were likely to be instantly cast into a basement or shot out into the garden. The walls bore mirrors that created distortions, adding a bizarre quality to the opulence of the decorations. With an almost inspired prescience, Winstanley topped his house with a huge lantern, and the opulent dwelling was known as Winstanley's Wonders.

Situated between Audley End and the house in which King Charles had installed Nell Gwynn at Newport, Winstanley's Wonders achieved what its owner intended: it attracted the frivolous attention of the courtiers and, aping them, the local gentry. Winstanley charged entrance fees to his house and, as a consequence, the shillings of every curious person willing to travel and submit to the discomfiture of the owner's sardonic humour further enriched him. Other money-making schemes included novelty playing cards and making engravings of noblemen's houses. In London he ran a 'Mathematical Water-Theatre' known as Winstanley's Waterworks, a series of moving tableaux with breathtaking effects from water spouts and fountains, the most sensational combining fire and water.

By 1695, the fifty-one-year-old Winstanley was both famous and rich, investing money in ships, two of which were wrecked on the Eddystone. The loss of the second, the *Constant*, prompted him to visit Plymouth where he learned of the difficulties of building a lighthouse on the notorious reef. Imaginative as ever, Winstanley saw the opportunity to engross his glory by building the most fantastic wonder; beyond the fame of the mountebank, there now beckoned the fame of the philanthropist.

Obtaining his patent and lease, and armed with a design of his own devising, Winstanley recruited skilled workmen, labourers and boatmen. Work commenced in July the following year but by October little progress had been made, owing to the difficulties of access to the rocks and the problems encountered in anchoring the structure to so bleak a spot. Winstanley had selected the western rock for his tower and his men had succeeded in laboriously drilling into it a dozen holes. Nevertheless, by the winter Winstanley had gained invaluable experience and made a careful study of the tides.

Despite the hammerings of summer gales and the necessity to remove all tools every evening, the following year iron bars were fixed into the rock and bedded in with molten lead. Onto these the first courses of masonry were laid. To his more obvious skills Winstanley now added leadership: he inculcated in his men a deep hatred of the unyielding rock, it became something to be subdued and to this end he cajoled, wheedled, and joked, sharing with the men the hardship and constant drenching. He was very far from being a fop.

England was now at war with France and such was the importance of the Eddystone project that the Admiralty provided Winstanley with a man-of-war for protection on working days. One morning, at

the end of June 1697, HMS *Terrible* did not arrive; in her stead a French privateer sent in a boat, took Winstanley prisoner, and carted him off to France. It is said that when Louis XIV heard of the incident he ordered Winstanley to Versailles, stating that 'France was at war with England not with humanity'. Charmed by Winstanley, the Sun King ordered his release and he was returned during an exchange of prisoners in late July. In spite of this diversion, by the end of the season there was on the rock 'a solid body or rough kind of pillar twelve foot [sic] high and fourteen diameter'.

In 1698 real progress was made, the lighthouse took the form of a solid masonry drum around 5 metres in diameter and height. On top of this was the tower, a series of wooden stories with living accommodation for keepers, topped by a flat roof with an open gallery. By this time the workmen were able to live in the tower and work proceeded apace. On one occasion a June gale confined them to the rock for eleven days, but this delay served to prove the strength of the structure and, in due course, on 14 November 1698, Winstanley himself ascended into the elaborate glazed lantern tower set above the domed roof. Inside his octagonal lantern, 3 metres in diameter, Winstanley raised his lit taper to the candelabra. On distant Plymouth Hoe the citizens rushed to see the eighth wonder of the world on their own doorstep: Winstanley had lit the Eddystone and built the first true rock lighthouse in the world.

As if resentful of this triumph, a gale blew up, confining Winstanley and his workmen to the lighthouse. 'We put up the light on the 14th of November 1698,' he wrote. 'Which being so late in the year it was three days before Christmas before we had a relief to get ashore again, and were almost at the last extremity for want of provisions, but by good providence then two boats came with provisions and the family that was to take care of the light, and so ended this year's work.'

The following spring, when Winstanley visited the lighthouse, the keeper and his family, he found that the winter weather had taken its toll. The waves had washed right over the tower and much of the cement pointing had been torn away. He decided that major changes were needed, and that year the lighthouse was more or less rebuilt. The light was shut down, the wooden tower dismantled and the stone base was enlarged by encasing the original and the jointing was covered with iron bands. Winstanley then erected a larger tower, raising the height of the structure by 12 metres. To add to its magnificence every flat surface of the building was inscribed and decorated. Winstanley also exercised his ingenuity in fitting the lighthouse with features that ranged from the fantastical to the surprisingly practical and useful. His proud description of the lighthouse lists many of these: 'An Engine Crane yt [that] parts at joynts to be taken off when not in use, the rest being fasten'd to ye side of ye house to save it in time of storms, and it is to be made use of to help landing on ye Rock, which, without [it], is very difficult…a very fine Bedchamber, with a Chimney and Closet, ye Room being richly Gilded and Painted and ye outside Shutters very strongly Barr'd…. The State Room being 10 square 19 foot wide and 12 foot high, very well Carv'd and Painted, with a Chimney and 2 Closets…. The Airry or open Gallery where is Conveniency to Crane up Goods and a great Leaden Cestern to hold ye rain Water…. The Lanthorn [lantern] yt holds ye light is 8 square 11 foot Diameter 15 foot high…having 8 great Glass windows…and conveniency to burn 60 Candles at a time besides a great hanging Lamp…great wooden Candlesticks or Ornaments but ye irons yt bars them is very useful to stay a ladder to clean ye glass…a vessel to let float on ye water to take in Small things from a Boat on ye West side of ye Rock, then there is no landing on ye other side…a moving Engine Trough to cast down Stones to defend ye landing Place in case of need.'

Winstanley quickly produced a drawing of the lighthouse, prints were made and sold in great quantities at his Water Works and at Littlebury, a best-seller still being reprinted in the 1760s. He also built large models of the lighthouse at his shows. Along with this hype went wild stories of life at the lighthouse, tales of the tremendous size of the seas and of how a rowing boat had been lifted by a wave and carried through the open gallery during a gale. The most sinister were insisted upon as true, related by the keeper: that in heavy weather the tower shuddered under the impact of the seas.

By now the utility of the lighthouse was indisputable and its value was underwritten by the opinions of mariners. Nevertheless, Winstanley was unable to ignore the doom-laden prophesies of his critics or the goading of those who claimed the extravagant decoration was an affront to the puritan God who still dwelt in the sceptical souls of the citizens of Plymouth. For them the posturing and powdered character of Winstanley represented the distant and decadent court of the son of the Great Malignant, Charles I. Winstanley responded in typical fashion, declaring in public that he wished for nothing more than to be inside the lighthouse during 'the greatest storm there ever was'.

Fate took him at his words. In November 1703 there was a fortnight of Atlantic gales causing great concentrations of ships in anchorages and roadsteads, all waiting for a moderation that would allow them to proceed with their voyages. On 25 November there was a lull in the weather and, early on 26 November, the fifty-nine year old Winstanley headed out with his workmen to the Eddystone, to carry out repairs.

That night a deep depression raced up the English Channel, bringing with it a ferocious storm. Across southern England thousands of buildings were damaged and trees uprooted. Daniel Defoe

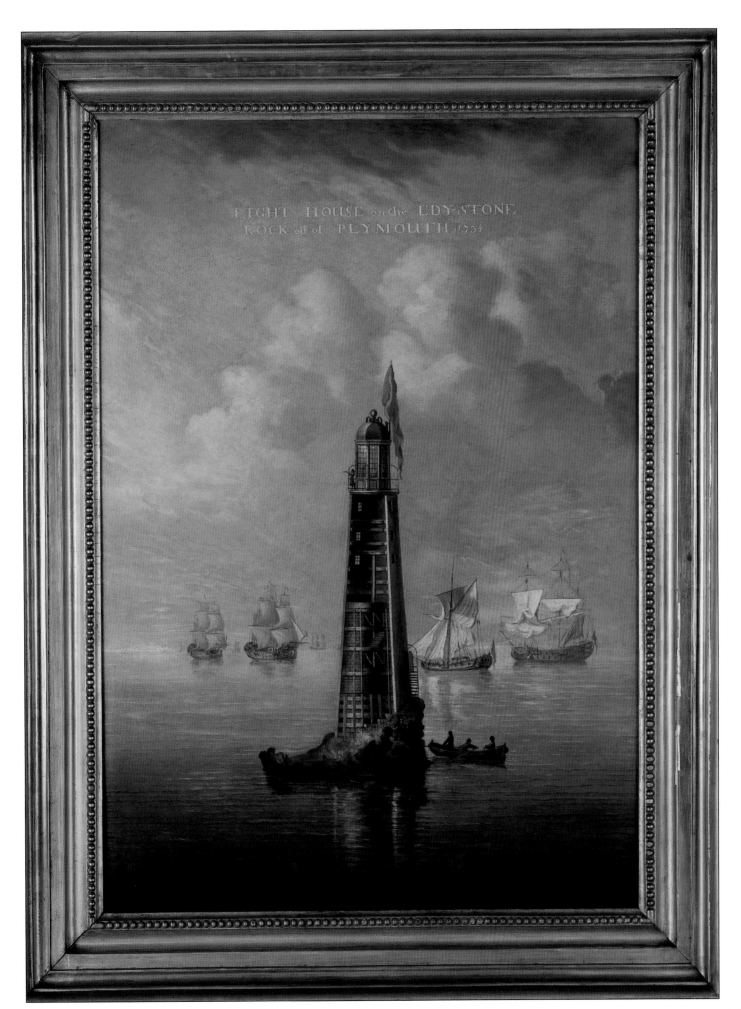

LIGHT HOUSE on the EDY-STONE
ROCK off of PLYMOUTH 1734

171

recorded over 150 ships destroyed and more than 8,000 sailors drowned. By daybreak on 27 November there was nothing left of the Eddystone Lighthouse but a few bent bars of iron projecting from the rock.

No doubt the Jeremiahs in Plymouth shook their heads and clucked their tongues, but Winstanley's tower had failed not through an excess of decoration, but through a weakness in its foundations. In death Winstanley not only played the heroic, he also proved philanthropic, for he had spent £8,000 on the project that had then yielded only half that in dues. Moreover, to prove the wisdom of his attempt and to justify his faith, just two nights after the loss of the Eddystone, a large merchant vessel, the *Winchelsea*, having endured the weeks of severe weather on her homeward passage from the American colonies, came to grief on the unmarked rocks, driving straight onto them in expectation of seeing the lighthouse. Only two men got away in a boat. It was clear that a new lighthouse had to be built on the Eddystone, though Trinity House declined the challenge.

Perhaps inspired by Winstanley two men next came forward. They were Colonel John Lovett, a member of the Irish Parliament, and his friend John Rudyerd, a silk merchant of London. Lovett intended to invest his wife's dowry of £5,000 in the lighthouse and expected a return of £700 a year. Trinity House obtained an Act of Parliament in 1706 for rebuilding the light and obtaining the dues, granting Lovett a lease for 99 years at £100 a year rent.

John Rudyerd was to be the designer; he was a mysterious amateur in a field yet to be dignified as 'structural engineering'. His ideas, possessing some modicum of practicability, were approved by the force and conviction of Lovett but Rudyerd himself seems to have possessed something of a persuasive quality. Perhaps Rudyerd's idea was not as fantastical as Winstanley's and appealed to Trinity House on the basis that he took a shipwright's approach – his design was based on a timber cone. Work began in July 1706 and Rudyerd was assisted by Smith and Norcutt, two shipwrights from the Naval Dockyard at Woolwich.

Rudyerd had Winstanley's experience to build on and grasped the fact that no matter how massive the structure, it would not survive unless it was securely anchored to the rock. He dressed the surface of the rock as smooth as his men were able, then had thirty-six large dovetailed holes, each almost a metre in depth, together with two hundred minor holes, drilled into the rock. The larger holes were filled with melted tallow, then wrought-iron bolts were driven into them and wedged. Red-hot pewter was next poured in to displace the tallow and to fill every possible interstice in the cavity. Horizontal oak beams were then secured to produce a level platform upon which sixteen courses of stone, alternated with timber, were laid. These in turn were sheathed with oak. Upon this secure and heavy foundation a wooden tower was raised, carefully jointed by Smith and Norcutt, providing accommodation for the keepers and tapering to the lantern floor 21 metres above the rock. This use of timber ensured the action of the waves was unable to disturb the joints, while the lack of projections allowed seawater a smooth passage over its surface.

Installing three keepers to tend the light, Rudyerd lit his tower on 28 July 1708, although the structure was not properly completed until the following year. Sadly Rudyerd died in 1713, three years after his partner, and their lease was sold to a syndicate of Lovett's business associates. One of these was Robert Weston whose family kept an interest in the light until the lease expired.

By 1723 shipworm had damaged the timbers and repairs were carried out then and afterwards under the direction of John Holland, a shipwright from Plymouth Dockyard. Then, having stood for almost half a century, during the night of 1/2 December 1755 the top of the lantern caught fire, possibly from a leak in the chimney of the keeper's stove below. Hall, the keeper on watch, who was eighty-four years old (some accounts say ninety-four) but said to be 'of good constitution and active for his years', did his best to put out the fire by throwing water ineffectively upwards from a bucket. An account of the fire written by the Superintendent of Plymouth Dockyard, possibly from the evidence of the other keepers, reads: 'About Nine that Night Wm Hall…went up the Lantern and found it so full of Smoak he could not see the Candles'. Hall 'endeavoured to put out the Fire with Water in two Caske there, a quarter part full, he extinguished the Fire in one of the Pillars, and did all he could to put out the Whole, but for want of more help could not effect it, tho' he frequently call'd the other Two Men to come and assist him, and Short often answered he was coming, he did not come till Hall had been there near three-quarters of an Hour and Cupola was all afire, they were soon after obliged to retire down stairs, and from thence to the Rocks as the Fire was encreasing very fast, the Wind Blowing fresh at NE they remained on the Rocks with the Melted Lead and pieces of Burning Timber frequently falling upon them, till about three the next afternoon, when some men in a Cawsand Boat got them off.'

Whilst fighting the fire, the leaden roof melted and a gobbet of molten lead fell into the old man's open mouth. Notwithstanding this, Hall's efforts were little short of heroic but, with the fire above him all the time and gradually burning downwards as if consuming a gigantic candle, it finally drove the keepers out onto the rock. The fire was observed from the shore by a Mr Edwards, 'a man of some fortune and more humanity'. He is said to have sent off the 'Cawsand boat' which arrived at the lighthouse later in the day. The sea was too rough for the boat to approach the rock so the crew threw ropes and dragged the keepers through the waves to safety. The lighthouse continued to burn for five days and was completely destroyed.

Hall lived for twelve days after the incident. He was attended by a Doctor Spry of Plymouth who, when carrying out a post-mortem, found a flat oval piece of lead weighing seven ounces in Hall's stomach. Spry wrote an account of the case to the Royal Society, but the Fellows were sceptical as to whether any man, let alone one of such an age, could live for so long in this condition. This so incensed Spry that, for the sake of his reputation, he performed many experiments on dogs and fowls, pouring molten lead down their throats to prove that they could survive, at least for a while! As for the lead specimen, it resides today in the National Museum of Scotland in Edinburgh.

The Plymouth Superintendent speculated on the cause of the fire, considering it possible that the keepers had contributed to it: 'Whether this Accident proceeded from their [the keepers] Drinking too much of three Pints of Gin received with the Provisions and Candles that Evening, or having too great a fire in the chimney I cannot discover, but must observe at the time the Fire was discovered that there was but one Buckett in the [Light] House'.

In addition to the reluctance of the other keepers to go immediately to the unfortunate Hall's assistance, this interpretation of the cause of the fire has a further shred of circumstantial evidence attached to it: whether motivated by fear or guilt, one of the keepers ran away as soon as he gained the shore and was never heard of again.

After experiencing the benefit of a light for fifty-two years, mariners were anxious to have it replaced as soon as possible. Trinity House ordered a light vessel moored off the Eddystone to guard the position until a new lighthouse could be built. Robert Weston, then the principal proprietor and

Rear Admiral Richard Beechey (1808-1895) took up marine painting after retiring on naval half-pay. Beechey had specialised in surveying and, in common with most hydrographical surveyors, was a competent artist. His depiction of Smeaton's Eddystone on a brisk day is particularly fine.

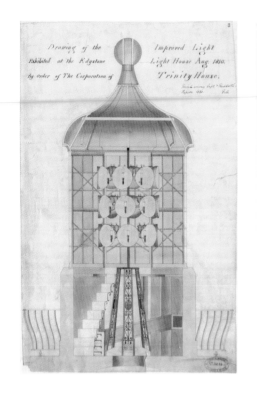

Drawing of the Improved Light Exhibited at the Eddystone Light House Aug. 1810. By order of The Corporation of Trinity House.

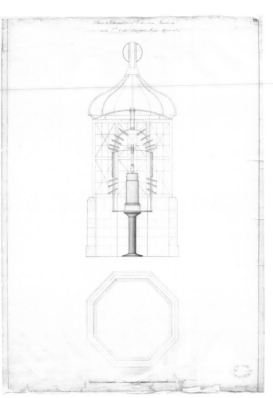

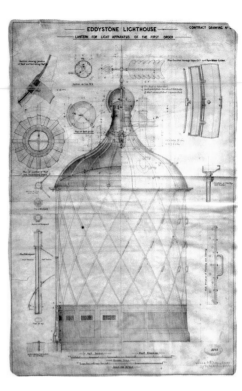

EDDYSTONE LIGHTHOUSE

LANTERN FOR LIGHT APPARATUS OF THE FIRST ORDER

CONTRACT DRAWING

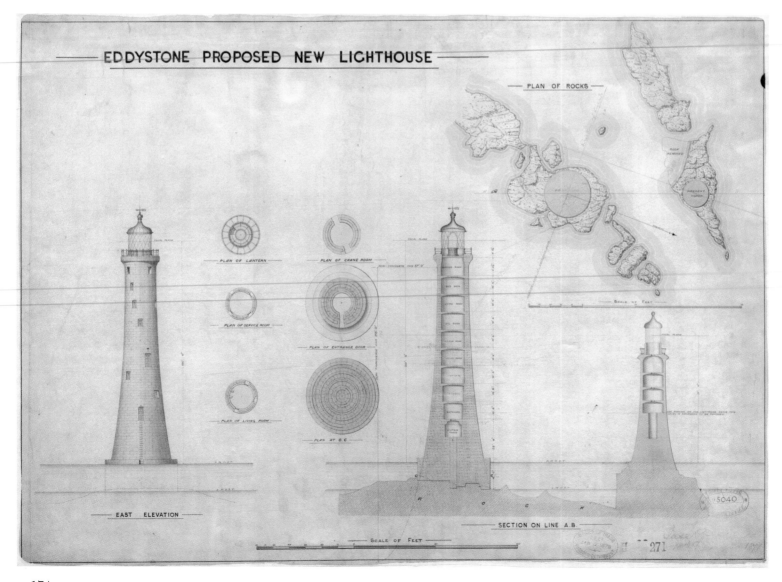

EDDYSTONE PROPOSED NEW LIGHTHOUSE

PLAN OF ROCKS

PLAN OF LANTERN

PLAN OF CRANE ROOM

PLAN OF SERVICE ROOM

PLAN OF ENTRANCE DOOR

PLAN OF LIVING ROOM

PLAN AT C.C.

EAST ELEVATION

SECTION ON LINE A.B.

SCALE OF FEET

SCALE OF FEET

271

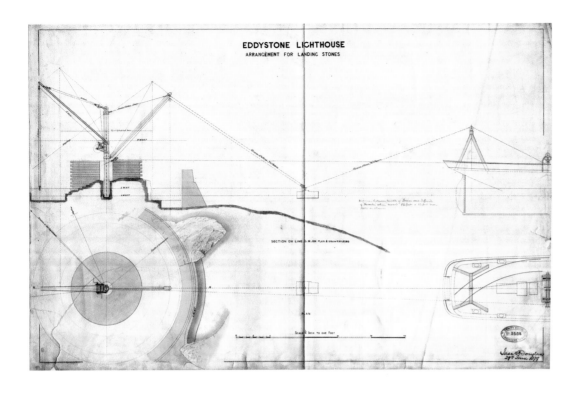

EDDYSTONE LICHTHOUSE
ARRANGEMENT FOR LANDING STONES

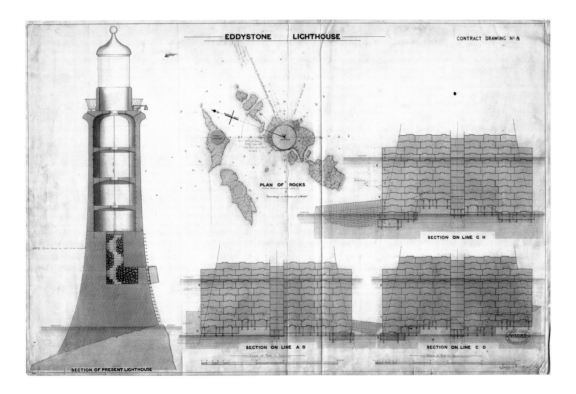

EDDYSTONE LICHTHOUSE

CONTRACT DRAWING Nº 4

PLAN OF ROCKS

SECTION ON LINE C H

SECTION ON LINE A B

SECTION ON LINE C D

SECTION OF PRESENT LIGHTHOUSE

eager to maintain his income from the light-dues, was obliged to comply and a small herring buss was fitted out on the Thames. Next Weston called in the Yorkshireman, John Smeaton, who had been recommended by the Royal Society and had already acquired a reputation for the design and construction of harbours, bridges, and land-drainage schemes. Smeaton, the 'father' of English civil engineering, travelled to Plymouth to survey the task. After prolonged planning, he decided to construct a tower based on the shape of an English oak tree, but made of stone rather than wood. For such a task he needed not only masons, but also the toughest of labourers, and he set about recruiting Cornish tin miners. To avoid men being abducted from the rock by unscrupulous commanders of men-of-war, Trinity House arranged with the Admiralty to have a medal struck for each workman to prove them exempt from the naval press.

Smeaton had given considerable thought to his design, making a model of the rock's surface

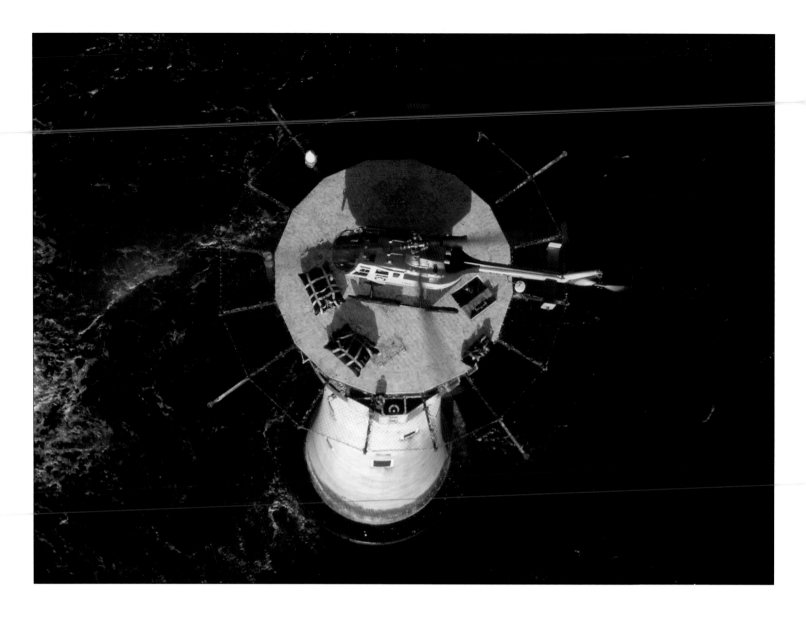

in order that the closest possible union could be made with the lowest course of stone blocks, exploiting Rudyerd's work and dovetailing both the rock and the lowest stones. In this way he sought to combine the virtues of Rudyerd's structure with a non-flammable, monolithic tower. The tapered base, reminiscent of the bole of the oak tree, was intended to give a low centre of gravity to the structure, and to deflect and dissipate the energy of the breaking waves. To achieve unity Smeaton extended the system of dovetailing, said to be derived from the kerbstones of London, so that the stones of each course, radiating out from a central keystone, each locked into its neighbour.

Smeaton and his workmen, led by shipwright Josias Jessop who had lately tended Rudyerd's tower, began work on 3 August 1756. After wrangling with Weston, Trinity House had finally decided to provide a lightvessel itself, but denied use of it to Smeaton for his men's quarters. Instead Smeaton made use of the buss Weston had originally intended for a lightvessel, and this provided him and his two teams of a dozen men with a floating workshop and accommodation anchored near the reef.

After months of preparatory work, the first stone, weighing 2.25 tons, was lowered into place at eight o'clock on the morning of Sunday 12 June 1757. It took all day to secure in position. Smeaton took enormous care with the building operations, devising ingenious ways of lifting the stones and perfecting the logistics of the complex operation. He also capitalised on available time, organising two shifts of workmen so that one could be constantly at work on the rock. But it was painstaking work, particularly in the first stages, and would take three summers to complete. Local granite known as 'moorstone' was used for the foundations and facing, infilled with softer but more easily worked Portland stone. Smeaton had also invented a quick drying cement, essential in the wet conditions on the rock, made from lime and volcanic ash. Each course was 'dressed' and offered up to its neighbour ashore, so that no delays would be encountered on the rock. In addition to the dovetails between blocks in the same course, tapered oak wedges held the courses together and, in the upper part of the tower, marble 'joggles' were fitted. To maintain strength in the upper storeys, two iron chains were placed around the tower at the level of the vaulted floors and sealed in lead. Bedevilled by a thousand setbacks, Smeaton finally informed Trinity House of his success and a light was first shown on 16 October 1759. Smeaton was watching from Plymouth Hoe 'and saw the light quite clearly through his telescope'.

Lit by a candelabrum of twenty-four candles and tended by three keepers, Henry Edwards, Henry Carter, and James Hatherley, Smeaton's literally ground-breaking tower was the triumph to which Winstanley had aspired. In contrast to Winstanley's inscriptive mania, Smeaton had a quotation from the 127th Psalm cut into the wall of one of the rooms: 'Except the Lord build the house, they labour in vain that build it'. An essentially modest man, in 1791 Smeaton published his *Narrative of the Building of the Eddystone Light* saying that it had given him more trouble to write the account than to build the lighthouse.

Weston's lease expired in 1806 and Trinity House assumed direct responsibility for the light, appointing an agent at Plymouth, along with fitting out a tender for the support of the lighthouse. It was soon realised that, splendid though the tower was, the light source was poor and in 1810 oil lamps were installed, greatly improving matters, so much so that it was the late 1870s before necessity compelled Trinity House to undertake further work when it was discovered that the rock on which the lighthouse stood was being undermined. It was decided to replace Smeaton's tower.

The task was no longer daunting and no time was lost. Huge advances had been made in the construction of offshore rock towers, particularly in Scotland, where Robert Stevenson had adopted Smeaton's basic principles and improved upon them. One such improvement was the adoption of a specially fitted out steamer, the *Hercules*, which carried the shaped blocks of stone from the dressing yard ashore to the site. Mooring to a set of buoys laid for the purpose, *Hercules* hooked up a running wire from the crane set in the centre of the site to her own stern gantry. Each stone block, on a small bogey running on rails down the ship's deck, was hoisted and swung across to its assigned position. The ship also served as accommodation and floating workshop.

This work was overseen by James Douglass, Engineer-in-Chief of Trinity House, a talented and experienced lighthouse constructor. His father, Nicholas, had preceded him in the office and James had known the life from childhood. At twenty-one he was appointed chief assistant to his father during the building of Bishop Rock and he went on to build the Smalls and Wolf Rock. Like Winstanley, James Douglass was an inspiring leader who had gained the respect of his workmen by sharing their privations and dangers. In turn, the on-site supervision was carried out by James's son, William. During the work William, like Smeaton before him, fell from the tower. He would have been killed on the rocks below had not a wave caught him and swept him into the sea where he was rescued by a boat.

Although constructing the tower was much easier than it had been for Douglass's predecessors, the new Eddystone Lighthouse was to be built on the stable central ridge of the reef – under water even at low tide. Thus, the first task was to construct a coffer dam to provide dry conditions for establishing the base of the tower. This took almost a year but once it was completed and a ceremonious start had been given to the project, work proceeded quickly, assisted by the *Hercules* which handled the huge blocks of granite (averaging 2 to 3 tons) with ease.

A topping out ceremony was held on 1 June 1881, attended by the *Hercules* and the Trinity House Yacht, the *Galatea*, aboard which were all the Elder Brethren. It was a fine day as the last of 2,171 blocks was laid by HRH The Duke of Edinburgh, the then Master of Trinity House, to the cheers of people surrounding the rock in small craft. Finally, on 18 May 1882 Douglass's magnificent tower, a mass of 4,668 tons of granite, was finally crowned by a large oil-lit biform optic blazing out over the surrounding sea. Douglass had estimated

that the project would take five years and cost £78,000. In the event it was completed in three and a half, and cost only £59,000. Douglass was knighted 'on the occasion of the completion of the new Eddystone Lighthouse, with which your name is so honourably connected'.

Smeaton's tower was dwarfed by this new structure, which rose to twice its height. Upon the proposal for its demolition being made known, the people of Plymouth raised the funds for it to be dismantled and re-erected on the Hoe, where it may still be visited.

Not only the first rock station, the Eddystone was also to be the first remote lighthouse to be

automated. To achieve this a helipad must first be constructed above the lantern. This was completed in 1980 and enabled work to be carried out in most weathers. Again a lightvessel was laid to provide a temporary aid to navigation, then, on Tuesday 21 July 1981, the light was shut off and the three keepers, Gordon Phillips, Larry Walker, and Leslie Harriman were withdrawn by helicopter. The work of automation was completed and the light was reintroduced on 18 May 1982, one hundred years to the day since the inauguration of Douglass's tower. Finally, in 1999, just over three hundred years after the candles on Winstanley's tower were first lit, the Eddystone Lighthouse was modernised and converted to solar power, its functional control being carried out many miles away in Harwich.

John Argent (1834-1916) painted a number of marine scenes connected with Trinity House. This one is of Douglass's Eddystone Lighthouse standing tall alongside the stump of Smeaton's tower that had been dismantled and rebuilt on Plymouth Hoe.

St Anthony's Head Lighthouse

The western county of Cornwall appears to project bravely into the Atlantic, a granite massif with ancient, almost mystical associations in the English psyche. Arthurian connections with Tintagel may be spurious, but they are enduring, as are hints that the lost kingdom of Lyonesse lies beneath the sea somewhere between Land's End and the Isles of Scilly. In this legend we begin to receive a rather different perception of Cornwall not as a bastion, but as a retreating salient, worn by the relentless attrition of the sea, leaving in its wake the outcrops of rock that mark the summits of those once proud hilltops. The Isles of Scilly possess a remote beauty, but their western edge, rising from the deep Atlantic, is a wild tumble of rocks and reefs that have claimed the lives of seafarers since mankind's first maritime adventures. Less obvious, but no less dangerous, is the reef of the Seven Stones to the northeast of the islands, and the 'steeple' of the Wolf Rock to the south of Land's End. The former is marked by a lightvessel, the latter by a spectacular lighthouse.

These seamarks, now so much a part of Cornwall's heritage, were once perceived as impositions, warding ships off the shore and depriving a poor and indigent population of the proceeds of wreck. 'Lord send us a mild winter, or a good wreck', ran the old Cornish prayer. Tales of deliberate

Latitude	*50° 08.43'N*
Longitude	*005° 00.90'W*
Established	*1835*
Height of tower	*19m*
Height of light above MHWS	*22m*
Character	*IsoWR15s*
Range	*16/14Nm*
Fog Signal	*Horn(1)30s*

wrecking are, like those of smuggling, difficult to corroborate in detail. To what extent locals tied lights to the tails of a bullock and drove the animal along the coast to mislead mariners we shall never know; that they robbed drowned sailors and plundered their wrecks, would seem too obvious for comment. When returning from the Mediterranean in October 1707, Admiral Sir Clowdesley Shovell's flagship, HMS *Association*, and two of her squadron, were lost on the Scillies in heavy weather. Shovell, a huge fat man, was washed ashore half dead upon the sand where he was discovered by a local woman. The sight of his emerald-studded ring proved too much for her; she swiftly smothered him before cutting off his finger and stealing the ring. It was afterwards recovered but Shovell's heartless murder symbolises that of countless other less prominent seamen.

It was not only the headlands and off-lying dangers that required marking, but also the entrances to Cornwall's greatest harbour. Like Plymouth, Falmouth is a flooded ria and formed an important haven of refuge. Until their final demise at the onset of the Second World War, the last commercial sailing ships sailed from Australia with their cargoes of grain, bound around Cape Horn and on to 'Falmouth for orders'. For a long period Falmouth was the port of despatch for the Post Office Packets that maintained contact with North America and the West Indies, and it was to Falmouth that Admiral Collingwood sent Lieutenant Lapenotiere and the schooner *Pickle* with news of the great victory off Cape Trafalgar and the death of Nelson. From here, Collingwood knew, Lapenotiere could take a government post-chaise and race to the Admiralty in London.

To guard the port, Henry VIII built two of his coastal castles and a beacon long stood upon the Black Rock that encumbers the entrance to Carrick Road, but it was 1835 before Trinity House built a lighthouse upon St Anthony's Head to the east.

Although situated on the mainland, access to the site was, and remains, difficult. To overcome this the builder, James Walker, constructed the new tower of granite blocks, each of which was cut and pre-assembled, as though for a rock station, before delivery, piece by piece, by boat from Penzance. Landed, it was quickly assembled on location. Below the main optic a red fixed light was fitted to shine over a narrow sector covering the Manacles, a dangerous reef lying in the approaches to Falmouth off the eastern coast of the Lizard peninsula.

Thirty years after the lighthouse was established a fog signal in the form of a large bell was added, its hammer operated by clockwork. In 1882 an even larger bell, weighing two tons and 1.5 metres in diameter was installed, suspended from the lantern.

In 1954 St Anthony's Lighthouse was converted to run on mains electricity and a new form of fog signal – a number of electrical emitters similar to those used for public address systems – replaced the bell. The lighthouse was automated in 1987 and modernised in 2000 when the character was changed from occulting to isophase, having equal periods of light and darkness. Due to the isolated nature of the station St Anthony's Lighthouse has retained much of its original elegant character and care was taken during the modernisation to maintain the old-world air.

The Lizard Lighthouse

Latitude	49° 57.61'N
Longitude	005° 12.13'W
Established	1619
Height of tower	19m
Height of light above MHWS	70m
Character	Fl3s
Range	26Nm
Fog Signal	Siren(1)30s
DGPS	306.0KHz 150M

The distinctive twin towers of the Lizard Lighthouse mark the most southerly point of mainland Britain. It stands as a passage-mark for vessels transiting the English Channel and heading for Falmouth. Below the headland jagged ridges of rock run out nearly a quarter of a mile from the shore and over two hundred wrecks have been claimed here, clear evidence of the difficulties in coastal navigation in the past.

As early as 1570 Sir John Killigrew of Arwenack, Falmouth, was granted a patent by Elizabeth I to build a coal-fired light on land he owned at the Lizard. However, Killigrew's motive, light-dues, ran contrary to the aspirations of less influential inhabitants: enrichment from occasional wrecks. Local opposition scotched the plan. Sir John's grandson applied for a patent in 1619 together with his cousin, Lord Dorchester. They presented the project as charitable – the applicants would build the lighthouse at their own expense and take only voluntary contributions from the owners of ships passing the point. The patent was issued, signed by the Duke of Buckingham, then the Lord High Admiral and, incidentally, the King's catamite. The patent took the terms of the application literally, with no compulsory dues set, but demanded a rent of 'twenty nobles by the year' for a term of thirty years. Moreover, because of the fear of such a light attracting the attentions of enemies during time of war, the owners were instructed to extinguished the light on the approach of the enemy.

Killigrew and his partner, Robert Thynne, set to work building the lighthouse. Local people were reluctant to help, as Killigrew reveals in a letter to his cousin: 'They affirm I take away God's grace from them. Their English meaning is that now they shall receive no more benefit by shipwreck, for this will prevent it. They have been so long used to reap by the calamity of the ruin of shipping as they claim it hereditary…. Custom breeds strange ills.' Despite all the difficulties with his contentious neighbours, Killigrew finished his tower by Christmas 1619 at a cost of £500. Once operating, Killigrew found it to consume ten shillings worth of fuel each night but, he added in his report to Dorchester, 'I presume it speaks to most parts of Christendom'. Alas, 'Christendom' seems not then to have extended to Cornwall, whose inhabitants had, in Killigrew's opinion, grown 'idle in the assurance of gain by shipwreck' and, despite the benefit, shipowners offered nothing for the upkeep of the light. By 1620 the mounting costs of maintenance was bankrupting Killigrew and the light was extinguished for periods during 1620 and 1621, whereupon more wrecks occurred. In 1623 Killigrew appealed to the King. Despite opposition from Trinity House who had ascertained that the 'most capable ship-masters stated [the light] could not be seen in hazy weather while in clear conditions the headland was itself visible' but they calculated that a modest due would yield £400 per annum. In 1624 Sir William Monson, a distinguished naval officer, strongly advocated the provision of lighthouses generally and at the Lizard in particular, citing the difficulties of Cavendish who, on his return from his circumnavigation, had told Monson that 'falling in with our Channel, somewhat short of the Lizard…[Cavendish] was so taken with so great a storm that he could not make the land and…endured more hazard and trouble in two

nights upon our coast than in his long navigation'. There was much more, but it did not alter Trinity House's opinion. Then it was alleged that Killigrew himself had removed cargo from a wreck. Perhaps money troubles induced by the failure of the lighthouse had driven him to it, but in his defence he stated to Dorchester that he had rights 'which custom and descent gave me'. Custom did indeed breed strange ills.

Unsurprisingly in this atmosphere of parochial ambiguity the scheme foundered. In 1630 a new patent was applied for as 'a thing all seamen desire', but nothing came of it and Killigrew's tower became derelict. Nothing was done until 1748, when Richard Farish, in concert with Thomas Fonnereau, the owner of Lizard Point, sent a proposal to Trinity House to build four light towers on the site. Trinity House responded positively but suggested that two towers would be more economical. Thus the Lizard would form one of a group of three distinctive major landfall lights, St Agnes in the Scillies having a single light, and the Casquets in the Channel Islands, three.

Farish set about collecting support for his petition from seafarers but died in 1750. He assigned his interest in the light to Fonnereau and the following year it was agreed that Trinity House would obtain a patent for the light and grant Fonnereau a lease for sixty-one years at £80 per annum, after which the light and the land would belong to the Corporation without compensation to the owner. Fonnereau objected strongly to this, and to the provision that the lights would be extinguished in wartime and the dues scrapped for the duration. Moreover, the two Elder Brethren, Captains Carteret and Smith, who proceeded to the Lizard to 'mark out the most proper spot', did so at Fonnereau's expense. A legal wrangle ensued, but the two towers were quickly erected at the cost of £3,000 and were first lit on 22 August 1752. Litigation rumbled on until 1771 when the utility of the lighthouse was well established and Trinity House won the case and assumed responsibility for the lights.

Originally crowned by coal fires in brick hearths, the glazed screens – with their small panes of leaded glass and heavy wooden frame – that protected the light also lessened its power. However, they reduced coal consumption in high winds whilst allowing the smoke to escape through their open tops. A drawing of these structures shows a wooden balcony attached to the outside of the tower, which may well have been added in order to clean the glazings.

A cottage stood between the towers, in which an overseer lay on a sort of couch, with a window on either side commanding a view of the lanterns. When the bellows-blowers relaxed their efforts and the fires dimmed, he would remind them of their duty by a blast from a cow horn.

In 1812, Argand lamps and reflectors were installed at the Lizard at a cost of £5,000. This improved both the quality and efficiency of the lights. The accommodation was also modified at this time so that a covered passage linked the two towers. The later addition of a revolving light made one tower redundant and, in due course, it was converted into the fog-signal house, an addition that increased the establishment of the station to eight keepers – a circumstance that caused the number of children living on the station at one time to reach forty-five.

In 1878 Lizard Lighthouse became one of the earliest electric-powered stations and today possesses the only large engine room surviving from that period. A century later the Lizard operated as an area control station for a brief period until it was itself fully automated in 1998, whereupon the keepers were withdrawn on 16 April. The automation involved replacing the compressed-air fog horn – the last one in the Service – with an electric signal. Since then, whilst continuing its vital role, the station has become a popular visitor centre and is, as are all accessible automated lighthouses, 'kept' by a visiting attendant.

Fleet Prison, but his profits were remitted to his family by way of the Court of Chancery. Smith's family did rather well out of this arrangement until 1836 when, empowered by Parliament to acquire all outstanding leases, Trinity House bought out the unexpired nine and a half years for the handsome sum of £40,676.

The lighthouse was manned by four men, two at a time on a monthly roster. They were provided with food whilst on station, but not when ashore, where they were free to seek other employment to augment their not ungenerous annual pay of £30. An alleged incident at the Longships in which wreckers kidnapped the keeper in order to compromise the light was an apocryphal Victorian

Below left: The earliest lighthouse on the Longships, built by Smith and Wyatt and first lit in September 1795.

Below right: Elevations and sections of Douglass's taller replacement tower, completed in 1875.

invention. A novel, making a high moral point, 'recorded' how, after her father's removal, the keeper's daughter maintained the light, standing on the family bible to do so. This fictive nonsense was typical of the mid-Nineteenth-Century romance that surrounded lighthouses and is interesting only in that it demonstrates a shift in cultural perception. After the Act of Parliament of 1836 the lighthouse was no longer regarded as a symbol of decadent exploitation, but, rather, of staunch – and by implication British – reliability. Moreover, the keepers themselves personified this dignified image, exemplified by the courage of Grace Darling and her father. Sadly for fiction, there were no families at the Longships – cottages were built for them at Sennen on the mainland nearby.

Wyatt's lighthouse suffered from not being high enough and, if not swept by waves, its light was reduced in intensity from spray in the air. The matter was addressed in 1875 when Sir James Douglass built the present circular tower of grey granite alongside Wyatt's tower, only demolishing the former when he had completed his work so that not a night passed without the light.

The modern isophase optic causes a red light to be shown over the rocks on the landward side where an inshore passage may be passed in fine weather. In 1974 a helipad was constructed on the lantern-top and fourteen years later, in 1988, the station was automated, its control eventually passing to Harwich.

Round Island Lighthouse

Latitude	*49° 58.70'N*
Longitude	*006° 19.35'W*
Established	*1887*
Height of tower	*19m*
Height of light above MHWS	*55m*
Character	*Fl10s*
Range	*23Nm*
Fog Signal	*Horn(4)60s*
Racon fitted	

The lighthouse on Round Island, situated in the northern part of the Scillonian archipelago was built in 1887 during the era of high Victorian endeavour. The granite island is about 40 metres high and its precipitous sides challenged the construction almost as much as wave-swept rocks for the sheer rock face made the unloading of building materials difficult. Despite its elevation, during severe gales in January 1984, seas smashed the lower doors of the fog-signal house.

Until its automation in 1987, this was a popular station with keepers and boasted a small vegetable garden. Although technically a 'rock' station the size of the island provided ample room for a helicopter landing pad when aircraft were introduced to the Service in 1969. Boat access is still obtainable from a landing place and a flight of steps cut into the rock.

Round Island is one of the few stations using red as its main light colour and, in order to cope with the weaker propagation qualities of red as opposed to white, Round Island formerly bore an enormous hyper-radial optic – a glittering structure of bronze astragals and prismatic glass. Such a magnificent apparatus was fitted to only two other lighthouses at the beginning of the Twentieth Century, though similar optics were in use elsewhere. It was replaced in 1967 with a more modern apparatus which, in turn, was replaced during the automation of the lighthouse in 1987 when the present equipment was installed and the light was altered to white.

Bishop Rock Lighthouse

The difficulties and dangers that beset the navigators of previous ages cannot be exaggerated. In thick weather they sought the entrance to the English Channel with great trepidation, proceeding largely 'by guess and by God', fearfully aware that the Isles of Scilly posed a terrifying threat to their safe passage. The risks were recognised early in maritime history and Trinity House had in fact taken on the building and running of a lighthouse in the islands by 1690. Early illuminants were not very effective and the lighthouse at St Agnes was really too far away from the western extremity of the reefs to warn incoming ships of their presence before it was too late. The early Eighteenth Century wrecking of Admiral Shovell's *Association* has already been mentioned, but there were literally hundreds of other losses.

Although St Agnes had been kept up to date, insofar as improvements in lighting apparatus were concerned, it was clear that a light was required on the western reefs of the Scillies as urgently as it was upon the Wolf Rock. In 1847 James Walker, Trinity House's Engineer in Chief, began work on an

Latitude	*49° 52.34'N*
Longitude	*006° 26.29'W*
Established	*1858*
Height of tower	*49m*
Height of light above MHWS	*44m*
Character	*Fl(2)15s*
Range	*24Nm*
Fog Signal	*Horn(N)90s*
Racon fitted	

Far left: Walker's iron-lattice structure was erected on Bishop Rock between 1849 and 1850. It was intended to offer minimal resistance to the passage of heavy seas but was destroyed the night before the installation of the optic.

Left: Back to the drawing board: Walker's eventual design of 1850 returned to the basic principles established by Smeaton.

iron, screw-pile tower inspired by the durability of the wooden-lattice structure on the Smalls Reef off Pembrokeshire (see page 223). Walker was against building a solid granite tower arguing that the rock ledge was too small and the elements too powerful. He demonstrated that the wind pressures at times exceeded 7,000lb per sq.ft, and as many as thirty gales a year were not unusual in the area.

The work went well and by December 1849 the tower was ready to receive the optic the following spring. On 5 February 1850 a furious gale hit the islands and upon its abatement nothing was left of Walker's iron tower – what worked with resilient timber could not be replicated in unresisting iron. Undaunted, Walker returned to Smeaton's method and found an area of rock that gave him a diameter of 12 metres. He surrounded it with an iron caisson and, by pumping out the water granted his workmen a measure of protection against the elements and enabled them to defy the tide. Walker's on-site supervisor was the then young James Douglass who insisted on sharing the discomforts of the workforce, living with them at their camp on the neighbouring islet of Annet and joining them in their diet of 'limpets and puffins' eggs' and, in the evenings, enjoying concerts to which he contributed flute solos.

Some 2,500 tons of granite blocks had to be sent out from the mainland where they had been dressed and offered up, each to its neighbour. Despite these preparations the task took seven years to accomplish and cost £34,560, but it convinced Walker that if he could achieve success here, he could do so at the Wolf. Moreover, James Douglass earned himself the experience and reputation that were to make him the doyen of English lighthouse constructors. On 1 September 1858 the light was 'put in' to crown the 37 metre tower. Its provision did not prevent shipwrecks – in 1875 a German immigrant ship, the *Schiller*, ran ashore with the loss of some 350 souls – but it did reduce them.

However, like the Longships Lighthouse, it was found that Walker's tower was not high enough to avoid being obscured by spray at times, nor to escape damage; during one particularly powerful storm, waves thundered up the side of the lighthouse and tore away the 550lb fog bell from its fastenings on the gallery. In 1881, in response to a report from the Principal Keeper, Douglass made a detailed inspection of the lighthouse and reported extensive damage and weakness in the structure. It was decided to strengthen the tower and, at the same time, to increase the elevation of the light by 12m.

The window embrasures, set in the thick tower walls, provided storage space for the keepers' fruit and vegetables, enclosed, as they were, by inner and outer glazings.

Right: Cramped quarters housing cooking facilities, entertainment and communications equipment also provide living space for the three keepers on Bishop Rock.

Below: A lighthouse keeper's only privacy was behind the drawn curtains of his curved bunk. Additional bunk space above was available for visiting mechanics.

This complex and bold plan effectively entailed the building of a new lighthouse around the old one, completely encasing it. But the real weakness in Walker's structure was its foundation, which had given rise to the keepers' anxieties, and this Douglass proposed to strengthen and enlarge with massive blocks of granite sunk into the rock and held there by heavy bolts. He constructed an enormous cylindrical base, providing the lighthouse with an excellent buffer onto which the force of the waves could be spent before hitting the tower itself. This stone casing, averaging a metre in thickness, was carried up as far as the new masonry required for the increased height of the light. The weight of the additional granite was 3,200 tons, making a total weight of 5,700 tons. Work was completed in October 1887 at a cost of £66,000.

The original light was provided by a multi-wick paraffin burner surrounded by a massive biform optic floating in a bath of mercury and weighing over two tons. So delicately balanced was this huge apparatus, that it could be turned with a finger, and so effective was it, that it remained in service until 1973, when the lighthouse was converted to electric operation. In 1976 a helipad was constructed above the lantern thus enabling keepers to be relieved by helicopter.

Bishop Rock Lighthouse was converted to automatic operation during 1991, the keepers being withdrawn on 21 December 1992. Subsequently, control was assumed at Harwich. The lighthouse continues to provided a departure for, and landfall light after, the long crossing of the North Atlantic Ocean. For much of its history the Bishop Rock lighthouse was the eastern terminus for the unofficial but prestigious Blue Ribband of the Atlantic, awared for the fastest transatlantic crossing by the great passenger liners of the past.

Peninnis Lighthouse

Peninnis is situated on St Mary's Island in the Isles of Scilly, enabling small vessels to enter St Mary's Road and the little port of Hugh Town. It is a small automatic light contained in a steel tower and was established in 1911 when the old lighthouse on St Agnes was discontinued. Originally powered by acetylene, it was re-engineered and converted to electricity in 1992. Peninnis was one of the very early gas-powered stations and had a unique gas-driven optic.

Latitude	*49° 54.24'N*
Longitude	*006° 18.15'W*
Established	*1911*
Height of tower	*14m*
Height of light above MHWS	*36m*
Character	*Fl20s*
Range	*17Nm*

Sevenstones Lightvessel

It is not inappropriate to mention the automatic lightvessel which marks the Sevenstones, an isolated group of steep rocks about a square mile in area to the northeast of the Isles of Scilly. Like the major lighthouses in the vicinity, it provides a passage mark for vessels navigating the mandatory Traffic Separation Scheme now in force for vessels passing north or south between the Scillies and Land's End. In 1967 the tanker *Torrey Canyon* infamously ran aground on the Sevenstones reef despite warnings from the then manned lightvessel. The incident marked the beginning of public awareness in the fragility of the ecosystem and the collective responsibility we all share for the condition of our planet.

The Sevenstones is the most exposed lightvessel station in the world and, though only rarely, she has been known to drag her anchor. The depth of water and the heaviness and length of her moorings makes her return to station a difficult task for the crew of the attending Trinity House Vessel. The early establishment, in 1841, of a lightvessel in this dangerous and remote location shows the determination of the Trinity House of the day to embrace the responsibilities laid upon it by the Act of 1836 and to cast off its unsympathetic image of the previous century. In 1841 the Brethren had investigated the locale for

Latitude	*50° 03.58'N*
Longitude	*006° 04.28'W*
Established	*1841*
Height of light above MHWS	*12m*
Character	*Fl(3)30s*
Range	*23Nm*
Fog Signal	*Horn(3)60s*
Racon fitted	

potential sites for aids to navigation during a voyage in the Trinity House Vessel *Argus*. Although Captains Welbank and Hayman considered the Sevenstones inaccessible, they thought a lightvessel might lie to moorings there – and there, not without difficulty, she has lain ever since.

Pendeen Lighthouse

Latitude	*50° 09.90'N*
Longitude	*005° 40.20'W*
Established	*1900*
Height of tower	*17m*
Height of light above MHWS	*59m*
Character	*Fl(4)15s*
Range	*16Nm*
Fog Signal	*Siren(1)20s*

The north coast of Cornwall is an inhospitable shore and the grave of many ships; it was devoid of any lighthouse until the latter part of the Nineteenth Century when increasing concern was felt for seamen in the wake of Samuel Plimsoll's advertisement of their hapless plight in Parliament. During this period Trinity House continued its rolling programme of establishing aids to navigation in the form of an increasing number of buoys, beacons, lightvessels and, of course, lighthouses. They adopted the principle of having a major light at twenty-mile intervals to facilitate constant cross bearings in clear weather. Accordingly it was decided to construct a lighthouse on the north coast of Land's End, a poorly

served area with coasters and fishing vessels plying offshore and in and out of the port of St Ives. The site chosen was Pendeen. The lighthouse and fog signal were designed by Douglass's successor, Sir Thomas Matthews, the works being undertaken by Arthur Carkeek, of Redruth, with Messrs Chance of Birmingham supplying the lantern.

The buildings were to occupy a large area and before construction could begin the cap of the Point had to be removed and the whole headland flattened. A huge retaining wall was built on the seaward side and, by the beginning of 1900, Carkeek's men had only reached the half-way mark although the lantern makers were ready to install their apparatus. However, work thereafter progressed more rapidly and the light was commissioned on 26 September 1900.

Within the tower itself are two rooms and above the upper of these is the lantern. This originally contained a five-wick Argand lamp, to which oil was pumped from the room below. In 1926 an electric lamp was fitted within the huge 2.5 ton lens mounting which, like others of its vintage, floated in a trough containing three quarters of a ton of mercury.

Pendeen Lighthouse was automated in 1995, the keepers leaving the station on 3 May. The original optic has been retained but a new lamp plinth with a two position lamp changer has been installed, along with an emergency light and a new fog signal and fog detector. The lighthouse is now monitored and controlled via a telemetry link from Harwich.

Godrevy

Latitude	*50° 14.51'N*
Longitude	*005° 23.96'W*
Established	*1859*
Height of tower	*26m*
Height of light above MHWS	*37m*
Character	*FlWR10s*
Range	*12/9Nm*

Little more than three miles to the north of St Ives, Godrevy Island is the home of rock-pipits, gulls, terns, shags, oystercatchers and other waders, and is partly covered by grass where it slopes down to the sea on the landward side. In springtime, carpets of brightly coloured primroses, sea thrift and heather adorn its thin soil but, although the island is close to the mainland, it is exposed to the full force of Atlantic gales. Moreover, its proximity to the coast causes it to be constantly within the turmoil of the tides and the backwash from the shore. The sea state was so frequently poor that the station acquired a reputation for its late relief of the keepers.

A dangerous reef, called the Stones, extends outwards towards St Ives, and many vessels have been lost there. On 30 November 1854, the iron screw steamer *Nile* was wrecked on the Stones with the loss of all passengers and crew and, in 1859, under public and mercantile pressure, Trinity House finally decided to erect a lighthouse on Godrevy. James Walker designed the station, and its welcome lights shone out on 1 March of that same year, a main navigation light with a subsidiary red-sector light over the Stones. Two keepers were originally appointed to the lighthouse to maintain both lights and fog signal.

Walker's white octagonal tower, 26 metres high, is made from rubble stone bedded in mortar and is sited, together with its adjoining keepers' cottages, almost in the centre of the largest of the rocky islands that make up the Stones reef. The cost of the station was £7,083. The original optic revolved on rollers on a circular race and was rotated by a clockwork motor powered by a large weight running down a cavity in the wall of the tower. The station was also equipped with a bell fog signal, and this was struck once every 5 seconds.

Enormous difficulties were experienced in relieving the two keepers who maintained the station. Godrevy was never manned with the three men considered essential elsewhere and the folly of this, combined with the difficulties of boatwork, was emphasised in 1925 when one of them was taken

Below: An attempt was made to link Godrevy to the mainland by means of an aerial runway but it was not a success. With boat access also difficult, Godrevy was one of the earliest lighthouses to be converted to an automatic system.

ill with pneumonia on Christmas Day. The condition of the weather had been steadily deteriorating along with that of the sick keeper and at last his mate fired the rockets for assistance and the St Ives lifeboat was launched. It was almost dark when the lifeboat crew, displaying their customary gallantry, approached the landing. Even on the lee side 'it was a boiling pot. The sea roared and crashed with violence over the rocks and landing place, and the wind howled…. The moon, hidden by ugly black clouds made it eerie as the dark overhanging rocks towering towards the blackness of the sky…seemed as if they would crash and bury everything…. We saw the lifeboat approach the landing bow first with a kedge anchor over the stern. Suddenly the…large bulk of the lifeboat loomed up above our heads…. The sea passed on and…it was then that they shouted for my mate to jump, which he did and was hauled inboard by the bowman. Just then a heavy sea broke astern of the lifeboat, lifting [it]…high above the landing, and it appeared as if only a miracle could avert the disaster of the lifeboat crashing to pieces on the rocks, but by clever seamanship

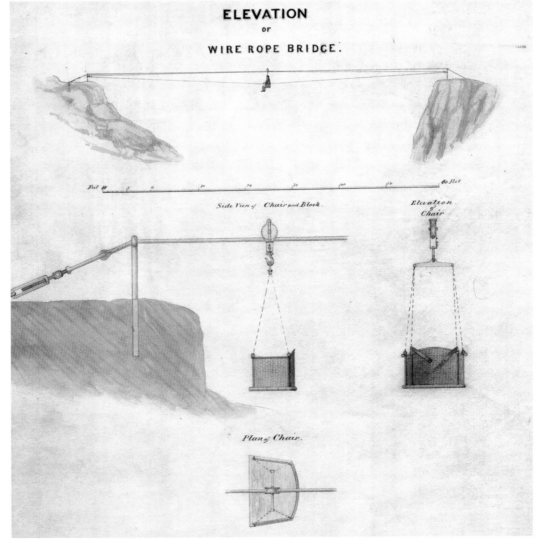

ELEVATION
OF
WIRE ROPE BRIDGE.

she was hauled out quickly [on the kedge line] to the centre of the gully....'

The author of this account, Mr W.J. Lewis, was obliged to remain alone on the island for eight days, despite a failed attempt to get another man ashore on Boxing Day. Lewis fought sleep and the depression of his solitary confinement when, 'the mind seems conducive to the supernatural and shocks are frequent with unreal objects formed by a vivid imagination.... For eight days and nights the lights and fog signal were kept going single-handed with eight hours' broken sleep during the lone vigil.' Later the Trinity House Board 'observed with much satisfaction' Lewis's conduct and, having highly commended him for his devotion to duty, awarded him £5.

The establishment of Pendeen, with its powerful fog signal reduced the importance of Godrevy and, in 1933, its fog signal was discontinued and the light was automated. Run from acetylene accumulators operated by a solar-sensitive operating valve, only the light remained and the keepers could be withdrawn. In 1995 Godrevy Lighthouse was converted to solar power and is today controlled from Harwich.

Trevose Head Lighthouse

Latitude	*50° 32.92'N*
Longitude	*005° 2.07'W*
Established	*1847*
Height of tower	*27m*
Height of light above MHWS	*62m*
Character	*Fl 7.5s*
Range	*21Nm*
Fog Signal	*Horn(2)30s*

It was an old sailors' saw that: 'From Padstow Bar to Lundy Light, is a Sailor's grave by day or night'. Looking down over Padstow Bar is Trevose Head and it had been an obvious site for a lighthouse since 1809. The position was further considered by Trinity House in 1813 and again in 1832, but it was not until 1 December 1847 that an oil light backed with reflectors, was first lit there.

The lighthouse is situated on the northwest extremity of the headland, with gigantic cliffs of grey granite rising sheer from the sea to a height of over 45 metres. The area, like so much of the Devon and Cornish coastline, is constantly threatened by sea mists that diminish even the most powerful lights. This makes it difficult to understand why a fog signal was not installed at that time.

Prior to 1882 there were two fixed lights at Trevose Head, a higher one in today's tower and, to seaward of it, a lower light. An entry in the Channel Pilot of 1859 gives the details for Trevose as follows: 'Trevose Head lights – two fixed bright lights, at different elevations. The highest of these lights burns at an elevation of 204 feet above the level of high water, and illuminates 274 degrees of the compass...and is visible for 19 miles. The lower light, which is placed about 50 feet in advance, or to seaward of the higher light, burns at an elevation of 129 feet above the level of high water, and illuminates about 176 degrees of the compass...visible for 16 miles.'

In 1882 the low light was discontinued and an occulting light was installed in the high tower. On 31 August this was tested and found satisfactory by James Douglass. On 1 August 1912 the station was 'visited by Captain Clarke and Sir Thomas Matthews, Engineer-in-Chief, and Mr Hood on exhibition of the new light flashing every five seconds – all found in good order. The work on the new fog signal progressing favourably.' On 6 February 1913 the new fog signal was put in to service at an inauguration ceremony attended by the then Deputy Master, Captain Sir Acton Blake, Elder Bretheren Captains Crawford and Marshall, and Sir Thomas Matthews.

The new fog signal had been developed by Lord Rayleigh, who was scientific adviser to Trinity House between 1869 and 1919. Rectangular in shape the horn was 36 feet long with the aperture 18 feet by 2 feet, it being intended that this shape would give a wide horizontal spread of sound. It must have been successful because it remained in use until replaced in 1963 by a Super-typhon with eight horns. ('Lord Rayleigh's Trumpet' is replicated, usually by a tuba, every time Malcolm Arnold's popular march *Padstow Lifeboat* is played.)

ELEVATION NEXT THE SEA.

72 TREVOSE LIGHT, NORTH CORNWALL.

Following: The complications arising from the fitting of helipads above the lantern are clearly seen here on the Eddystone. In fact the apparent confusion of the helical astragal supports resolves itself as each aligns with its inner neighbour when viewed from the centre, thus the radiation of the light is minimally impeded.

During the 1912/13 modernisation, a first order catadioptric optic was put into service and it was into this lens, in around 1920, that a Hood paraffin vapour burner was installed. This innovation utilised vaporized oil at high pressure, burnt within a gauze 'autoform' mantle. The incandescent light produced was of 198,000 candle power, and produced a red flash every 5 seconds with a nominal range of 25 miles; the 3.6 tonnes lens was operated by a clockwork motor driven by weights.

Trevose Lighthouse was automated in 1995 and the keepers were withdrawn on 20 December. The existing optic was retained but the rotation speed was slowed to extend the character, while the red screens were removed to give a white light. The Super-typhon was replaced by an electric omni-directional signal operated by a fog detector. The light is controlled by a photocell mounted on the lantern and telemetry links the station with its distant monitors at Harwich.

The Bristol Channel

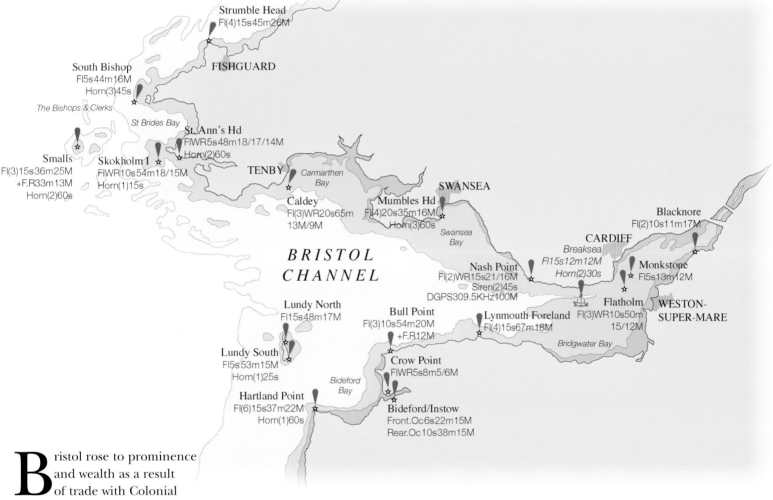

Strumble Head
Fl(4)15s45m26M

FISHGUARD

South Bishop
Fl5s44m16M
Horn(3)45s

The Bishops & Clerks

St Brides Bay

St. Ann's Hd
FlWR5s48m18/17/14M
Horn(2)60s

Smalls
Fl(3)15s36m25M
+F.R33m13M
Horn(2)60s

Skokholm I
FlWR10s54m18/15M
Horn(1)15s

TENBY

Carmarthen Bay

Caldey
Fl(3)WR20s65m
13M/9M

Mumbles Hd
Fl(4)20s35m16M
Horn(3)60s

SWANSEA

Swansea Bay

Blacknore
Fl(2)10s11m17M

CARDIFF

Breaksea
Fl15s12m12M
Horn(2)30s

Monkstone
Fl5s13m12M

BRISTOL CHANNEL

Nash Point
Fl(2)WR15s21/16M
Siren(2)45s
DGPS309.5KHz100M

Flatholm
Fl(3)WR10s50m
15/12M

WESTON-
SUPER-MARE

Lundy North
Fl15s48m17M

Bull Point
Fl(3)10s54m20M
+F.R12M

Lynmouth Foreland
Fl(4)15s67m18M

Bridgwater Bay

Lundy South
Fl5s53m15M
Horn(1)25s

Crow Point
FlWR5s8m5/6M

Bideford Bay

Hartland Point
Fl(6)15s37m22M
Horn(1)60s

Bideford/Instow
Front.Oc6s22m15M
Rear.Oc10s38m15M

Bristol rose to prominence and wealth as a result of trade with Colonial North America, the West Indies and Canada, and especially as a consequence of the slave trade – Bristol 'guineamen' purchased their human cargoes from the chiefs and traders of west Africa, before carrying them to the sugar and cotton plantations across the Atlantic and returning to England with Caribbean produce. As shipping grew, so did shipbuilding. All that now remains of Bristol's maritime industry and endeavour is one of her most remarkable products, the auxiliary steamship *Great Britain*. Brunel's innovative and ground-breaking vessel has been restored to the dry dock in which she was built and, incidentally, close to where the Trinity House Vessel *Vestal* was constructed in 1947. Today there is no ship-construction in Bristol and the commercial docks have migrated downstream to Avonmouth, were general, bulk and liquid cargoes continue to be handled.

On the coast of South Wales, the once busy coal-exporting ports of Newport, Cardiff, Barry, and Swansea, are much reduced in capacity. Nevertheless, cargoes do still move in and out of Welsh ports, iron ore feeds the steel works at Port Talbot and oil the refineries of Milford Haven.

Facing: Blacknore Lighthouse in the Severn Estuary.

205

Hartland Point Lighthouse

Latitude	*51° 01.28'N*
Longitude	*004° 31.50'W*
Established	*1874*
Height of tower	*18m*
Height of light above MHWS	*37m*
Character	*Fl(6)15s*
Range	*22Nm*
Fog Signal	*Horn(1)60s*

Feared for generations of seamen as a point of great danger, the great carboniferous cape of Hartland Point was known to the Romans as 'the promontory of Hercules' because it seemed to them to defy the elements with its splendour. Hartland Point Lighthouse marks the passage between the Devon coast and the off-lying island of Lundy and its establishment was part of Trinity House's great lighthouse-building programme of the second half of the Nineteenth Century. Constructed in 1874 under the direction of Sir James Douglass, it was built on the extremity of the point at a height just below the altitude at which cloud formed. The stability of this location is constantly threatened by the undermining action of the sea to such an extent that rock had to be broken from the cliff head behind the lighthouse; falling to the beach below it formed a 'soft-defence' against which the waves would dissipate their energy – estimated at 36 tonnes per square metre in heavy weather. Under this force of attrition it is not surprising that the procedure had to be repeated at frequent intervals as the deposits were washed away whenever a northwesterly gale coincided with a high spring tide. Eventually it was decided to construct a permanent barrier, and in 1925 a sea wall 30 metres long and 6 metres high was built. In 2001 the approach road fell away and today access is limited to a narrow footpath or by helicopter.

Prior to automation in 1984 the station was manned by four keepers, who lived with their families in dwellings attached to the lighthouse. The accommodation was demolished when the station was modified in order to allow for the construction of a helipad next to the tower.

Crow Point Lighthouse

Crow Point Light is a 'house' only by courtesy, for it provides a local guide to small vessels navigating the Taw and Torridge estuary in north Devon. It is a small steel lattice structure with the light just 7.6 metres above Mean High Water. Crow Point was established in 1954 as an automatic acetylene-powered light, converted to solar power in 1987 and further modernised in 2001.

Latitude	*49° 56.23'N*
Longitude	*006° 18.44'W*
Established	*1954*
Height of tower	*7m*
Height of light above MHWS	*8m*
Character	*FlRW5s*
Range	*5/6Nm*

Instow Leading Lights

Behind the sand dunes of Hartland Bay, the Rivers Taw and Torridge meet. In order to debouch into the sea, they have to force their way through the sand heaped up by the prevailing onshore winds. The intricate navigation of this passage may only be made at high water and it relies upon the provision of two leading lights. These were established at Instow, opposite the haven's entrance.

Instow Rear Light

Latitude	*51° 03.48'N*
Longitude	*004° 10.28'W*
Established	*1820*
Height of tower	*9m*
Height of light above MHWS	*38m*
Character	*Oc10s*
Range	*15Nm*

Instow Front Light

Latitude	*51° 03.58'N*
Longitude	*004° 10.59'W*
Established	*1820*
Height of tower	*18m*
Height of light above MHWS	*22m*
Character	*Oc6s*
Range	*15Nm*

BIDDEFORD
HIGH LIGHT

NW   SECTION   SE

Left: The wooden structure of the high leading light at Instow, near Bideford.

Bull Point Lighthouse

Latitude	*51° 11.93'N*
Longitude	*004° 12.00'W*
Established	*1879*
Height of tower	*11m*
Height of light above MHWS	*54/48m*
Character	*Fl (3) 10s +F.R*
Range	*20/12Nm*

On the northern headland of Hartland Bay lies Bull Point lighthouse. Below its main light, which serves as a passage light for vessels navigating in the Bristol Channel, red sector lights warn of the off-lying dangers of the Rockham Shoal and the Morte Stone. Built in 1879 it is, like so many stations established at that time, notable only for years of quiet service to the seafaring community; that is until 18 September 1972 when the Principal Keeper reported ground movement in the area of the engine room and the passage leading to the lighthouse. In the early hours of Sunday morning, 24 September, 15 metres of the shale cliff face crashed into the sea and a further 15 metres subsided steeply, causing deep fissures to open up inside the boundary of the lighthouse compound. Walls had cracked and the generator and fog-signal house partly collapsed, putting the fog signal out of action. By 1530 on 25 September, a Trinity House Vessel had been ordered to attend, and she laid a buoy off the point; meanwhile a lightvessel was prepared at the Trinity House Depot, Swansea. On 26 September the Bull Point lightvessel was laid on station to provide an adequate fog signal until a replacement could be set up on the headland above.

As a temporary arrangement, an old Trinity House light tower, formerly situated at Instow but at the time in use at Braunton Sands, was borrowed back from the Nature Conservancy Board, to whom it had been given. Relocated, an optic was installed and it served as Bull Point's lighthouse for nearly two years. After a few weeks it was augmented by a make-shift hut housing three temporary diaphone fog signals, whereupon the lightvessel was withdrawn.

Construction work on the new lighthouse began in 1974; it was designed and built so that all the equipment from the old lighthouse, which dated from the 1960s, could be reused with only minor modifications. The plant from the collapsed generator and fog-signal house was salvaged, overhauled and re-installed. The overall task cost £71,000.

In 1988, following the Navaid Review, the station was converted to automatic operation. Ironically, one consequence was the removal of a fog signal at Bull Point. In 2001 the station was further updated, being linked with Harwich.

Lynmouth Foreland Lighthouse

Twenty miles east of Bull Point Lynmouth Foreland Lighthouse was established by Trinity House in 1900 as a further aid to navigation in the Bristol Channel. The round white tower is 15 metres high, set on the extremity of the headland some two miles east of Lynmouth. Because of the orientation of the building just below the cloud level with high ground rising behind it, the lighthouse only sees the sun for the three months of high summer. It proved a gloomy place for the keepers and their families and for this reason service at Lynmouth Foreland was limited to three years.

    The station is also isolated. Sent to relieve a sick keeper during the cold winter of 1962, Bill O'Brian recalled: 'From Barnstaple to Lynmouth the snow was piled high and there was only a single track. I got to Lynton but there was no way to get out to the lighthouse. You have to go over a hill and it was absolutely covered in snow. I phoned the Swansea depot to say I had better stay in a hotel and...I was in that hotel for a week. The taxi driver who usually [carried out] the Lynmouth reliefs had a toboggan, so we piled all the gear on the toboggan and pulled it along. We got to Lynmouth and I was there for a fortnight. The water froze solid everywhere, the toilets, even the drinking water which was in the big tanks just off the lighthouse. We had to hammer the ice and carry two buckets back to the lighthouse. The water would splash on your boiler suit and freeze instantly. That will tell you how cold it was. It was quite horrendous. The end of the month came and we were overdue again. I had to spend two months stuck there.'

    Electric power was provided in 1975 and in 1994 Lynmouth Foreland Lighthouse was fully automated to be controlled from Harwich. While the privations endured on the remote, offshore rocks acquired a certain glamour, and the withdrawal of their keepers a degree of emotional regret, the abandonment of this gloomy establishment caused little grief.

Latitude	*51° 14.70'N*
Longitude	*003° 47.14'W*
Established	*1900*
Height of tower	*15m*
Height of light above MHWS	*67m*
Character	*Fl(4)15s*
Range	*18Nm*

The Lundy Lighthouses

At the mouth of the Bristol Channel lies the Island of Lundy. Once densely populated by puffins, or sea-parrots, the island takes its name from the old Norse word for this attractive little auk. It is a rugged mass of dark granite, its original shale cap eroded to leave a residual trace at its southern extremity. The island is surrounded by rocks, though an anchorage exists on the eastern side in a sheltered bay. Some 3.5 miles in length, Lundy is narrow, never more than three quarters of a mile wide, and lies on a north/south axis. Two lighthouses, one at either end, now mark the island and form passage marks for shipping in the Bristol Channel.

In 1786 a syndicate of Bristol merchants obtained a patent for a lighthouse on the island but, although they began construction, the work was given up. Then, in 1819, Trinity House proposed the erection of a lighthouse on the rocky summit of Chapel Hill. The architect was Daniel Alexander, the builder Joseph Nelson and the Superintendent of Works James Turnbull. Their granite tower, finished in 1822 to a height of 29 metres, cost £10,277 and rose above the adjoining keepers' dwellings. Two lights were shown from the tower; the lower a fixed white light, the upper a white light that flashed every minute. This flashing characteristic was intended to be an innovation in lighthouse optics; unfortunately the light revolved so quickly that no period of darkness was detectable between the flashes so, in effect, it also appeared as a fixed light. Moreover, although they were shown from elevations of 155 and 164 metres respectively, from a distance of only five miles the two lights merged into one.

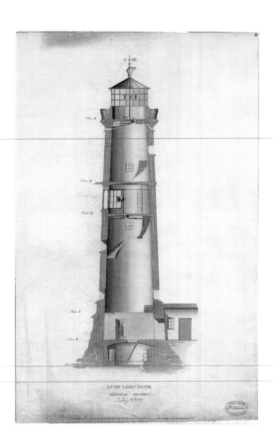

But it was not only the fixed light that caused problems at Lundy. The siting of the lighthouse on the island's summit yet again caused it to be frequently obscured by low, orographic cloud, forming when warm, wet air is forced to rise as it is blown over high ground. Condensing, the water vapour forms dense horizontal clouds beneath which the visibility may be perfectly good. A fatal combination of these two limitations contributed to a disaster on the evening of November 1828. The French ship *La Jeune Emma*, bound from Martinique to Cherbourg, was approaching in thick weather. Uncertain of his position, the sudden appearance of the fixed white light induced her master to conclude that he was off the Île d'Ouessant (Ushant), many miles away to the south. A few seconds later *La Jeune Emma* piled onto the rocks at the base of the cliffs, an appalling wreck which cost the lives of thirteen of the nineteen souls on board. One of the dead passengers was a niece of the late Empress Josephine and it may have been this that prompted the public outcry that focused on the poor light, rather than the shipmaster's faulty navigation. To confound its critics Trinity House established a fog signal station on the western side of the island, half way down the cliff below the light. This consisted of two embrasures and a powder store and was fitted with two muzzle-loading cannon that were fired in fog or misty weather.

Over the succeeding years Trinity House was bombarded by complaints about the Lundy light, but it was not until 1897 that they abandoned the place in favour of two new lighthouses, erected on the north and south extremities of the island. Even this did not prevent disaster. In May 1906 the new British battleship HMS *Montagu* was conducting early radio trials in fog when she struck the west side of Lundy and, although her guns and most of her stores were salvaged, she became a constructive total loss at a cost to the long-suffering taxpayer of £1-million. More recently, in 1980, the German coaster *Kaaksburg* was lost on the east side of the island.

Not surprisingly the keepers were often involved in the business of succouring survivors cast ashore by shipwreck. In February 1892 the Principal Keeper, John McCarthy, organised the throwing of a rocket line to the French ship *Tunisie*. Using an old coal sack McCarthy and his men rigged up an extempore breeches buoy and rescued all twenty-one of her company. For this McCarthy, his two Assistant Keepers and some itinerant labourers were each awarded fifteen shillings by the RNLI for their 'gallant and successful exertions', to which the Board of Trade added a further £3.

Lundy South Lighthouse

The South Lighthouse is a compact station with a white circular tower. When helicopter reliefs were introduced a summit of rock to the east of the lighthouse, flattened in 1897 to enable the light beam of the new tower to sweep out to sea in that direction, made an excellent landing pad. The station was a popular one, for in the summer Lundy's tiny population is regularly augmented by holidaymakers seeking the solitary beauty of the cliffs, the wild flowers and the bird life. Regular visitors to the lighthouse broke the monotony of watch-keeping and the island possessed a lively pub. Stores were landed by the local Trinity House Vessel, lifted out of her motorlaunches by means of a wire hoist which ran from a gantry on the boundary wall down to anchors in the bay far below. Lundy South was manned until its automation in 1994, when it was converted to solar power.

Latitude	*51° 09.69'N*
Longitude	*004° 39.29'W*
Established	*1897*
Height of tower	*16m*
Height of light above MHWS	*53m*
Character	*Fl5s*
Range	*15Nm*
Fog Signal	*Horn(1)25s*

Lundy North Lighthouse

Latitude	*51° 12.08'N*
Longitude	*004° 40.57'W*
Established	*1897*
Height of tower	*17m*
Height of light above MHWS	*48m*
Character	*Fl15s*
Range	*17Nm*
Racon fitted	

The more remote North Lighthouse is set on a narrow plateau overlooking an offshore reef known as the Hen and Chickens. On the surrounding cliffs large colonies of guillemots, razorbills and kittiwakes nest in the spring while, on the rocks below, Atlantic Grey seals may be seen basking on warm days. Until 1971, when electric generators were installed, a paraffin vapour burner, surrounded by a huge optic, provided the station's main light.

Like its sister station to the south, Lundy North received stores by way of a long wire hoist. The 300 metre wire ran from the cliff top to an anchorage point of a large rock, named Seal Rock. Along it ran a traveller controlled by smaller wires from the winch-house next to the gantry high above. Boat reliefs at this station were often hazardous. A flat landing-place had been constructed at the foot of a long flight of steps, alongside which the motorlaunch of the local Trinity House Vessel would lie. A heavy swell usually rolled around the northern headland a few yards away, and the use of a stern anchor was frequently called for. On one occasion an incoming swell lifted the 6-tonne boat onto the landing. Just as the coxswain and boat officer were contemplating their predicament, the next wave carried them off again.

In 1969 relief was taken over by helicopter, which was able to land in conditions of reasonable visibility on a flat patch of grass on the high ground behind the lighthouse. The keepers were withdrawn from Lundy North in 1976 and it was monitored and controlled from the South Lighthouse until 1985 when it was fully automated. Further modifications were carried out in 1991 on conversion to solar power. A new proprietary lantern manufactured by Orga was installed on the disused fog-signal building and thus the tower of 1897 fell out of use.

Blacknore Point Lighthouse

Blacknore Point Lighthouse, a minor passage light beacon in the Upper Bristol Channel, is a small iron-lattice tower built by Trinity House in 1894 to assist shipping moving into and out of the Avon. The lighthouse was converted to automatic electric operation in 1941 with what was probably the world's smallest biform optic. Blacknore Point was further modernised in 2000 when control was taken over in Harwich.

Latitude	51° 29.07'N
Longitude	002° 47.93'W
Established	1894
Height of tower	11m
Height of light above MHWS	11m
Character	Fl(2)10s
Range	17Nm

Monkstone Lighthouse

This granite tower was built in 1839 on the Monkstone, a flat granite rock lying near Flatholm Island near Cardiff, which breaks surface at low water spring tides. The Upper Bristol Channel is subject to the second largest tidal range in the world and thus to very strong tidal streams. This area is strewn with great sandbanks that, though passable at high water, rise out of the sea six hours later. It is extremely hazardous, even to powerful modern ships, most of which embark pilots when entering or leaving the locality. The Monkstone beacon therefore not only marks the precise location of the rock after which it is named, but also provides an important visual reference mark.

     The beacon was unlit before about 1925 when it was strengthened and fitted with an iron lantern in which automatic acetylene lighting apparatus was set up. In 1993 it was further updated, the gas installation being replaced by a prefabricated red glass-reinforced plastic unit housing a new solar-powered light.

Latitude	51° 24.86'N
Longitude	003° 05.92'W
Established	1839
Height of tower	23m
Height of light above MHWS	13m
Character	Fl5s
Range	12Nm

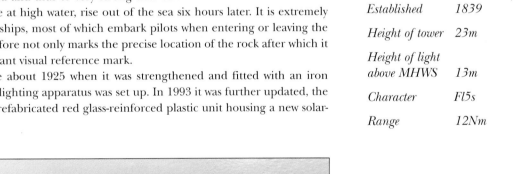

Flatholm Lighthouse

Latitude	*51° 22.50'N*
Longitude	*003° 07.05'W*
Established	*1737*
Height of tower	*30m*
Height of light above MHWS	*50m*
Character	*FlWR(3)10s*
Range	*15/12Nm*

The island of Flatholm lies between the busy channels where the Bristol Channel meets the Severn estuary. Flatholm Lighthouse warns shipping of the presence of the island itself, the adjacent island of Steepholm, and the many off-lying shoals and dangers. The need for a lighthouse on the island had been discussed for many years by leading shipmasters and by members of the Society of Merchant Venturers of Bristol. In 1733 John Elbridge, a senior member of the society, forwarded a petition to Trinity House enumerating the dangers to navigation and the general desire for a light on the island. However, Trinity House informed Elbridge that no application had been made to the Crown for a light, at the same time taking steps to ensure that no light was erected other than in its own name.

In April 1735 William Crispe of Bristol informed Trinity House that he had leased Flatholm Island for ninety-nine years from John Stuart, Earl of Bute. Crispe wished to build a lighthouse at his own expense, but in the name of Trinity House. However, he may have excited the jealousy of his fellow citizens for, at their meeting on 9 May, the Merchant Venturers rejected Crispe's scheme. Then, at the end of 1736, sixty soldiers were drowned when a military transport was wrecked near Flatholm and this reinvigorated further agitation to establish a lighthouse on the island. On 17 March 1737 William Crispe attended at the Hall of the Merchant Venturers with new proposals. The merchants agreed to support a petition to Trinity House and this was submitted on 2 April. In this petition Crispe stated that the society of Merchant Venturers required the following tolls: 'For all Bristol ships to or from foreign parts $1\frac{1}{2}$d per ton both inward and outward, according to their reports of tonnage at the Custom House, and double these dues on foreign ships. For all coasting vessels to or from Ireland 1d per ton: vessels from

St. David's Head or Lands End up the Bristol Channel (market boats and fishing boats excepted) one shilling for every voyage inward and one shilling outward.'

The Merchant Venturers insisted that Crispe should, himself, lay out not less than £900 for the building of the tower. Crispe agreed to this and to paying the legal expenses of Trinity House in obtaining the Crown patent for the light. In return he would expect to be granted a lease at a yearly rental of £5. At their next meeting on 9 April 1737 the Court of Trinity House agreed to apply for a patent in Crispe's name and in consequence to grant him a lease from the kindling of the light until Lady Day 1834, when the lease would expire. Crispe's annual yearly rental would be £5 for the first thirty years, followed by £10 for the remainder of the term. The lease was finally signed, the tower swiftly built and a coal-fired light was first shown on 1 December 1737.

Owing to the cost of the structure William Crispe took on a partner, Benjamin Lund. However, their joint funds were insufficient even with loans secured from John Elbridge and they were very soon bankrupt. To settle their debts they surrendered their lease to Caleb Dickenson. In due course Dickenson and his successors undertook the entire management of Flatholm lighthouse including the collection of light-dues.

On the night of 22 December 1790 a violent gale caused considerable destruction in the west of England and Flatholm Lighthouse suffered some damage. The senior tenant keeper reported to Dickenson, 'We expected every moment to be our last. At three o'clock on the morning of the 23rd the tower was struck by lightning. The man attending the fire was knocked down and narrowly escaped falling through the stairway. The iron fire grate was smashed to pieces and the top of the tower considerably damaged.' Until repairs were effected a fire was maintained on the headland in front of the lighthouse.

However, Bristol traders continually complained of the inadequacy of the light, saying that the owners of the lighthouse enjoyed a large income from it yet refused an additional £100 a year to make it a reasonable aid to shipping. On 17 November 1819 Trinity House signed an agreement with William Dickenson, the then principal lessee of the lighthouse, by which they undertook to alter and maintain the light for an annual payment of £400 for the remainder of the lease. The Corporation then took over the tower and premises and their surveyor prepared plans for the alterations. The massive circular stone tower was now increased in height from 21 metres to 27 metres in order to make a suitable base for the lantern which held an Argand lamp supported by reflectors. The new light, petitioned for over so many years, was first exhibited on 7 September 1820 as a fixed white light.

In July 1822 an Act of Parliament was passed empowering Trinity House to purchase outright the leases of any coast lights. This was a precursor of the more powerful and influential act of 1836 by which acquisition was compulsory. The value of the remaining twelve years of the lease was computed at £15,838.10 which was accordingly paid to William Dickenson and his executors, and Trinity House took absolute possession of the light from 21 March 1823. In 1825 further modifications resulted in the installation of a fountain oil lamp and the raising of the lantern by another 1.5 metres. Another improvement was made in 1867 when a new lantern was installed and this remained in use until 1969. The light was converted to occulting in 1881 by the installation of a clockwork operated mechanical hood which 'doused' the light. Subsequent alterations were the installation of a Douglass multi-wick burner in 1904 and its replacement by a Hood paraffin vapour burner in 1923. In 1908 a powerful compressed-air fog signal having two horns was installed in a separate building erected for the purpose.

In February 1902 Flatholm was the scene of a remarkable phenomenon. During the night a shower of mud fell on the island and the glazing of the lighthouse was covered with a dirty white coating that stuck to the glass like glue and proved difficult to remove. A quantity of fine dust, believed by meteorologists to have been carried in the atmosphere from the Sahara Desert, fell on an area of about 2,000 square miles of southwest England. Much of it had been transformed into mud by rainfall.

Until 1929 Flatholm Lighthouse had been manned by keepers living with their families in cottages next to the lighthouse, but at this time it was converted to a rock station. An additional keeper was appointed, increasing the number to four, thus enabling the men to serve three months on duty followed by one month's leave. In more recent years, the lighthouse was manned by two sets of three keepers each working one month on the lighthouse followed by one month ashore.

Flatholm Lighthouse was automated in 1988 and the keepers were withdrawn. In 1997 it was modernised and converted to solar power, being controlled from Harwich.

Nash Point Lighthouse

Latitude	*51° 24.03'*
Longitude	*003° 33.06'*
Established	*1832*
Height of tower	*37m*
Height of light above MHWS	*56m*
Character	*FlWR(2)15s*
Range	*21/16Nm*
DGPS	*309.5KHz 100M*

Nash Point Lighthouse stands upon the coast of South Wales and was originally built to warn shipping off the Nash Bank, a long and dangerous ridge of sand extending to the west. In 1830 an application for a lighthouse on Nash Point by Thomas Protheroe of Newport was supported by 439 shipowners and shipmasters from the Bristol Channel ports. Trinity House instructed Joseph Nelson to erect two towers, whose transit would lead vessels clear of the Nash Sand.

The two circular towers were completed in 1832. Set just over 300 metres apart, they had thick walls and stone galleries. The eastern, or high, lighthouse is 37 metres high and the western, or low, lighthouse, 25 metres high. The high light was painted with black and white stripes, its lower partner was white; both towers showed a fixed light, red over the Nash Sand, and white over the clear water. The low light was abandoned in the mid 1920s and an occulting light with white and red sectors was installed in the high light. In 1959 the black bands on the tower were painted white.

In 1977 it was found that the tuberous thistle (*Cirsium tuberosum*), a very rare plant, was growing around the lighthouse and so the area within the compound was declared a Site of Special Scientific Interest.

In the late 1980s as the general automation programme progressed, Nash Point lighthouse became one of the area monitoring stations. The keepers took on responsibility for Flatholm, Mumbles, and even the distant Eddystone. Such remote control was a foretaste of things to come and, inevitably, in 1998 Nash itself was fully modernised. On 5 August the keepers handed over control of the station and its out-stations to Harwich. Nash Lighthouse had been the last manned lighthouse in Wales.

Mumbles Lighthouse

Standing guard at the western side of Swansea Bay, the Mumbles Lighthouse overlooks the shallow patch of the Mixon Shoal, half a mile offshore to the southward. This unmanned lighthouse is built on the outer of two small islands off the Mumbles Head and is accessible by foot at certain states of the tide or by boat at high water.

The Swansea Harbour Trustees were given the power to provide a lighthouse on Mumbles Head in the Harbour Act of 1791. In July 1792 the Trustees contracted for the erection of the lighthouse and work began. Unfortunately, in October 1792, the half-finished structure collapsed. In 1793 the plans of the local architect William Jernegan were accepted and, empowered by an Act of Parliament, in March 1794 Trinity House granted to Swansea Town Council a ninety-nine year lease, at £5 per annum. The lighthouse was finally completed and lit in the autumn of 1794.

Mumbles Lighthouse originally displayed two open coal fire lights one above the other to distinguish it from St Ann's Head Lighthouse off Pembrokeshire, which had two lights on separate towers, and Flatholm Lighthouse with its one light. The coal lights in braziers were expensive and so difficult to maintain that by 1802 they had been replaced with a single oil-powered light consisting of Argand lamps and reflectors set within a cast-iron lantern. Evidence of the original two coal-fired lights remains in the two-tiered structure of the tower.

Among various changes to the equipment through its two centuries of life are the fitting of a dioptric light in 1860, an occulting mechanism in 1905 and automation in 1934. The fort or battery which surrounds the southern side of the lighthouse was built in 1860 by the War Department during the scare occasioned by the building of the French ironclad warship *Gloire*. Until recent times Mumbles lighthouse was under the management of the British Transport Docks Board but on 1 November 1975 Trinity House assumed responsibility for the station, the property being transferred without any payment being made by either side.

In 1987 a lantern taken from Lightvessel No 25, which had formerly belonged to the port of Dundee and had lain anchored at the Abertay station off the east coast of Scotland, was placed on the

Latitude	*51° 33.98'N*
Longitude	*003° 58.20'W*
Established	*1794*
Height of tower	*17m*
Height of light above MHWS	*35m*
Character	*Fl(4)20s*
Range	*16Nm*
Fog Signal	*Horn(3)60s*

tower to improve servicing conditions. In 1995 the Mumbles Lighthouse was converted to solar power, with solar module arrays mounted in frames on the roof of the fort. A pair of biformed lanterns replaced the main light and a new emergency light, fog detector, and control and monitoring equipment were installed, enabling control from Harwich.

Caldey Island Lighthouse

Caldey Lighthouse is on the highest point of Caldey Island, three miles off Tenby. It provides a passage light along the Welsh coast that is encumbered by the St Gowan shoals to the southwest, and the Helwick Sand to the southeast. A buoyed passage for small craft lies between the Caldey and the mainland.

Like several other British islands, Caldey has become a place of spiritual retreat and a hermit was first recorded here in the Sixth Century. Later, a small community grew up around a chapel where the Old Priory now stands. In 1131 Caldey was donated to the Benedictine monks by its then owners, the Abbey of Tiron in France but, in 1536, during the Reformation, the order was expelled from the island. However, in 1906 an Anglican Benedictine brotherhood bought the island and erected the present monastery. In the 1920s the island, its farm and its monastic establishment, were sold to the Order of the Reformed Cistercians.

The island, a low escarpment one-and-a-half miles long and less than three-quarters wide, rises to the south where it drops sharply away to the sea. Here stands the lighthouse. Built by Trinity House in 1828 to the design of Joseph Nelson, its Argand light, consisting of twenty burners and reflectors, was first lit on 26 January 1829. It throws red sectors over shoals off the island. Flanking the tower and connected to it are two dwellings that were occupied by the keepers and their families prior to the conversion of the station to automatic unmanned acetylene operation in 1927, when they were sold into private ownership.

The modernisation of Caldey Lighthouse was completed in November 1997 when it was powered by mains electricity and handed over to Harwich.

Latitude	*51° 37.86'N*
Longitude	*004° 41.00'W*
Established	*1829*
Height of tower	*16m*
Height of light above MHWS	*65m*
Character	*Fl(3)WR20s*
Range	*13/9Nm*

St Ann's Head Lighthouse

St Ann's Head Lighthouse is the oldest on the Welsh coast and stands on the western side of the entrance to Milford Haven. In addition to providing a landfall mark for the Haven, the lighthouse is an important guide for coastal traffic with red sectors warning of the St Gowan Shoal and giving a clearing bearing for Linney Head, off which lie two dangers, Crow and Toe Rocks.

In 1485 Henry Tudor landed at Mill Bay, a little north of St Ann's Head, on his way to Bosworth Field. Here he wrested the crown from Richard III, ending the Wars of the Roses and establishing the Tudor dynasty on the English throne. After his coronation as Henry VII, he built a chapel to commemorate the landing and this is thought to have been the St Ann's Chapel that is recorded in Sixteenth Century portolans as a landmark for Milford Haven, the entrance of which is difficult to make from the west.

In 1662 Trinity House, incorporated by Henry's son a century-and-a-half earlier, approved, in principal, a coal-fired light at St. Ann's Head to guide shipping bound for Milford. It was to be

Latitude	*51° 40.85'N*
Longitude	*005° 10.35'W*
Established	*1714*
Height of tower	*13m*
Height of light above MHWS	*48m*
Character	*FlWR5s*
Range	*18/17/14Nm*
Fog Signal	*Horn(2)60s*

supported by voluntary payment of dues, but the owners extracted dues illegally from shipowners and the light was ordered extinguished by Parliament in 1668. This legal technicality proved a dangerously pettifogging expedient, for there was not one single lighthouse on the entire west coast of England or Wales, contemporary charts showing St Ann's Head bearing a tower 'without fire'.

This appalling situation lasted for almost half a century when, prompted by a petition, on 15 March 1713 Trinity House obtained a patent for a new lighthouse at St Ann's Head. The owner of the land, Joseph Allen, was granted a lease for ninety-nine years at an annual rent of £10 for the erection of two lights. At the termination of the lease Allen's successors were to 'peaceably' leave the land and light to Trinity House. To maintain his lights Allen was permitted to collect from shipmasters arriving in Milford Haven a due of one penny per ton of cargo on British vessels and twopence on foreign vessels. It has been suggested that Allen may have brought the old tower, topped by a coal brazier, back into service and added another tower. At all events two lights were first exhibited on 24 June 1714, before the lease was actually signed, a measure of the urgency of the matter. The adoption of two lights was to distinguish St Ann's from the single light as St Agnes in the Isles of Scilly and to provide a transit clearing the Crow and Toe Rocks.

In June 1800 the lessees accepted the opinion of Trinity House that the installation of reflected Argand lamps mounted within lanterns would improve the benefit to navigation, a view to which the lessees agreed, whereupon Trinity House undertook the work. The Brethren met the cost of £2,600, being repaid out of the light dues, and also undertook the management of the lights at a charge of £140 per annum. On the first of his 'lighthouse tours', Robert Stevenson visited St Ann's in 1801, commenting approvingly: ' The light is from Argand burners with parabolic silvered copper reflectors each twenty and a half inches in diameter. In the one lantern there are sixteen reflectors and in the other eleven and though they are only about one hundred paces distant from each other there is a distinct keeper at each lantern, so that they are in the most complete state of cleanliness and good order. Their construction is simple and extremely well adapted for the purpose of a lighthouse.'

More details of contemporary lighthouse management exist for St Ann's owing to the reversion of the lease to Trinity House in 1813. Net profits to the Corporation at the time were £5,339 after deducting the cost of maintaining the lights (£1,205) and the collection of the dues (£1,147).

The lower front light was rebuilt in 1844 when cliff erosion endangered the old tower, the new one being situated 9 metres or so from the cliff edge. This is the present lighthouse; the high or rear light was discontinued in 1910, to be later converted into a Coastguard station. The modern light throws a red sector over the off-lying dangers.

As an area control station between 1983 and 1998, St Ann's lighthouse was manned by four keepers and supported helicopter operations to the offshore lighthouses on the 'Western Rocks' of the Smalls, Skokholm and South Bishop after their automation. The automation of St Ann's Head followed, being completed on 17 June 1998, whereupon the keepers were withdrawn. Although now monitored and controlled from distant Harwich, St Ann's lighthouse remains an operating base for Trinity House's maintenance teams and the attendant charged with the 'keeping' of all these stations.

Skokholm Lighthouse

Extending some twenty miles west of St Ann's Head lies a dangerous area of islands and rocks terminating in the Smalls reef. The whole locality is subject to strong tides and exposed to the full fury of onshore gales, which may strike at any time in the year. It is equally hazardous in calm conditions if fog, mist or haze reduce the visibility. The area is guarded by three major lighthouses known colloquially as the 'Western Rocks'.

Skokholm Lighthouse stands on the southwest point of the small island of Skokholm. The island has high cliffs rising sheer from the sea and upon which a variety of bird life is to be found; resident and visiting species include the storm petrel, fulmar, guillemot, razorbill, puffin, gannet and the Manx shearwater.

The lighthouse was built in 1916, following the construction of a necessary landing place. On completion of the lighthouse the landing continued to be used for disembarking stores and supplies, these being carried the mile from landing to lighthouse on two small trucks running on a narrow-gauge railway. The trucks were originally pulled by a donkey, which instinctively knew when a relief day was due. The animal would deliberately hide, often standing motionless under an overhanging rock, the colour of which blended perfectly with the donkey's grey coat. Other accounts mentioned the animal standing in a small lake on the island, stolidly defying the keepers. On any other day the donkey would oblige its masters and come at a call. The pony which replaced him acquired an even more annoying habit: every time he was summoned to pull the trucks, the animal would upset them and scatter coal and stores all over the place. In due course a tractor was landed on the island.

Skokholm lighthouse was automated in 1983 and converted to solar power in 1998. Although keepers have long since left the station, the island, now a bird sanctuary, is occupied by ornithologists. Shortly before its solarisation the light was changed from red to white with the installation of new

Latitude	51° 41.62'N
Longitude	005° 17.18'W
Established	1916
Height of tower	18m
Height of light above MHWS	54m
Character	FlWR10s
Range	18/15Nm
Fog Signal	Horn(1)15s

equipment. This led to the injury and deaths of birds who were disorientated and attracted by the white light as they had not been by the red. Thus, when solar power was installed, red shades were introduced to cover the island sector and thereby overcame the problem.

Smalls Lighthouse

The Smalls is a low, wave-swept reef to the west of which lies deep water. A place as forbidding as the Wolf Rock, the low eminence of the westernmost of the two principal rocks attracted interest as a potential site for a lighthouse as early as the 1770s. Reports of the dangerous hazard to shipping posed by the Smalls reef were well known in Liverpool where the harbourmaster, Captain William Hutchinson, was a keen advocate of lights and had built several to facilitate the navigation of the Mersey.

This encouraged John Phillips, an assistant dock-manager, a man full of schemes, constantly in financial difficulties, and also acting as agent for the Skerries Lighthouse. Mindful of the dues he was collecting for the Skerries, Phillips conceived the idea of building a lighthouse on the Smalls and drafted a specification. This called for a fixed white light with a range of a dozen miles, supported by a less powerful fixed green light above it, to guide vessels passing close to the rock and seems to have been the first proposal for a coloured light in England. In August 1774 he was granted a lease by the Treasury. Advertising for designs for a structure in which to install his light, Phillips chose that submitted by Henry Whiteside, a young musical-instrument maker also at Liverpool. The comparison with Winstanley is irresistible and Whiteside does not disappoint.

Born in Liverpool 1748, Whiteside was apprenticed to a cooper, became skilled at wood carving and, in around 1770, became 'a maker of violins, spinettes and upright harpsichords'. Attracted by Phillips's idea, he planned an octagonal timber building, some 5 metres in diameter, which would stand upon legs of wood and cast iron. These would extend over a span of 7 metres at the rock, the whole structure being 20 metres high. The 'house' would consist of a lower living room, subdivided into compartments for accommodation and storage, with a lightroom and lantern above.

Latitude	*51° 43.28'N*
Longitude	*005° 40.15'W*
Established	*1776*
Height of tower	*41m*
Height of light above MHWS	*36/33m*
Character	*Fl(3)15s +F.R*
Range	*25/13Nm*
Fog Signal	*Horn(2) 60s*
Racon fitted	

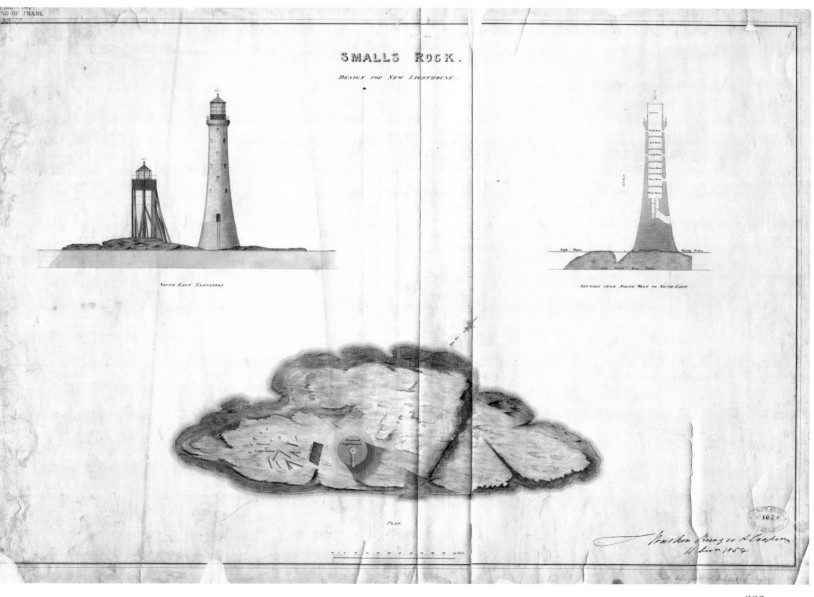

Having raised the necessary funds, Phillips, Whiteside, and a party of Welsh miners landed on the Smalls in 1775. The first iron rod had hardly been driven into the rock before the wind and sea rose, their boat had to sheer off, and five men were left stranded. They clung to the iron rod for two days and nights before they were rescued. Notwithstanding this setback, during the following weeks holes were excavated for the first piles, and ring-bolts were set into the rock to which a hut 'big enough to lodge twelve men' was lashed. During the following winter Whiteside set up the whole of his structure at Solva, a small Welsh haven 25 miles away. Here he abandoned the cast-iron legs, replacing them with additional heavy wooden piles.

By 1 September 1776 the whole thing had been transferred to the Smalls, erected and the twin lights lit. The miners also toiled laboriously to set a coal hole and wooden fresh-water tank into the rock. By December the alarmed keepers reported the structure too weak and, in January 1777, Whiteside and his blacksmith arrived on the rock, only to be nearly overwhelmed by a succession of gales. Fearing for all their lives, Whiteside sent off messages in three bottles. One reached Galway, another was handed to Phillips's local agent at St David's, a man named Williams.

Phillips had no resources to strengthen the lighthouse, withdrew Whiteside, the smith and the keepers, and abandoned the light. He was compelled to hand over his interests to a syndicate of Liverpool merchants. Persuaded of the utility of the lighthouse they now approached Trinity House and, in due course, the Brethren advanced sums for the repairs and reinforcement of the tower. On 3 June 1778, after the passing of an Act of Parliament, Phillips was granted a ninety-nine-year lease at an annual rent of £5 and the single white light was reinstated by September. Despite these shaky beginnings, Whiteside's extraordinary tower, re-braced several times, lasted until 1861. Its success seems to have lain in its resilience which, as we have noted, became a point of interest for subsequent experiments in lighthouse design by James Walker.

Nevertheless, the tower was subject to further damage and in October 1812 the light was again shut down until repair work could be carried out the following spring. A heavy sea had broken in through one of the windows and the keepers had smashed the others to permit the water free movement through the lighthouse, rather than cause irreparable damage to the structure. Again, this time in 1831, the deck and two sides of the house were beaten in and the iron cooking stove was flattened. For eight days the keepers cooked over the lighthouse's Argand lamps.

At the end of the Eighteenth Century a strange incident took place when one of the two keepers on the Smalls died from natural causes. So anxious was his colleague not to be charged with murder, that the wretched man made a coffin from the interior woodwork, placed his mate's corpse inside it and lashed it to the outer part of the lantern. Here it remained for three weeks until the tender arrived. The plight of the solitary keeper is supposed to have persuaded those responsible in succeeding years that there should never be less than three men on an isolated station, the only exception to which was made at Godrevy in north Cornwall.

In 1823, having improved the lighting apparatus, Trinity House sought to buy out the lease on the Smalls, but the compensation claimed by the lessees was considered exorbitant at £148,430. In 1836 when obliged to purchase the remaining 54 years, the profits on the Smalls had doubled to £11,142 and the compensation, judged by a local jury, had risen to £170,468.

In 1859 James Douglass began the construction of a new lighthouse designed by Walker and based on Smeaton's Eddystone. Girded by red and white painted bands, it was built in two years – a prodigious feat. The new light was 'put in' on 7 August 1861, supported by a fog signal. Whiteside's crude yet strangely durable 'raft of timber' was demolished, though traces of his oak piles remain to this day.

During the late 1960s considerable improvements were made on the Smalls. In 1969 a concrete helipad was built over the station's oil and water tanks and this was used until 1978 when the top of the tower was fitted with an elevated helipad and the station prepared for automation. This was completed in 1987 and the Smalls was, for a few years, monitored and controlled from St Ann's. In 1997 the red and white bands were removed, the tower blasted back to bare stone and control was vested in Harwich.

South Bishop Lighthouse

Latitude	*51° 51.14'N*
Longitude	*005° 24.66'W*
Established	*1839*
Height of tower	*11m*
Height of light above MHWS	*44m*
Character	*Fl5s*
Range	*16Nm*
Fog Signal	*Horn(3)45s*
Racon fitted	

South Bishop Lighthouse is situated on a outcrop of rock in St George's Channel five miles southwest of St David's Head, Pembrokeshire. The lighthouse acts primarily as a passage mark, but also stands guard over the scattered archipelago of rocks and islets known as the Bishops and Clerks.

An application was first made to Trinity House in 1831 for a light at South Bishop by shipping interests trading to Cardigan. This was supported in 1834 on behalf of those shipowners using the Bristol and St George's Channels and, in due course, James Walker began building on the largest of the rocks, known as the South Bishop. Work was completed in 1839. Unusually South Bishop still uses the original lantern, the oldest to survive unaltered in a working lighthouse in England and Wales, though its light source was converted to electricity in 1959, diesel generators being fitted on station. A new fog signal was installed during these modifications.

In 1971 a helipad was built on a flat area of lower rock, though this is occasionally swept by a sea at high tide. Automated and de-manned in 1983, the control of the station passed from St Ann's to Harwich and the station is now powered by the sun, the installation of solar modules being completed in 2000.

South Bishop Lighthouse stands on the migration route of several bird species. Many are attracted by the brilliance of the light and they are prone to dash themselves against the lantern. Trinity House, with the Royal Society for the Protection of Birds, built special bird perches around the lantern and this has appreciably reduced the mortality rate.

Left: Trinity House operates a twin-engined MBB 105D helicopter capable of lifting underslung loads such as the neoprene bags, seen here, in which diesel oil, and occasionally fresh water, are delivered to an offshore lighthouse. Such transfers are made either from the shore, or the helideck of a Trinity House Vessel.

Strumble Head Lighthouse

Latitude	*52° 01.75'N*
Longitude	*005° 04.35'W*
Established	*1908*
Height of tower	*17m*
Height of light above MHWS	*45m*
Character	*Fl(4)15s*
Range	*26Nm*

Strumble Head Lighthouse stands imposingly on Ynysmeicl (St. Michael's Island), an islet about five miles west of Fishguard, separated from the mainland by a very narrow gap through which the sea boils in stormy weather.

Like much of this exposed western coast, Cardigan Bay became the grave of many sailing ships. They were driven into its great bight by strong onshore westerly gales that were usually accompanied by poor visibility. Before realising their predicament, their masters found themselves embayed with insufficient sea room to beat offshore.

Strumble Head Lighthouse was built in 1908 by Trinity House for the greater safety of shipping using the then new harbour at Fishguard from which ferries run to Ireland.

The original revolving lens system weighed four-and-a-half tons and floated on a bath of mercury to reduce friction. A massive clockwork mechanism rotated it, driven by a quarter-ton weight which, suspended on a cable, dropped slowly down a cylinder running from top to bottom through the tower. This had to be re-wound every twelve hours. Strumble Head was also equipped with an explosive fog signal. The charges for this were kept in a stone magazine, detached from the dwellings, which may still be seen, complete with its timber-lining.

Despite the footbridge to the mainland across the narrow sound, Ynsymeicl's isolation and topography created difficulties comparable with more remote stations. Supplies were swung across by means of a jackstay suspended between two winches, one on the mainland clifftop, the other beside the lighthouse. The handrail of the footbridge and steps also doubled as an oil pipeline to carry oil into the tower basement.

The optical system was replaced by more compact equipment when Strumble Head lighthouse was fully electrified in 1965. Fifteen years later the lighthouse was converted to unmanned automatic operation and later linked to Harwich.

Above left and right: Access to Strumble Head Lighthouse was, at first, provided by an aerial runway, later replaced by a permanent footbridge. Notwithstanding this attachment to the Welsh mainland, stores were occasionally delivered by boat from the local Trinity House Vessel.

Following: The lighthouse at Skokholm seen from the southwest.

229

North Wales and the Irish Sea

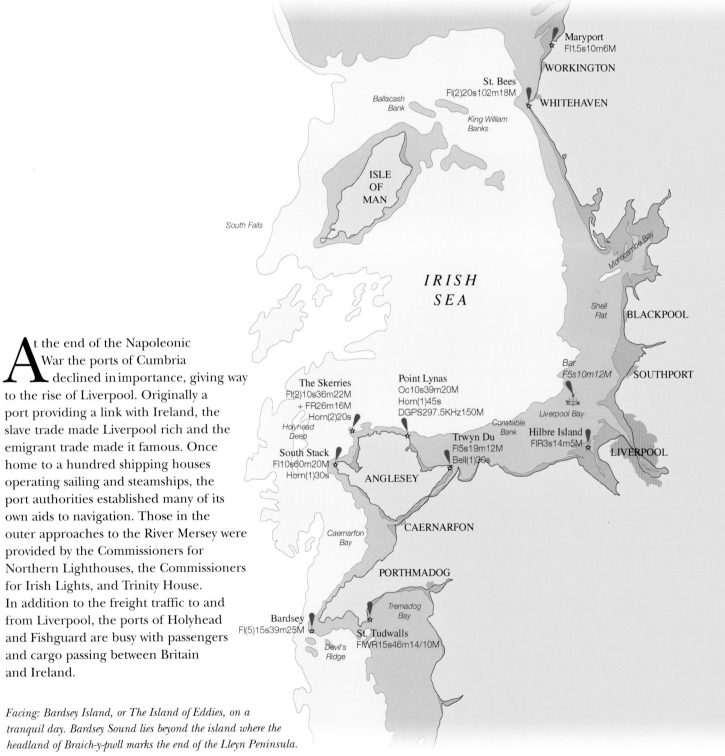

Maryport
Fl1.5s10m6M

WORKINGTON

St. Bees
Fl(2)20s102m18M

Ballacash Bank

WHITEHAVEN

King William Banks

ISLE OF MAN

South Falls

Morecambe Bay

IRISH SEA

Shell Flat

BLACKPOOL

Bar
F5s10m12M

SOUTHPORT

The Skerries
Fl(2)10s36m22M
+ FR26m16M
Horn(2)20s

Point Lynas
Oc10s39m20M
Horn(1)45s
DGPS297.5KHz150M

Holyhead Deep

Constable Bank

Liverpool Bay

Hilbre Island
FlR3s14m5M

South Stack
Fl10s60m20M
Horn(1)30s

Trwyn Du
Fl5s19m12M
Bell(1)30s

LIVERPOOL

ANGLESEY

Caernarfon Bay

CAERNARFON

PORTHMADOG

Tremadog Bay

Bardsey
Fl(5)15s39m25M

St. Tudwalls
FlWR15s46m14/10M

Devil's Ridge

At the end of the Napoleonic War the ports of Cumbria declined in importance, giving way to the rise of Liverpool. Originally a port providing a link with Ireland, the slave trade made Liverpool rich and the emigrant trade made it famous. Once home to a hundred shipping houses operating sailing and steamships, the port authorities established many of its own aids to navigation. Those in the outer approaches to the River Mersey were provided by the Commissioners for Northern Lighthouses, the Commissioners for Irish Lights, and Trinity House. In addition to the freight traffic to and from Liverpool, the ports of Holyhead and Fishguard are busy with passengers and cargo passing between Britain and Ireland.

Facing: Bardsey Island, or The Island of Eddies, on a tranquil day. Bardsey Sound lies beyond the island where the headland of Braich-y-pwll marks the end of the Lleyn Peninsula.

St Tudwal's Lighthouse

Latitude	*52° 47.89'N*
Longitude	*004° 28.21'W*
Established	*1877*
Height of tower	*11m*
Height of light above MHWS	*46m*
Character	*FlWR15s*
Range	*14/10Nm*

Evidence of a once busy local coastal trade, St Tudwal's Lighthouse was built to serve the schooners that carried general cargo and slate from the quarries of North Wales. Standing on the higher of a pair of small islands just off the coast near Aberdaron, St Tudwal's Lighthouse and its dwellings were built in 1877, following the purchase of the island by Trinity House for the sum of £111 the previous year. The completed light threw a red sector over offshore dangers, including Carreg-y-Trai, or Half-Tide Rock, which lies just off the island.

In 1922 St Tudwal's Lighthouse, together with several other stations of secondary importance, was fitted with automatic acetylene equipment which included a flash-control unit and light developed by the Aga company. This was effectively controlled by a 'sun-valve' invented by the Swedish inventor, Gustav Dalén. Blinded by a gas explosion in a quarry while testing the flammable nature of acetylene, this remarkable man also invented the popular Aga cooker, a task he undertook during his convalescence. His sun-valve, which automatically shut off the supply of gas to the lamp at daylight and reversed the process at sunset, took advantage of the differential expansion of matt-black and plated rods. Sunlight is reflected from the plated rods onto a central matt-black rod secured at its head, thus confining it to downward expansion where it operates a small valve controlling the flow of gas. Dalén was awarded the Nobel prize for his contribution to the safety of navigation.

The keepers were withdrawn and thirteen years later their redundant dwellings were sold off. In 1995 the gas equipment was replaced by more modern and sustainable solar power, Dalén's wonderfully efficient sun-valve being replaced by a photo-electric cell.

Bardsey Island Lighthouse

Although a place of ancient Celtic pilgrimage and known as 'the island of twenty Thousand Saints', the Welsh name for Bardsey Island is Ynys Enlli (Island of Eddies). Set at the extremity of the Lleyn Peninsula, the rips and overfalls which, at certain states of the tide boil through Bardsey Sound between the island and Braich-y-Pwll, made the navigation of sailing vessels hazardous here. Even today, a combination of strong wind and opposing tide can whip up vicious seas sufficiently dangerous to cause damage to modern power-driven ships.

Originally a refuge for Christian Celts fleeing from Saxon incursions, the island supported an abbey that was home to many pious monks. The patron saint of the island, St Dolmers, died there in 612 AD and lies among many other hallowed Celtic holy men and women of his day. Although the northern end of the island rises to a considerable height, the southern extremity is flat and in 1821 a square tower was erected by Trinity House under the supervision of Joseph Nelson. The tower alone cost £5,470, while its lantern added another £2,950 to the bill. In 1910 the lantern was raised to increase its visible range, whereupon the Cardigan Bay lightvessel to the south was discontinued. Painted red and white, the lighthouse exhibits a racon and fog signal. In 1987 it was converted to automatic operation, run from a control station at Holyhead. In 1995 control was transferred to Harwich.

Like South Bishop, Bardsey lies on the migration route of birds and similar measures have been taken here to reduce bird mortality.

Latitude	*52° 44.95'N*
Longitude	*004° 47.95'W*
Established	*1821*
Height of tower	*30m*
Height of light above MHWS	*39m*
Character	*Fl(5)15s*
Range	*26Nm*

South Stack Lighthouse

Latitude	*53° 18.39'N*
Longitude	*004° 41.91'W*
Established	*1809*
Height of tower	*28m*
Height of light above MHWS	*60m*
Character	*Fl10s*
Range	*20Nm*
Fog Signal	*Horn(1)30s*

Situated on an offshore 'stack' at the foot of Holyhead Mountain, the South Stack is separated from the mainland by a narrow gut through which the sea surges. This dramatic location first attracted notice as a potential site for a lighthouse in 1665. Although applied for, no patent was granted and the matter lay in abeyance until 1809 when work was put in hand to erect a lighthouse to the design of Daniel Alexander. To begin four hundred steps had to be cut in the cliff and a hemp cable flung across the chasm; along this a sliding basket was rigged to convey men and materials to the stack, a factor contributing to the then considerable cost of £12,000.

In 1828 an iron suspension bridge was built to link the stack to the mainland. On Tuesday 25 October 1859 an exceptionally bad storm blew up, known as 'the Royal Charter gale' on account of a notorious wreck on the opposite coast of Anglesey. On his way to the lighthouse, Assistant Keeper Jack Jones was crossing the suspension bridge when he was struck by a rock dislodged by the wind from the cliff above. Knocked almost senseless with concussion and covered in blood, Jones dragged himself to

Above: A coloured aquatint by William Daniell (1769-1837) a Royal Academician who made a tour around Great Britain between 1814 and 1825 depicting a number of lighthouses. This shows the lighthouse on the South Stack in January 1815. Note the rope catwalk over the 'gut'; it was replaced by an iron bridge in 1828.

the tower but his feeble cries failed to attract the attention of the Principal Keeper, Henry Bowen. Bowen found Jones next morning, but he was too late. Three weeks later the unfortunate keeper died of a compound fracture of the skull.

In 1840 an unusual step was taken at South Stack to provide at least a partial solution to the problem of fog obscuring the elevated light when a 'railway' was laid down the face of the cliff below the lighthouse. A subsidiary light was lowered down this to shine out over the sea beneath the assumed level of the average sea fog. It proved of only limited use and was withdrawn in the mid 1870s when a new oil lamp was fitted in the lighthouse lantern. This was replaced in 1909 by an incandescent burner which in turn was updated in 1927. In 1938 electric power was provided and the old iron bridge was replaced by an aluminium span in 1964. When the light was automated in 1984, the keepers handed over control to Holyhead, leaving the station on 12 September.

In 1977 another new footbridge had been designed and fitted by Laings and Mott Macdonald following a joint initiative between Trinity House and the Welsh Development Agency. The lighthouse has since become a popular visitor attraction. In 1999, controlled from Harwich, the station was fully modernised with new lamps and a fog signal operated by a fog detector.

Skerries Lighthouse

Latitude	*53° 25.26'N*
Longitude	*004° 36.43'W*
Established	*1717*
Height of tower	*23m*
Height of light above MHWS	*36/26m*
Character	*Fl(2)10s*
Range	*22/16Nm*
Fog Signal	*Horn(2)60s*
Racon fitted	

The crucial 'turning point' for vessels entering or leaving Liverpool Bay is the Skerries Reef, off Holy Island. Not surprisingly a profitable lighthouse was sought by a speculator in 1658. Henry Mascard's petition was rejected, largely on the grounds of impossibility, but Winstanley's success on the Eddystone changed matters entirely. In 1709 another petition by shipowners led by Captain John Davison claimed that 'many ships were cast away...for want of a light on the Welsh coast'. The Attorney General, Sir Edward Northey, ruled that Trinity House did not have exclusive rights to erect lights and advised the Crown that Davison's petition should be granted. The Skerries were leased by a William Tench and it was Tench who, in July 1714, received a sixty-year lease at a rent of £5 per annum, payable to the Crown. Tench could charge dues of one penny per ship and twopence per ton of cargo, and promptly despatched his son with the first workmen to supervise the works. Sadly their vessel was wrecked and all were drowned, a tragedy that delayed matters for a couple of years. On 4 November 1717 Tench had erected a light-tower 11 metres in height, upon which he lit a coal fire in an open grate. Tragically, having lost his heir, Tench now found it impossible to levy dues and he died a debtor in 1729. Appraised of this circumstance and in a misguided attempt to right a wrong, Parliament granted the lighthouse to Tench's daughter in perpetuity. In due course this was to prove an embarrassment to Trinity House.

At a salary of £15 a year, Tench had employed a married couple to tend the light. This couple had to haul between 80 to 150 tons of coal up the tower in a single year, consumption depending upon the strength of the wind. One windy night in 1739 the keeper's wife was terrified when a black man walked into the dwelling. He was the sole survivor of a wreck that had shortly before driven ashore on the off-lying rocks.

In February 1804 the coal light was replaced. The tower had been raised and an oil lamp was fitted behind glazings. From its early unprofitable start, the Skerries soon proved lucrative, thanks to the enormous upswing in trade with America following the end of the Napoleonic War. Between 1827 and 1833, with annual running costs of £350 and the administration of light-dues collection amounting to £1,604, the net profit of the Skerries lighthouse was an average £12,525. Keen to buy out the lease in 1834, Trinity House's approach was rejected outright by the then owner, Morgan Jones. Even five years after the Act of 1836, Jones resisted compulsory purchase, maintaining his perpetual right to ownership. In the event the matter was finally settled by the enormous payment of £444,984.

Alterations to the building and installation of a fog signal were carried out in the Nineteenth Century and conversion to electricity took place in 1927. Sixty years later the keepers were withdrawn upon the automation of the station, when control was taken over by Holyhead. Ten years later this passed to Harwich.

Point Lynas Lighthouse

Latitude	*53° 24.98'N*
Longitude	*004° 17.35'W*
Established	*1779*
Height of tower	*11m*
Height of light above MHWS	*39m*
Character	*Oc10s*
Range	*20Nm*
Fog Signal	*Horn(1)45s*
DGPS	*297.5KHz 150M*

By the 1760s, following Britain's success in Canada during the Seven Years War, the growing economic vigour of the American colonies encouraged the expansion of Liverpool and the establishment of a pilotage service for the River Mersey. As a practical necessity a boarding station was located at Point Lynas on the coast of Anglesey. Here the pilots initially occupied a lookout station in a farmhouse. In 1779 William Hutchinson, the innovative and 'scientific' harbourmaster at Liverpool, who early undertook the observation of tides and the computation of tide tables, established a lighthouse with oil lamps and reflectors of his own devising. Sadly none of these provisions prevented the wreck of the *Rothesay Castle*. As a consequence, in 1835, the Mersey Docks and Harbour Company built a new crenellated lighthouse at

Point Lynas at a cost of £1,165. Today the interior of this lighthouse is almost unaltered from its original state, with its kitchen range and sink.

Trinity House assumed responsibility for the light on 2 April 1973. Now fully automatic, powered by mains electricity backed up by stand-by generators, a fog detector initiates the fog signal should the visibility close in.

Trwyn Du Lighthouse

Several wrecks occurred in the northern entrance to the Menai Strait during the 1820s, most notably that of the Rothesay Castle on Puffin Island in 1830, while Red Wharf Bay, lying between Puffin Island and Point Lynas, was an anchorage frequently used by ships waiting to clear the Skerries in southwesterly gales. The pilots of Liverpool recommended a lighthouse in the vicinity and, by 1838, Trinity House had complied, erecting a tower on a reef off Trwyn Du (Black Head), at a cost of £11,589. The black-and-white banded lighthouse, which still sounds a bell as its fog signal, was converted to automatic acetylene operation in the 1920s.

In 1996 Trwyn Du Lighthouse was converted to solar power.

Latitude	*53° 18.76'N*
Longitude	*004° 02.37'W*
Established	*1838*
Height of tower	*29m*
Height of light above MHWS	*19m*
Character	*Fl5s*
Range	*12Nm*
Fog Signal	*Bell(1)30s*

Right: Trwyn Du Lighthouse.

Hilbre Island Lighthouse

Latitude	53° 22.98'N
Longitude	003° 13.63'W
Established	1927
Height of tower	3m
Height of light above MHWS	14m
Character	FlR3s
Range	5Nm

Hilbre Island Light provides a port-hand mark for the Hilbre Swash, a channel in the River Dee estuary. This small automatic beacon passed from the jurisdiction of the Mersey Docks and Harbour Company to that of Trinity House in 1973. It was converted from acetylene gas to solar power in 1995.

St Bee's Lighthouse

Upon the shoulder of Cumbria, south of the small harbours of Maryport, Workington, Whitehaven, and Silloth, sandy beaches and grassy foreshores give way to cliffs around the high promontory of St Bee's Head. In 1718 these ports were engaged in a vigorous trade to North Wales, the Isle of Man, Liverpool, Ireland and beyond, and Trinity House obtained a patent to erect a lighthouse on the headland.

Latitude	54° 30.81'N
Longitude	003° 38.11'W
Established	1718
Height of tower	17m
Height of light above MHWS	102m
Character	Fl(2)20s
Range	18Nm

SAINT BEES LIGHTHOUSE.

SOUTH WEST ELEVATION.

Thomas Lutwige was granted a ninety-nine-year lease at an annual rent of £20 on the undertaking that he erected and maintained a lighthouse at his own expense. The lighthouse was to be funded by dues of three half-pence per ton on vessels trading to the nearby ports.

St Bee's lighthouse seems to have attracted complaints of inadequacy early in its history and these were to persist for some time. When Robert Stevenson visited the lighthouse in 1801 he was appalled. The ramshackle old tower was surmounted by a coal fire in a small open grate. Stevenson claimed that 'in storms so small a body of fire cannot be kept up as it ought to be'. Despite its inadequate performance this pitiful light consumed 130 tons of coal a year. In 1814 another commentator wrote that the building was 'of the meanest description and provided with a very bad light supplied by a coal fire. I imagine a light in this situation is admitted to be of very little use or such a one as this could not scarcely be submitted to or escape the vigilant observation of the Trinity House.'

One wonders how long this relic would have been 'submitted to' had fire not destroyed the primitive coal-fired light, the last in the whole of Great Britain. On 17 January 1822 the conflagration caused the tragic death of the keeper's wife and five of his children. The keeper himself escaped, being found just inside the lighthouse door where the fresh air had sustained him and unlike his family, had prevented him from suffocation.

Joseph Nelson was despatched by Trinity House to build a circular tower and, at a total cost of £2,322, to crown it with an optic of oil-powered Argand lamps and reflectors optic. In 1866 Nelson's tower was superseded by a new lighthouse and dwellings, erected further inland. This was built under the supervision of James Douglass who installed a large optic providing an occulting light. De-manned and automated in 1987, St Bee's was further modernised in 1999 when control was moved to Harwich.

Maryport Lighthouse

Latitude	*54° 43.06'N*
Longitude	*003° 30.56'W*
Established	*1796*
Height of tower	*4.7m*
Height of light above MHWS	*10m*
Character	*Fl1.5s*
Range	*6Nm*

An important port in the latter part of the Eighteenth Century, Maryport is thought to have possessed a small lighthouse in 1796. Five years later Robert Stevenson reported that the light was an oil lamp with two reflectors.

The present small lighthouse was converted to acetylene operation in 1946 and taken over by Trinity House in 1961. In 1996 a new aluminium tower was built and the light was connected to mains electricity.

Gibraltar

T rinity House has provided advice, engineering expertise and keepers to a number of stations outside the United Kingdom. Actively involved in the building of the lighthouses on the Great Basses Reef off Sri Lanka, providing the keepers at Cape Pembroke in the Falkland Islands and, more recently, the lighthouse on Sombrero Island in the West Indies, it remains responsible for the lighthouse on Europa Point, Gibraltar.

Europa Point Lighthouse

Under powers granted by an Act of Parliament in 1838 Trinity House was made responsible for a proposed lighthouse at Gibraltar and, under the Merchant Shipping Act of 1894, the Corporation became the General Lighthouse Authority for the colony and has remained so since the change in Gibraltar's political status.

Europa Point Lighthouse was built and lit in 1841, a single-wick oil lamp being augmented by a fixed dioptric lens and catoptric mirrors. In 1864 this was replaced by a four-wick burner and a new lens. At this time a red sector was introduced to shine over the Pearl Rocks on the western side of the entrance to Gibraltar Bay. In 1894 a more powerful light was fitted with an occulting rather than a fixed character, and an explosive fog signal of two reports every five minutes was added. An incandescent burner was fitted in 1905 and a Hood paraffin vapour burner with a single incandescent mantle superseded it in 1923.

Between 1954 and 1956 extensive structural alterations were carried out and the station was powered by electricity. A revolving-lens system of over 60,000 candle-power was installed and an additional fixed red sector light over the Pearl Rocks was added in a new storey added below the main lantern. The fog signal was replaced by a compressed-air horn.

In February 1994 automation was completed. An automatic, three-position lamp changer was fitted within the existing optic, along with an electrical fog signal. All the monitoring systems were then run through a simple reporting station linked to the Gibraltar Post Office which acts as control station.

Latitude	*36° 06.67'N*
Longitude	*005° 20.62'W*
Established	*1841*
Height of tower	*20m*
Height of light above MHWS	*49m*
Character	*Iso10s +OcR10s +F.R*
Range	*19/15/17Nm*
Fog Signal	*Horn(1)20s*

Following: South Stack Lighthouse.

Postscript

I t would be wrong to leave the reader with the impression that Trinity House has faded into the depths of its long and eventful history. Today, the Corporation is a thriving organisation that has a clear vision about the future while it remains true to the best traditions of its past. Much progress has been made in the furtherance of the Corporation's charitable aims, including substantial and regular grant support to a wide range of UK maritime charities.

Education in seamanship has also become a major and on-going charitable objective. Through its Scholarship Cadet Scheme, Trinity House has already provided full sponsorship to over 100 cadets in their four-year training for Merchant Navy Officer qualification. Added to this is the evolutionary path on which Trinity House continues to discharge its duty as a General Lighthouse Authority, by providing the right mix of visual, audible and electronic aids to navigation – many now powered by solar energy – to meet the modern needs of all classes of vessel.

The technological feat of automating lighthouses has often been misrepresented as the occasion of their demise or closure. Doubtless there will come a time when the role of lighthouses is significantly reduced and Trinity House is already preparing for that time by keeping the Lighthouse Estate intact and producing plans for its future conservation and management through alternative uses. The largest shore stations including Lizard, Portland Bill and South Stack Lighthouses, have already been made accessible to visitors and a selection of the lighthouse keepers' cottages at stations in England, Wales and the Channel Islands are being made available for holiday letting.

The steps currently being taken by Trinity House, such as the conservation plan published for Lizard Lighthouse – probably the first of its kind worldwide – will ensure a better understanding of the historic and cultural significance of Britain's lighthouses, most of which have stood for centuries. Many of our properties are living icons of local and national history and their trademark silhouettes on the coastal landscape compete with castles and churches, whilst the construction of the magnificent offshore pillar rock towers, such as Eddystone, Wolf and Bishop Rock Lighthouses, must surely stand out as one of the great stories of our social heritage.

Lighthouses will remain pivotal to the cultural and economic identity of coastal communities long after their use as seamarks. In the meantime, Trinity House will ensure that the best examples of our lighthouse heritage remain in public ownership for the access, education and enjoyment of future generations.

Rear Admiral Sir Patrick Rowe KCVO CBE
Deputy Master of the Corporation of Trinity House

Index

Bibliography

Lighthouses General

Bowen, J.P., *British Lighthouses* (1947)

Hague, Douglas and Rosemary Christie, *Lighthouses, their Architecture, History and Archaeology* (1975)

Naish, John, *Seamarks, Their History and Development* (1985)

Nicholson, Christopher, *Rock Lighthouses of Britain* (1995)

Renton, Alan, *Lost Sounds* (2001)

Stevenson, D. Alan (ed), *English Lighthouse Tours, 1801, 1813 and 1818, from the diaries of Robert Stevenson* (1946)

ibid., *The World's Lighthouses Before 1820* (1959)

Sutton-Jones, Kenneth, *Pharos, The Lighthouse Yesterday, Today and Tomorrow* (1985)

Woodman, Richard, *View from the Sea* (1985)

Lighthouse Keepers

Lane, A. J., *It was Fun While It Lasted* (1998)

Parker, Tony, *Lighthouse* (1975)

Lighthouses of Northeast England

Armstrong, Richard, *Grace Darling – Maid and Myth* (1965)

Darling, William, *The Journal of William Darling, Grace Darling's Father; from 1795 to 1860* (1886)

Morrison, Paul G., and Tony Rylance, *Coquet Island, Northumberland* (1989)

Smedley, Constance, *Grace Darling and her Times* (1932)

Watt, Grace, *The Farne Islands, Their History and Wild Life* (1951)

Lighthouses of East Anglia

Chaplin, Captain W.R. *The History of the Lowestoft Lighthouses* (unpublished t/s)

Long, Neville, *Lights of East Anglia* (1983)

Underwood, Charlie, *The Great Light, The Orfordness Lighthouses* (1993)

Lighthouses of the Strait of Dover

Beazeley, Alexander, *On Coast Fog Signals,* Lecture to the RUSI, 24 May 1872

Boyle, Martin, *Beachy Head* (1999)

Byng Gattie, G. *Memorials of the Goodwin Sands* (1890)

Douglass, James Nicholas, *The Electric Light Applied to Lighthouse Illumination* (excerpt, Minutes of Proceedings of the Institution of Civil Engineers, vol. LVII, session 1878-79, part iii)

Goldsmith-Carter, George, *The Goodwin Sands* (1953)

Lane, Anthony, 'Disaster at the South Goodwin', *Bygone Kent,* vol. 13 No 1, January 1992

ibid., 'Brake Lightvessel: a story of two collisions', *Bygone Kent,* vol. 14 No 6, June 1993

Lapthorne, W.H., *Historic Broadstairs* (3rd edition 1980)

Lewis, J. *The History of the Isle of Tenet* (1736)

Surtees, John, *Beachy Head* (1997)

Lighthouses of the South Coast and Channel Islands

James, Jude, *Hurst Castle, An Illustrated History* (1986)

Dunning, G.C., *The History of Niton, Isle of Wight* (1952) reprinted from the *Proceedings* of the Isle of Wight Natural History and Archaeological Society, vol. IV, part vi, (1951)

Newbury, Elizabeth, *St Catherine's Oratory, A Handbook for Teachers* (1987)

Boyle, Martin & Ken Trethewey, *Needles Point* (1996)

Chaplin, W.R., *Annals of the Caskets Lighthouse* (1965) (unpublished t/s)

Williams, Thomas, *Life of Sir James Douglass* (1900)

Lighthouses of Devon & Cornwall

The Lizard History Society, *The Lizard in Landewecdnack, a Village Story* (1996)

Majdalany, Fred, *The Red Rocks of Eddystone* (1974)

Mudd, David, *Cornish Sea Lights* (1978)

Palmer, Mike, *Eddystone 300 – The Finger of Light* (1998)

Tarrant, Michael, *Cornwall's Lighthouse Heritage* (1990)

Lighthouses of the Bristol Channel

Chaplin, Captain W.R. 'The History of Flat Holm Lighthouse', *The American Neptune,* vol. XX No 1 January 1960

Hague, Douglas B., *Lighthouses of Wales* (1994)

Lighthouses of the Irish Sea

Bardsey Island Trust, *Bardsey, Its History and Wildlife* (2nd edition 1995)

Boyle, Martin, *Skerries Rock* (1997)

Trinity House

Harris, G.G., *The Trinity House of Deptford Strond 1514-1660* (1969)

Tarrant, Michael, *Trinity House – The Super Silent Service* (1999)

Woodman, Richard, *Keepers of the Sea* (1983)

Acknowledgements

The Corporation of Trinity House wishes to acknowledge the contribution to this book made by: Bill Arnold, Matthew Black, Mike Berridge, Frank Biddle, David Brewer, Frank Celano, Ken Chapman, Howard Cooper, Dermot Cronin, Gerry Douglas-Sherwood, Terry Johns, Eddie Matthews, Brian Mayo, Bill O'Brian, Mike O'Sullivan, Paul Ridgway, Bill Summers, Dave Spurgeon, Breda Wall, Tom Whiston, Adrian Wilkins, Mike Williams, Jane Wilson and Richard Woodman.

Picture Credits

Page 248: Portland Lighthouse   *Page 251: Lynmouth Foreland Lighthouse*

Page 253: Lundy Old Lighthouse   *Page 254: Needles Lighthouse*

Page 255: South Bishop Lighthouse   *Right: Principal Keeper Eddie Matthews*

BISHOP ROCK LIGHTHOUSE
PROPOSED STRENGTHENING AND IMPROVEMENT

Drawing Nº 2/4

PROPOSED FOCAL PLANE

PRESENT ʃ FOCAL PLANE

32'-0"

142'-0"

110'-0"

Bed

oil

oil

Store

ENTRANCE ROOM

WATER TANK

Note – New Work shewn in Colour
Work to be removed, edged in Red.
Existing Masonry, not to be
disturbed, cross hatched.

H.W.S.T.

L.W.S.T.

ROCK

Jas N Douglass
25th May 1882

Scale   10   20   30   40 Feet